PERSPECTIVES

2

Daniel **BARBER**

Lewis **LANSFORD**

Amanda **JEFFRIES**

NATIONAL GEOGRAPHIC
LEARNING

Australia · Brazil · Mexico · Singapore · United Kingdom · United States

Perspectives 2a Combo Split
Daniel Barber, Lewis Lansford, Amanda Jeffries

Publisher: Sherrise Roehr

Executive Editor: Sarah Kenney

Publishing Consultant: Karen Spiller

Managing Editor: Claudienma Mimó

Senior Development Editor: Brenden Layte

Senior Development Editor: Lewis Thompson

Director of Global Marketing: Ian Martin

Product Marketing Manager: Anders Bylund

Director of Content and Media Production: Michael Burggren

Production Manager: Daisy Sosa

Media Researcher: Leila Hishmeh

Manufacturing Customer Account Manager: Mary Beth Hennebury

Art Director: Brenda Carmichael

Production Management and Composition: Lumina Datamatics, Inc.

Cover Image: This image, created by TED Prize winner JR, was on the cover of The New York Times Magazine's "Walking New York" issue. ©JR-art.net

© 2018 National Geographic Learning, a Cengage Learning Company

ALL RIGHTS RESERVED. No part of this work covered by the copyright herein may be reproduced or distributed in any form or by any means, except as permitted by U.S. copyright law, without the prior written permission of the copyright owner.

"National Geographic", "National Geographic Society" and the Yellow Border Design are registered trademarks of the National Geographic Society ® Marcas Registradas

For product information and technology assistance, contact us at
Cengage Learning Customer & Sales Support, cengage.com/contact
For permission to use material from this text or product,
submit all requests online at **cengage.com/permissions**
Further permissions questions can be emailed to
permissionrequest@cengage.com

Student Edition: Level 2 Combo Split A
ISBN: 978-1-337-29740-0

National Geographic Learning
20 Channel Center Street
Boston, MA 02210
USA

National Geographic Learning, a Cengage Learning Company, has a mission to bring the world to the classroom and the classroom to life. With our English language programs, students learn about their world by experiencing it. Through our partnerships with National Geographic and TED Talks, they develop the language and skills they need to be successful global citizens and leaders.

Locate your local office at **international.cengage.com/region**

Visit National Geographic Learning online at **NGL.Cengage.com/ELT**
Visit our corporate website at **www.cengage.com**

Photography Credits 4 (tl1) Denis Allard/REA/Redux, (tl2) © Christoph Otto, (cl) © Joey Schusler, (bl1) © Srdjan Stepanovic, (bl2) © Veronika K Ko, 5 (tl1) © Marla Aufmuth/TED, (tl2) © Wolfram Scheible/TED, (cl) © James Duncan Davidson/TED, (bl1) © James Duncan Davidson/TED, (bl2) © Mark Tioxon/TED, 6 (tl1) K H Fung/Science Source, (t12) © Prasad Ambati, (cl) © almalki abdulrahman/500px Prime, (bl1) © Murdo Macleod, (bl2) Randy Olson/National Geographic Creative, 7 (tl1) (tl2) (cl) (bl1) © TED, (bl2) © Ryan Lash/TED, 8-9 Denis Allard/REA/Redux, 10-11 Dinodia Photo/Passage/Getty Images, 12-13 (t) National Geographic Creative, 14 Boomer Jerritt/All Canada Photos/Getty Images, 15 DJTaylor/Shutterstock.com, 16-17 (t) © Marla Aufmuth/TED, 16 (cr) jsnyderdesign/DigitalVision Vectors/Getty Images, 18-19 imagebroker/Alamy Stock Photo, 20-21 © Christoph Otto, 22-23 Gary Conner/Photolibrary/Getty Images, 24-25 Bradley Garrett/eyevine/Redux, 26 Christopher Groenhout/Lonely Planet Images/Getty Images, 27 piola666/E+/Getty Images, 28-29 © Wolfram Scheible/TED, 31 Panther Media GmbH/Alamy Stock Photo, 32-33 © Joey Schusler, 34-35 Zuma Press, Inc./Alamy Stock Photo, 36-37 © Thomas Mukoya/Reuters, 38 Foto Arena LTDA/Alamy Stock Photo, 39 Ian Walton/Getty Images Sport/Getty Images, 40-41 © James Duncan Davidson/TED, 43 asiseeit/E+/Getty Images, 44-45 © Srdjan Stepanovic, 46-47 Wolfgang Rattay/Reuters, 48 Tom Cockrem/Lonely Planet Images/Getty Images, 50 UniversalImagesGroup/Getty Images, 51 Charoenkrung.Studio99/Shutterstock.com, 52-53 © James Duncan Davidson/TED, 54-55 Design pics Inc/National Geographic Creative, 56-57 © Veronika K Ko, 58-59 Bloomberg/Getty Images, 61 Vasin Lee/Shutterstock.com, 62 Past Pix/SSPL/Getty Images, 63 Buyenlarge/Archive Photos/Getty Images, 64-65 © Mark Tioxon/TED, 66-67 deimagine/E+/Getty Images, 68-69 K H Fung/Science Source, 70-71 Aaron Huey/National Geographic Creative, 73 Aurora Photos/Alamy Stock Photo, 74 Shaun Curry/AFP/Getty Images, 75 Huw Jones/Lonely Planet Images/Getty Images, 76-77 © TED, 78 Ammit/Alamy Stock Photo, 79 Pete Maclaine/Alamy Stock Photo, 80-81 © Prasad Ambati, 82-83 © Vasie Papadopoulos, 85 Toshiyuki Shirai/EyeEm/Getty Images, 86 © Mapping specialists Ltd, 87 Tobias Gerber/laif/Redux, 88-89 © TED, 90-91 RosalreneBetancourt 11/Alamy Stock Photo, 92-93 © Almalki abdulrahman/500px Prime, 94-95 NASA, 97 © Crossing Borders Education, 98 martin-dm/E+/Getty Images, 100-101 © TED, 102-103 Richard Newstead/Moment/Getty Images, 104-105 © Murdo Macleod, 106-107 © Johannes Stötter, 108 © Artez, 110 © Jason Larkin/Panos, 111 John Blanding/The Boston Globe/Getty Images, 112-113 © TED, 114-115 Lucas Vallecillos/Alamy Stock Photo, 116-117 Randy Olson/National Geographic Creative, 118 (bl) John Rensten/Stone/Getty Images, (br) Jim Richardson/National Geographic Creative, 119 (tr) Bettmann/Getty Images, (bl) Design Pics Inc/National Geographic Creative, (br) Alison Wright/National Geographic Creative, 121 Steve Vidler/Alamy Stock Photo, 122 Terry Williams/The Image Bank/Getty Images, 123 STR/AFP/Getty Images, 124-125 © Ryan Lash/TED, 126 Ableimages/David Harrigan/Getty Images, 151 (br)(bc) cTermit/Shutterstock.com, (bl) AFP/Getty Images, 152 (tr1) iStock.com/RapidEye, (tr2) Pavel_D/Shutterstock.com.

Text Credits 26 Text about "freeganism in Sydney" by Becky Khalil., 94 Text about "Getting your message out" there by Chris Hadfield.

Printed in the United States of America
Print Number: 03   Print Year: 2023

ACKNOWLEDGMENTS

Paulo Rogerio RoPaulo Rogerio Rodrigues
Escola Móbile, São Paulo, Brazil

Claudia Colla de Amorim
Escola Móbile, São Paulo, Brazil

Antonio Oliveira
Escola Móbile, São Paulo, Brazil

Rory Ruddock
Atlantic International Language Center, Hanoi, Vietnam

Carmen Virginia Pérez Cervantes
La Salle, Mexico City, Mexico

Rossana Patricia Zuleta
CIPRODE, Guatemala City, Guatemala

Gloria Stella Quintero Riveros
Universidad Católica de Colombia, Bogotá, Colombia

Mónica Rodriguez Salvo
MAR English Services, Buenos Aires, Argentina

Itana de Almeida Lins
Grupo Educacional Anchieta, Salvador, Brazil

Alma Loya
Colegio de Chihuahua, Chihuahua, Mexico

María Trapero Dávila
Colegio Teresiano, Ciudad Obregon, Mexico

Silvia Kosaruk
Modern School, Lanús, Argentina

Florencia Adami
Dámaso Centeno, Caba, Argentina

Natan Galed Gomez Cartagena
Global English Teaching, Rionegro, Colombia

James Ubriaco
Colégio Santo Agostinho, Belo Horizonte, Brazil

Ryan Manley
The Chinese University of Hong Kong, Shenzhen, China

Silvia Teles
Colégio Cândido Portinari, Salvador, Brazil

María Camila Azuero Gutiérrez
Fundación Centro Electrónico de Idiomas, Bogotá, Colombia

Martha Ramirez
Colegio San Mateo Apostol, Bogotá, Colombia

Beata Polit
XXIII LO Warszawa, Poland

Beata Tomaszewska
V LO Toruń, Poland

Michał Szkudlarek
I LO Brzeg, Poland

Anna Buchowska
I LO Białystok, Poland

Natalia Maćkowiak
one2one, Kosakowo, Poland

Agnieszka Dończyk
one2one, Kosakowo, Poland

The author and publishers would like to thank the following for their help: Artez; Sophie-chan; Emma Gore-Lloyd; Becky Khalil; Nick Robinson.

Perspectives teaches learners to think critically and to develop the language skills they need to find their own voice in English. The carefully guided language lessons, real-world stories, and TED Talks motivate learners to think creatively and communicate effectively.

In *Perspectives*, learners develop:

● AN OPEN MIND

Every unit explores one idea from different perspectives, giving learners opportunities for practicing language as they look at the world in new ways.

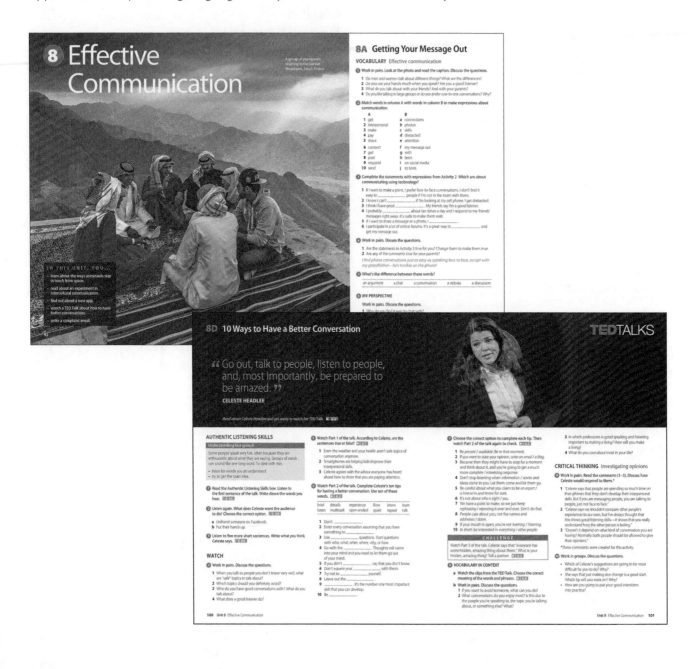

• A CRITICAL EYE

Students learn the critical thinking skills and strategies they need to evaluate new information and develop their own opinions and ideas to share.

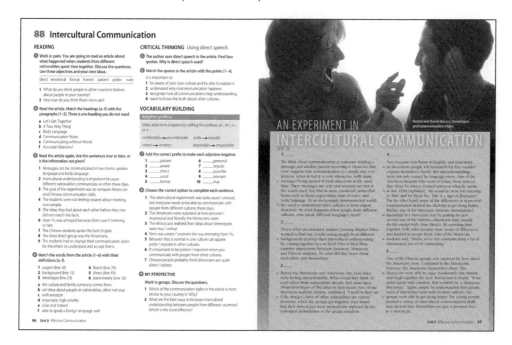

• A CLEAR VOICE

Students respond to the unit theme and express their own ideas confidently in English.

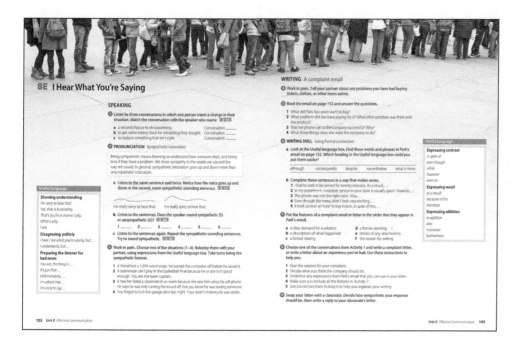

CONTENTS

GRAMMAR	**TED**TALKS		SPEAKING	WRITING
Talking about the present	This app knows how you feel—from the look on your face.	**RANA EL KALIOUBY** Rana el Kaliouby's idea worth spreading is that by teaching computers how to understand emotions on the faces of users, we can make more personal connections with the devices we use. **Authentic Listening Skills** Content words	Asking follow-up questions	A review **Writing Skill** Emphasis
Narrative forms **Pronunciation** *Used to*	Happy maps	**DANIELE QUERCIA** Daniele Quercia's idea worth spreading is that the fastest route may be efficient, but there are times when taking a different route can be more interesting and memorable. **Authentic Listening Skills** Understanding accents	Asking for and giving directions	A story **Writing Skill** *just*
Present perfect and present perfect continuous **Pronunciation** *For*	How I swam the North Pole	**LEWIS PUGH** Lewis Pugh's idea worth spreading is that sometimes we have to do extraordinary things to make people pay attention to important issues. **Authentic Listening Skills** Signposts	Agreeing and disagreeing	An opinion essay **Writing Skill** Giving your opinion
Making predictions **Pronunciation** Sentence stress with the future continuous and future perfect	Why I'm a weekday vegetarian	**GRAHAM HILL** Graham Hill's idea worth spreading is that cutting meat from our diet—even just part of the time—can have a powerful impact on the planet. **Authentic Listening Skills** Pausing **Critical Thinking** Persuading	Talking about hopes and goals	A social media update **Writing Skill** Interesting language
Present and past modals	Why the best hire might not have the perfect résumé	**REGINA HARTLEY** Regina Hartley's idea worth spreading is that our résumés tell employers about our experiences, determination, and ability to deal with life's challenges. **Authentic Listening Skills** Understanding contrasts	Job interviews **Pronunciation** *quite*	A cover letter **Writing Skill** Hedging

1 In Touch with Your Feelings

Hundreds of anonymous black and white photos make up a giant collage on the floor of the Pantheon in Paris, created by the French artist, JR.

IN THIS UNIT, YOU...

- talk about emotions.
- read about smiles.
- learn about the benefits of being outdoors.
- watch a TED Talk about an app that can "read" your facial expressions.
- write a review.

1A Show Your Emotions

VOCABULARY Describing emotions

1 Look at the photo and read the caption. What message do you think the artist is trying to communicate in this project?

2 MY PERSPECTIVE

Complete the sentence so it's true for you.

Happiness is <u>*diving under the water on a sunny day*</u> .

3 Match the sentences (1–9) with the follow-up comments (a–i).

1 I sometimes get **scared** when I'm on my own.
2 You must be **delighted**—that's great news!
3 I'm feeling more **relaxed** now that it's Saturday.
4 I got a little **confused** at the beginning of the movie.
5 My brother isn't normally this **nervous**.
6 Traveling to school on your own can be very **lonely**.
7 My parents started to dance. I was so **embarrassed**!
8 I'm feeling very **stressed** right now.
9 Please don't be **angry** with me.

a But it was great to see them having fun.
b It's been a very busy week, so it's nice to have some time off.
c I have so much work to do.
d I was only trying to help.
e I don't even like being at home without anyone else, really.
f He's doing a presentation in class this afternoon.
g I understood most of it, though.
h Sometimes I like having quiet time before a busy day, though.
i When did they tell you you're on the team?

4 Complete the questions with an adjective in bold from Activity 3.

1 Are you _____ of anything, like spiders, for example?
2 Have you ever been really _____ with your test results?
3 Do you get _____ if you cry in public?
4 Is it possible to feel _____ when you are with lots of people?
5 Do you get _____ before going to the dentist or speaking in class?
6 When you're feeling _____ , what do you do to relax?
7 Are you _____ about the meaning of any new words today?
8 If someone is late, do you feel _____ ?
9 Does reading make you feel _____ ?

5 PRONUNCIATION *-ed* adjectives

1 Listen and repeat. How many syllables does each word have? 🎧 1
2 Listen again. Do the adjectives end in /t/, /d/, or /ɪd/? 🎧 1

6 Work in pairs. Ask and answer the questions in Activity 4.

LISTENING

7 Work in pairs. Look at the photo and answer the questions.

1 What do you know about tigers?
2 Can photographers take photos like this safely? How?
3 How would you feel if you came face to face with a tiger in the wild?

8 Listen to descriptions of three National Geographic explorers' work. What emotions are the speakers describing? Why? 🎧 2

anger	excitement	fear
nervousness	unhappiness	worry

1 Matthew Luskin _____ , _____
2 William Allard _____ , _____ ,

_____
3 Chris Bashinelli _____

9 Listen again. Which explorer (Matthew, William, or Chris): 🎧 2

1 described an event with a happy ending for someone who wasn't the speaker?
2 did something he had never done before?
3 wasn't talking about his emotions?
4 was trying to solve a problem in his work?
5 was probably very tired?
6 was surprised at how he felt?

GRAMMAR Subject / object questions

10 Work in pairs. Can you remember the answers to these questions? Listen to William's story again and check your answers. 🎧 3

1 What does William Allard do?
2 Who killed Eduardo's sheep?
3 Who collected money for Eduardo's family?
4 How much did they collect?

Tigers live in Bangladesh, Bhutan, India, Indonesia, Malaysia, Nepal, Russia, and Thailand.

Subject / object questions

a *Who collected money for Eduardo's family?* **National Geographic** *readers collected money for him.*

b *How much did they collect? They collected* **over $7,000.**

Check page 128 for more information and practice.

11 Read the questions in the Grammar box. Then choose the correct option to complete the sentences.

1 The question word in question *a / b* asks about the subject of the answer (subject question).
2 The question word in question *a / b* asks about the object of the answer (object question).
3 To make *a subject / an object* question in the simple present and simple past we need an auxiliary verb, e.g., *do, does, did.*
4 *Subject / Object* questions in the simple present and simple past do not need the auxiliary verb *do* or *did.*

12 Use the prompts to write questions about Chris Bashinelli and Matthew Luskin's stories.

1 whose story / happen / in Mongolia?
2 what / the men / invite / Chris / to do?
3 what / Chris / say / about the experience?
4 what / Matthew / studying?
5 how many people / tigers / kill / before the expedition?
6 how many people / hide / in the tree?

13 Work in pairs. Discuss the answers to the questions in Activity 12.

14 Complete the questions about emotions.

1 How often _____ ?
   I laugh every time I'm with my friends.
2 What TV shows _____ ?
   Singing competitions on TV make me angry.
3 Who _____ ?
   My little sister cries the most in my family, definitely!
4 Which horror movies you've seen _____ ?
   Don't Breathe and *Krampus* were both scary, but *Don't Breathe* scared me the most!
5 When you feel confused about homework, what
   _____ ?
   I call a friend!
6 Who _____ you recently?
   My mom embarrassed me an hour ago!

15 Work in pairs. Ask and answer the questions in Activity 14.

16 Write five more questions about emotions to ask your classmates.
What makes you most excited about the future?

17 Work in groups. Ask and answer your questions.

Why do people smile?

🎧 4 **"Say cheese!"** In English-speaking countries, this is what you say to people to make them smile before you take their photo. "Service with a smile" is a common message for
5 store assistants and receptionists. Workers in call centers are even told to smile so they sound friendly when they speak to customers on the phone! The idea is that callers will notice if the phone operators aren't smiling. But why should we want people to
10 smile?

We've always known that smiling can express enjoyment, affection, or friendliness, but we're learning more and more about facial expressions, and realizing that their effect on our relationships is more
15 powerful than that. We know that smiling helps us connect with other people in social situations and get out of arguments and embarrassing situations. We know from studies that smiling regularly may even increase the chances of living longer. In fact, it's such
20 an important part of being human that we start it very young. You probably started smiling to show your happiness when you were just a few weeks old, but you've known how to smile for even longer. Unborn babies get used to moving their facial muscles by
25 smiling, in the same way they practice kicking using their leg muscles. And we aren't the only animals that

VOCABULARY BUILDING

Suffixes

We can make nouns from adjectives by adding suffixes.

adjective	suffix	noun
embarrassed	+ ment	embarrassment
friendly	+ ness	friendliness
depressed	+ ion	depression

1 Write nouns using *-ment*, *-ness*, or *-ion*. Use a dictionary if necessary.

1 nervous
2 sad
3 excited
4 disappointed
5 happy
6 exhausted
7 confused
8 lonely

2 Complete the sentences with a noun or an adjective from Activity 1.

1 Many people say that money can't buy _____, but I think it helps.
2 I felt very _____ at summer camp. It was my first time away from home and I didn't know anyone.
3 I had to sing on my own in the show. I felt so _____ that I couldn't sleep.
4 Emin studied hard for his tests. He didn't want to be a _____ to his parents.
5 There was a lot of _____ in the class. The teacher said the school trip was on Wednesday but the email said Thursday.

READING

3 Work in pairs. Try to make your partner smile. How easy is it? Then discuss the questions.

1 Look at the pairs of photos (a–c). Which smiles do you think are genuine (real)? Which smiles do you think are fake (not real)?
2 Why would you pretend to smile?
3 Are you good at recognizing genuine and fake smiles?

4 Make a list of things that make you smile. Compare your list with a partner.

when my team wins a game, chocolate,…

5 Read the article quickly. Choose the best subtitle.

1 How our bodies affect our emotions
2 The secret power of smiling
3 Smiling expresses many emotions

6 Read the article again. Are these sentences *true* or *false*, or is the information *not given*?

1 Some employees are taught to smile when they speak to people who can't see them.
2 You could stop a disagreement by smiling.
3 People who don't smile are more likely to get sick.
4 Other animals smile for the same reasons as humans.
5 Eating chocolate has a more powerful effect on our emotions than smiling.

b c

smile to communicate happiness—chimpanzees do it, too, suggesting that smiling existed before we did!

30 Have you ever been in this situation: you are angry with a friend but you can't stay angry because they're smiling at you? This is because smiles pass from person to person, and it's hard not to smile back. We actually lose some control of our own facial muscles when we look at someone smiling at us. When this

35 happens, we automatically copy their expression, and smiling like them may actually help us understand their emotions better.

Being happy makes us smile, of course. But smiling also makes us happy. Scientists can take pictures

40 of the brain to see what happens when a person is happy. They see the same effect when the person smiles, whether they're really happy or not. So a smile isn't just a sign to others; it is also a message to our brain telling it to feel happy. One study showed

45 that a smile can have the same positive effect on the brain as eating 2,000 bars of chocolate! So, even if you're feeling depressed, a fake smile can make all the difference. If you know someone who's always smiling, perhaps they're using it to control their

50 emotions. Why not control your emotions the same way? If you sometimes feel sad, worried, or angry, try smiling. You might feel better.

7 Summarize the article in no more than twenty words.

Smiling…

8 MY PERSPECTIVE

Work in groups. Discuss the questions.

1 Do you think smiling really is a good way to feel better?
2 What do you do if you aren't feeling very happy?
3 Who do you think smiles more, younger or older people, women or men? Why?
4 Do you know anyone who smiles too much / doesn't smile enough?

CRITICAL THINKING Rhetorical questions

9 Work in pairs. Read the Critical Thinking box and discuss the questions (1–4).

> Rhetorical questions are used to make a point, but a reply is not expected. They are often used to:
> - tell readers what information they can expect to read.
> - emphasize a point.
> - make a suggestion or persuade.
> - help readers relate the text to their own experience.

1 Look at the title of the article and list all the reasons that people smile.
2 Why is it a good idea to have a question as a title?

3 There are three more questions in the article. Underline them. Match the questions with three of the functions in the Critical Thinking box.
4 Write a question to include in the article for one of the other two functions.

10 Read about the "Pan Am smile." Then look at the photos again. Can you find the fake smiles more easily?

The "Pan Am smile" is named after the flight attendants of this old American airline. They were famous for their friendly customer service and for always smiling at the passengers. Everyone knew that these smiles weren't genuine but they were an expression of friendliness and had a positive effect on the passengers.

We all use Pan Am smiles because there are many situations where showing unhappiness would be rude. Smiling has the important social function of keeping people happy.

But how can you tell the difference between a genuine smile and a fake smile? In the nineteenth century, French scientist Guillaume Duchenne noticed that we use two sets of facial muscles to smile: around the mouth and around the eyes. Pan Am smiles only use the mouth, so the secret is to look at the eyes.

1C A Breath of Fresh Air

GRAMMAR Talking about the present

1 Read the sentences in the Grammar box. Underline examples of the simple present, present continuous, and present perfect.

Talking about the present

a *We've always known that smiling can express enjoyment, affection, or friendliness.*

b *We're learning more and more about facial expressions.*

c *We know from studies that smiling may even increase the chances of living longer.*

d *We aren't the only animals that smile to communicate happiness—chimpanzees do it, too.*

e *You're angry with a friend but you can't stay angry because they're smiling at you.*

f *If you know someone who's always smiling,…*

g *If you sometimes feel sad, worried, or angry, try smiling.*

Check page 128 for more information and practice.

2 Complete the rules by writing *simple present*, *present perfect*, or *present continuous*. Then match each rule with an example from the Grammar box.

1 The _____ is used:
- to talk about things that are always or generally true, e.g., scientific facts.
- to describe habits and routines (often with words like *sometimes* and *never*).
- with stative verbs, e.g., *enjoy*, *agree*, *think*.

2 The _____ is used:
- to talk about actions happening at or around the present time, or at the time of speaking/writing.
- to talk about changing situations.
- with *always* to describe actions that happen often. They may cause an emotional response in the speaker.

3 The _____ is used:
- to describe actions that started in the past and continue to the present.

3 Choose the correct options to complete the paragraph.

(1) *Are you feeling / Have you felt* stressed right now? Perhaps it's because you (2) *are always sitting / have always sat* in front of a computer screen these days. So what should you do? You could be the type of person who (3) *is usually reading / usually reads* a book, for instance, or (4) *plays / has played* video games for relaxation. Or perhaps you (5) *are believing / believe* that the answer to everyday stress is more time outside, surrounded by nature. (6) *Are you enjoying / Do you enjoy* getting away from cities, cars, and computers and heading into the mountains? It's true that we (7) *need / are needing* time off work to relax, though it (8) *becomes / is becoming* more and more difficult to get away. But people (9) *enjoy / have enjoyed* forests, parks, lakes, and rivers for thousands of years, so if life (10) *gets / has gotten* to be too much to cope with recently, think about taking a break out in the woods or a walk in the park, even if it's just for an hour or two.

4 Read about the effect nature can have on our brains. Complete the text with the best form of the verbs: simple present, present continuous, or present perfect.

A group of 22 students (1) _____ (take) a break from their everyday lives at the University of Utah. Normally, they (2) _____ (sit) in front of their computer screens studying psychology, but this week they (3) _____ (camp) with Professor David Streyer in the mountains of Utah. Streyer (4) _____ (spend) many years studying the effect of nature on our brains.

We (5) _____ (know) about the benefits of nature on the body for many years, but now we can see what nature (6) _____ (do) to the brain. Our stress levels (7) _____ (drop) just by looking at photos of nature. Many people (8) _____ (think) that little by little technology (9) _____ (destroy) our lives, but Streyer (10) _____ (believe) that after just two or three days away from modern life, we can start to think differently and in a healthier way.

5 Read about healing forests in South Korea. Correct the verbs that are wrong. Not all items have an error.

1 Nature is being very important in Korean culture for hundreds of years.
2 But most South Koreans live "digital lives" in large cities nowadays.
3 Their lives become more digital and more stressful every year.
4 Koreans work very long hours, and stress levels among workers and students go up in recent years.
5 The government has believed that the answer can be found in "healing forests."
6 These are places of natural beauty where people go to relax, to reconnect with nature, and to rest.
7 We now know that spending time outside reduces stress chemicals in the body and helps it to fight disease.
8 Currently there have been 37 healing forests in Korea, and they are becoming very popular.
9 Many of them are close to big cities like Seoul, where people can get to them easily.
10 People are often going there to walk, learn about plants, do yoga, or just relax under the trees.

6 Use the prompts to write questions using the best tense: simple present, present continuous, or present perfect.

1 you / go / out to the woods much recently?
2 where / you / usually / go / to spend time outdoors?
3 what / you / like / doing outdoors?
4 your parents / always / make / you do activities that you don't enjoy?
5 you / normally / feel / relaxed when you get home?
6 you / always / check / your cell phone, or can you leave it at home?
7 if / you / live / in a town or city, / you / be / happy?
8 you / plan / to go out in nature any time soon?

7 Work in pairs. Ask and answer the questions you wrote in Activity 6.

8 Work in groups. Discuss the questions.

1 Are young people spending as much time outside now as in the past? Why?
2 What are the advantages of doing outdoor activities?
3 What kinds of activities do you and your friends like doing outdoors?
4 What outdoor activities are popular with young people these days?

9 Design an ad for an outdoor activity center in your country. Answer these questions about the ad.

1 What type of activity center will it be—more like a healing forest or an adventure park?
2 What will get a lot of people interested? What will be good for young people's health and happiness?
3 How will you attract people to your center?
4 What photos or other images will you include?

10 CHOOSE

Choose one of the following activities.

1 On your own, write a radio ad for the activity center. Read it to the class.
2 In pairs, record or act out a TV ad promoting the activity center.
3 In groups, make a brochure (text and images) for your activity center.

1D This app knows how you feel— from the look on your face.

" I want to bring emotions back into our digital experiences. "

RANA EL KALIOUBY

Read about Rana el Kaliouby and get ready to watch her TED Talk. ▶ **1.0**

AUTHENTIC LISTENING SKILLS

Content words

It is difficult to listen for every word a speaker says. When we listen, it is easier to understand the important content words, because these are usually stressed. Content words usually give enough information for us to understand the meaning of a sentence.

1 Read and listen to the first sentence in the TED Talk. Notice how many of the content words are stressed. 🎧 **5**

Our <u>emotions</u> <u>influence</u> <u>every</u> <u>aspect</u> of our <u>lives</u>, from our <u>health</u> and how we <u>learn</u>, to how we do <u>business</u> and make <u>decisions</u>, <u>big</u> ones and <u>small</u>.

2 Look at the types of words that are usually stressed. Read this excerpt from the talk and underline the words you think will be stressed. Then listen and check. 🎧 **6**

Stressed	Not stressed	
adjectives	articles	pronouns
nouns	conjunctions	auxiliary verbs
main verbs	prepositions	
adverbs		

Our emotions also influence how we connect with one another. We've evolved to live in a world like this, but instead, we're living more and more of our lives like this… So I'm on a mission to change that. I want to bring emotions back into our digital experiences.

WATCH

3 Look at the emojis. Then discuss the questions in pairs.

1 What emotions do these emojis express?

2 Do you ever use emojis? Which ones? Where do you use them: email, text messages, social media?
3 Is it sometimes difficult to find the right emoji to express how you are feeling? Why?
4 What other ways can you use to express your feelings online?

4 Watch Part 1 of the talk. Are the sentences *true* or *false* according to Rana? ▶ **1.1**

1 It's difficult to connect emotionally with others in text messages, emails, etc.
2 Rana was with her husband in Cambridge.
3 The human face can show 45 emotions.
4 It's hard to teach a computer the difference between a smile and a smirk.
5 The computer studied lots of similar faces.

5 Watch Part 2 of the talk. Which emotions does Cloe demonstrate? ▶ **1.2**

1 a little bit happy
2 angry
3 confused
4 disgusted
5 nervous
6 no emotion ("poker face")
7 sad
8 scared
9 surprised
10 very happy

TEDTALKS

6 Watch Part 3 of the talk. Choose the correct option to complete each sentence. ▶ 1.3

1 Women in the *UK / US* are more expressive than men.
2 The most expressive age group is people *older / younger* than 50.
3 People with autism could *use their phones / wear special glasses* to help them understand other people's emotions.
4 Rana *can / can't* think of many other ways her technology could be used.

7 Work in pairs. Watch Part 3 of the talk again. What use of the technology that Rana mentions is your favorite? Why? ▶ 1.3

8 VOCABULARY IN CONTEXT

a Watch the clips from the TED Talk. Choose the correct meaning of the words and phrases. ▶ 1.4

b Work in pairs. Complete the sentences in your own words. Then compare your sentences with your partner.

1 I felt *homesick* once when I…
2 I get a sense of *curiosity* when…
3 The person in my family with the most *wrinkles* is…
4 The *characteristics* of a good friend are…
5 *Joy* for me is…

9 Work in groups. Think of different ways Rana's software could be used. Think about:

- advertising or social media
- entertainment (TV, movies, concerts, theater, etc.)
- health and medicine
- people with physical problems and learning difficulties
- shopping and fashion

10 Think about your ideas. Which ones could:

1 make tons of money?
2 help people with problems?
3 be a lot of fun?

CHALLENGE

Put comments a–d in order (1–4). The comment you agree with most is 1; the comment you agree with least is 4.*

a "This technology is fun, but I don't think it's necessary anymore. These days, we communicate more with webcams and video. We don't need the computer to read faces for us. We can read them ourselves."

b "We don't need to read faces when we communicate by phone. Why do we need it now?"

c "I think Rana's technology is amazing, but I worry that companies will only use it to sell more products to us."

d "I don't like the idea of my computer reading my emotions. It's a scary idea!"

*These comments were created for this activity.

Work in pairs. Compare your ideas. How do you think Rana would respond to the comments?

1E The Feel-Good Factor

SPEAKING

1 Work in pairs. Read about India's longest-running movie. Discuss the questions.

The Bollywood movie *Dilwale Dulhania Le Jayenge* is one of India's most successful movies. It was still showing at one cinema in Mumbai more than twenty years after it came out. It is a classic feel-good love story with a happy ending.

1 What does "the feel-good factor" mean?
2 Are there feel-good movies that people in your country watch more than once?
3 What are your favorite feel-good movies?

2 Check that you know the meaning of the words in bold in these sentences.

1 I don't think anyone could survive in space for that long, but the **special effects** were amazing!
2 The first movie was so scary, there's no way I'm going to watch the **sequel**.
3 It has a great **soundtrack** but some of the actors can't sing very well.
4 It's an emotional story about a group of soldiers during the Second World War. The **cast** is amazing—Tom Hanks and Matt Damon are in it.
5 The **plot** was really exciting. The **ending** was a complete surprise!
6 One **scene** made me laugh so hard that I cried!

3 Match the types of movie (a–f) with the sentences (1–6) in Activity 2.

a a comedy
b a drama
c a horror movie
d a musical
e a sci-fi movie
f a thriller

4 Listen to two friends talking about a movie. Choose the correct options. 🎧 7

Name of movie: *The Way We Were / The Way Way Back*
Starring: *Steve Carell / Collette*
Release date: *2003 / 2013*
Type of movie: *animation / comedy*
Set in: *a hotel / a water park*
Plot: An unhappy *teenager / father* goes on vacation with his family and makes new friends.
Recommended? *Yes / No*

5 Listen again. Which follow-up questions in the Useful language box do you hear? 🎧 7

Useful language

Asking follow-up questions

Who's in it?

What else has he / she been in?

What's the acting like?

When did it come out?

So what's it about?

What sort of movie is it?

Who directed it?

Where is it set?

Would you recommend it?

Using Emphasis

The special effects were really disappointing.

I couldn't put it down!

The sequel was even better!

Outdoor movie theater in the castle courtyard, Esslingen am Neckar, Germany

6 Match the questions you heard in Activity 5 with these answers about a different movie. Do you know the movie?

1 It's a sci-fi movie. It's the first in a series of four.
2 It was released in 2012.
3 She played one of the main characters in *X-Men: Apocalypse*.
4 It tells the story of a young woman who fights for her life in a competition.
5 In a country of the future called Panem.
6 It stars Jennifer Lawrence.

7 Work in pairs.

Student A: Tell Student B about a movie you've seen.
Student B: Ask follow-up questions to find out more.

A *I watched a great movie last night… Have you seen it?*

WRITING A review

8 Are the expressions in the Useful language box used to talk about books, movies, or both?

9 Read the review on page 149. How many stars does the writer give the novel?

10 Read the review again. List the book's good points and the reviewer's criticisms.

11 **WRITING SKILL** Emphasis

a Which sentence emphasizes more the way the person feels about the plot?
1 I really loved the plot.   **2** What I really loved was the plot.

b Find three more sentences in the review that add emphasis.

c Complete these sentences so that they are true for the movie you talked about in Activity 7.
1 One thing that I loved about the movie was…
2 What I found disappointing was…
3 What made me really think was…

12 Choose a movie or a book you know. Write a review that includes:

- introductory sentences that give basic information about the book or movie.
- a short description of the plot.
- the good and bad things about it.
- your opinion and emotional response to it.
- a sentence that tells the reader to read or watch it (or not).

13 Read other students' reviews. Which books or movies would you like to read / see?

Talking about movies and books

It stars…
It's set in…
It tells the story of… / It's about…
It was directed by…
It was released in…
It came out in…
It was published in…
The main character is…
The soundtrack was amazing.
The special effects were a little disappointing.
The sequel is even better / not as good.
It's a moving / inspiring / great / exciting / funny story.
I'd definitely recommend it.
I couldn't put it down.
It made me feel…
Unfortunately, I thought it was…

2 Enjoy the Ride

Students in Colombia cross the Rio Negro canyon using cables to get to school.

2A Getting from A to B

VOCABULARY Travel

1 MY PERSPECTIVE

Work in pairs. Discuss the questions.

1 What does this quote mean to you?

"Travel is the only thing you buy that makes you richer."

2 What are the benefits of travel? Do you want to be a traveler? Why?
3 Look at the photo and read the caption. Would you like to go to school like this? Why do you think the children don't have a safer way of traveling? How do you get to school?

2 Work in pairs. Discuss the questions.

1 How many ways of getting around can you think of? Make a list.
  go on your skateboard, take the bus…

2 Look at your list. Which form of transportation is the:

  • cheapest?   • fastest?   • most relaxing/stressful?

3 Complete the sentences with these pairs of words.

cruise + excursion	commute + ride	expedition + voyage
flight + destination	ride + route	trip + backpacking

1 When my parents _____ by car, they give me a _____ to school.
2 RY5608—that isn't our _____ . It's flying to the same _____ but it's a different airline.
3 Some passengers on the _____ stayed on the ship, but we went on an _____ around the old port.
4 We had an amazing _____ ! I'm glad we were _____ and didn't stay in a hotel. We saw more of the outdoors that way.
5 When I went for a bike _____ yesterday, I took a different _____ . I get bored going the same way all the time.
6 The _____ to the Antarctic lasted a year. After a difficult month-long sea _____ , the scientists started their research.

4 Cross out the item in each list that does **not** collocate with the verb(s).

1 **catch/miss** my bus, my train, ~~my car~~
2 **get** home, lost, school, from A to B
3 **get on/off** the bus, the car, the plane
4 **get to know** your way around, a trip
5 **get to** work, home, school
6 **go for** a trip, a bike ride, a drive
7 **go on** a flight, a journey, a travel
8 **take** a taxi, an hour, two miles

5 Complete the sentences with a word from Activity 3 or 4. Then finish them so they are true for you.

1 My _____ to school takes…
2 The best way for visitors to _____ to know my city is by…
3 If I _____ public transportation, I prefer to travel by… because…
4 The last long trip I _____ on was to…
5 If I could take a _____ anywhere, I'd choose… as my destination.

LISTENING

6 Listen to three people describe how they go to school. Complete the table. 🎧 **8**

	Where they live	How they travel	Time / distance they travel	What they do on the way
1 Santiago Muñoz				
2 Chosing	*The Himalayas*			
3 Daisy Mora				

7 Listen again. Who (Santiago, Chosing, or Daisy): 🎧 **8**

1 travels the farthest?
2 doesn't take long to get to school?
3 stays at school for a long time?
4 gets up early to get to school on time?
5 takes public transportation to get to school?
6 travels with a parent?
7 has a dangerous trip to school? (2 people)
8 is going to have an easier way to get to school soon?

GRAMMAR Adjectives ending in *-ed* and *-ing*

8 Read the sentences in the Grammar box. Underline the adjectives. Which adjectives describe the trips? Which adjectives describe how the people feel?

> ### Adjectives ending in *-ed* and *-ing*
>
> **a** *You might think it takes you a long time to get to school, but Santiago Muñoz has one of the most exhausting school commutes in the world… He's excited about having more time to spend with friends and getting more sleep!*
>
> **b** *They don't talk much, but it is never boring. It takes them six days and at the end they are exhausted.*
>
> **c** *For some students living along the Rio Negro, their trip to school is absolutely terrifying… If Daisy is scared, she doesn't show it!*

Check page 130 for more information and practice.

9 Choose the correct option to complete the sentences.

Participial adjectives are adjectives that are made from verbs. They usually end in *-ing* or *-ed*.

1 Adjectives that describe how a person feels end in *-ing* / *-ed*.
2 Adjectives that describe the thing that makes you feel an emotion end in *-ing* / *-ed*.

Students on the train in Kyoto, Japan

10 Match the *-ed* adjectives (1–8) with their meanings (a–h). Then complete *-ing* adjectives.

-ed adjective	meaning	-ing adjective
1 terrified	e	terrifying
2 exhausted		
3 annoyed		
4 disappointed		
5 depressed		
6 shocked		
7 worried		
8 confused		

a surprised because of something bad that happened suddenly
b unhappy and a little angry about something
c unhappy because something was not as good as you hoped or because something did not happen
d thinking about bad things that might happen
e very scared
f very sad and without hope
g unable to think clearly about or understand something
h very tired

11 Choose the correct option. Then work in pairs and tell your partner about one or two experiences you have had.

1 a destination you were looking forward to seeing but were a little *disappointed / disappointing* about when you got there

I was excited about a school excursion to the History Museum, but it was really boring. Everyone was really disappointed.

2 a *terrified / terrifying* experience you've had on a car trip
3 a day when you did so much walking that you were completely *exhausted / exhausting* at the end
4 the longest and most *bored / boring* trip you've ever been on
5 a trip when you were very *worried / worrying* that you wouldn't get to the destination on time
6 an *annoyed / annoying* delay on public transportation that you really didn't need
7 a *depressed / depressing* trip somewhere when you had a horrible time
8 an expedition that you'd be very *excited / exciting* to go on

12 Work in groups. Share your stories from Activity 11. Whose experiences have been the most exciting / boring / exhausting / frightening / disappointing?

URBEXERS LIFE ON THE EDGE OF THE CITY

Standing on the Forth Bridge, Scotland

VOCABULARY BUILDING Compound nouns

1 What places do visitors to your city or a city near you usually visit?

2 Use words in columns A and B to make compound nouns. Check the spelling in a dictionary.

A		**B**	
1	sight	**a**	site
2	a walking	**b**	station
3	a subway	**c**	transportation
4	a shopping	**d**	seeing
5	a construction	**e**	mall
6	public	**f**	tour
7	urban	**g**	roads
8	rail	**h**	top
9	a sky	**i**	park
10	a roof	**j**	exploration
11	an amusement	**k**	scraper
12	a view	**l**	point

3 Listen and check your answers to Activity 2. Underline the stressed part of each compound noun. Is there a general rule about where the stress is? 🎧 **9**

4 Which of the compound nouns in Activity 2 are things visitors might do, use, or visit? Which are buildings? Which are places the public doesn't usually go?

5 Use the compound nouns in Activity 2 to make eight sentences about your town or city.

READING

6 You are going to read an article about urban explorers (urbexers). Write three questions you'd like to find out about them. Does the article answer your questions?

7 Choose the correct ending to complete the sentences.

1 The article begins by talking about options for tourists because:
   a they are good examples of urban exploration.
   b they are very different from what urbexers do.
   c the writer wants to recommend some ways of exploring cities.

2 The places that urban explorers visit are:
   a always underground.
   b not used anymore.
   c not usually attractive to many people.

How do you get to know a city you've never been to before? For most people, the typical tourist options are enough. Take a bus tour to see the sights or, if you're feeling energetic, consider a walking tour. To get a taste of city life, use public transportation.

But there are people who want more than the standard tourist options. They are *urbexers*—urban explorers. They're interested in discovering parts of the city we normally see as less beautiful, the places tourists are not supposed to see: ghost subway stations that have been closed for years, shopping malls and amusement parks at night, abandoned* factories, construction sites, tunnels, and railroads. It's not for everybody. You can't be scared of heights or small spaces and you have to be willing to take risks.

Bradley Garrett is one of them. Urbexers don't follow the same routes as everyone else: "I've been to Paris six times and I've seen more of the city underground than I have above ground," he says. "If somebody asked me for a good restaurant, I'd have no idea."

It wasn't until Bradley and his urbexer friends had climbed to the top of London's tallest skyscraper, the Shard, and had managed to visit all of the city's fourteen abandoned subway stations that the police stopped them from exploring as a group. Bradley was studying urbexers for a book he was writing when they had to stop.

Bradley's best experience as an urbexer was in Chicago with friends when they climbed the Legacy Tower, a 72-story skyscraper. "We were sitting on a rooftop looking up at this building when someone suggested we try to get up. So we walked in and just got in the elevator after some residents had opened the door. When we made it up to the roof, it was the most incredible view I've ever seen."

Why do urbexers do it? Many enjoy the excitement of putting themselves in danger. Some enjoy the feeling they get from being alone in abandoned places. "I feel I'm the only person in the world," says Zhao Yang, a 29-year-old Chinese urbexer who explores places where people used to work, like old industrial sites and abandoned hospitals. Like many urbexers, Zhao is an avid photographer who takes his smartphone to record what he sees, and, like many, he also writes a blog about his experiences, but he prefers to explore alone.

This can be dangerous, of course, but if you're interested in exploring city spaces, there are safe ways of doing it. For example, it's easy to look at a map, identify an area that is new to you, and go there. Another way is to try to get lost in your own town. Or you could just set off for a walk without planning your route. Who knows what you might find!

abandoned *left; no longer used*

---

3 Bradley Garrett:
  a knows Paris very well.
  b doesn't like high places.
  c wouldn't be a very good guide for traditional tourists.

4 Bradley and his friends:
  a weren't allowed to go to London's abandoned underground stations.
  b can't explore together anymore.
  c didn't climb the Shard.

5 Garrett's trip to the top of the Legacy Tower was:
  a easy. **b** lonely. **c** well planned.

6 Zhao Yang:
  a investigates abandoned factories.
  b explores with friends.
  c doesn't want to tell anyone about his experiences.

7 The article ends by:
  a describing more activities that urban explorers do.
  b recommending other ways of exploring cities.
  c explaining the health benefits of urban exploration.

CRITICAL THINKING Selecting information

Writers have to think about the kind of information that will interest their readers.

8 Read the Critical Thinking box. Which questions does the article answer about urbexers and urban exploration?

  1 Does urban exploration happen all over the world?
  2 How long have people been exploring in this way?
  3 How many people do it?
  4 If I want to explore my local urban area, what can I do?
  5 Is the word "urbexer" in the dictionary?
  6 What are some of the stories that urbexers have?
  7 Why is urban exploration attractive to some people?
  8 What kind of places do urbexers visit?
  9 What personal qualities do urbexers need?

9 Work in groups. Discuss the questions.

  1 Did the article answer all your questions in Activity 6?
  2 What other information would you like to learn?
  3 How could you find out the answers to the questions that weren't answered?

10 Do you think the author did a good job? Did he choose the information that was interesting to you?

Sydney Opera House and the city, Australia

2C Sydney on $20

GRAMMAR Narrative forms

1 Work in pairs. Can you remember Bradley Garrett's adventure at the Legacy Tower? Retell the story using these words.

rooftop	the elevator	view

2 Check your ideas in Activity 1 with the article on page 25.

3 Choose the correct options to complete the sentences in the Grammar box.

Narrative forms

a *It wasn't until Bradley and his friends **had climbed / were climbing** to the top of the Shard and **used to manage / had managed** to visit all of the city's abandoned underground stations that the police **stopped / were stopping** them from exploring as a group.*

b *Bradley **studied / was studying** urbexers for a book he **wrote / was writing** when they had to stop.*

c *"We **had sat / were sitting** on a rooftop when someone **suggested / used to suggest** we try to get up the Legacy Tower. So we **walked / were walking** in and just **had gotten / got** in the elevator after some residents **had opened / were opening** the door."*

d *Zhao Yang explores places where people **were working / used to work**, like old industrial sites and abandoned hospitals.*

Check page 130 for more information and practice.

4 Read the sentences in the Grammar box and complete these rules with *simple past, past continuous, past perfect,* or *used to*.

When we tell stories or talk about actions or events in the past:

1 we use the _____ to describe an incomplete action or event when another action happened. The actions are often connected with *when, while,* or *as.* We also use it to give background information. It is not used with stative verbs (*know, love,* etc.).

2 we usually use the _____ to describe completed actions in the past. If actions happen one after another, we use this tense.

3 we use the _____ to emphasize that one past action finished before another past action. The actions are often connected with *after, before,* and *already.*

4 we usually use _____ to talk about situations, habits, and routines that were true in the past but are not true anymore.

5 Read about freeganism. What are the advantages of living like this? Would you like to live like this? What are the disadvantages?

Freeganism is a way of living and traveling that costs almost nothing. It's simply using your skills so you don't have to pay for things. People who practice freeganism are called "freegans," and they try to buy as little as possible because they want to save money and reduce their impact on the environment. They choose to eat food that has been thrown away and find alternatives to sleeping in hotels and paying for transportation when they travel.

6 Becky Khalil was a freegan in Australia for some time. Choose the correct option to complete what she says about traveling as a freegan in Sydney.

I (1) *used to think / was thinking* that Australia was a really expensive place, and the first time I (2) *went / had gone there*, I worked to pay for my living expenses. But while I (3) *had stayed / was staying* in Australia last time, I (4) *found / used to find* another way to live. I (5) *used to use / had already used* my working visa on my first trip, so I couldn't get a job this time. To make things worse, someone (6) *was stealing / had stolen* all my money during a train ride. So I (7) *became / had become* a freegan. Before, I (8) *used to buy / was buying* too much food and threw a lot of it away, but this time I (9) *had eaten / ate* leftover food from friends and shops, like day-old bread. I (10) *didn't spend / hadn't spent* anything on accommodations, less than $100 on travel, and less than $20 on food for six weeks!

7 Complete the rest of Becky's story with the best form of the verbs.

Most of the time, friends of mine (1) _____ (let) me sleep on their couches, but before my trip I (2) _____ (contact) a company that organizes "house-sitting" jobs, so sometimes I took care of houses when the owners were on vacation. To save money on bus fares, I (3) _____ (get) rides with people I knew, and while I (4) _____ (travel) around the country, I usually decided to camp. Once I went to sleep under the stars because I (5) _____ (be) too tired to put my tent up. Finding cheap or free food was much easier than I (6) _____ (expect) it to be. Even in winter, I enjoyed it because I (7) _____ (live) with other freegans and we (8) _____ (become) friends and helped each other. At the end of each day, stores gave us anything they (9) _____ (not sell). Believe it or not, we (10) _____ (eat) extremely well!

8 PRONUNCIATION *Used to*

Listen to these sentences. How is *used to* pronounced? Practice reading the sentences. 🎧 **11**

1 Our grandparents never used to throw their food away.
2 Did people use to travel a lot when your parents were young?
3 **A** Do you enjoy traveling by plane?
  B I used to, but not anymore.

9 Complete the sentences in your own words. Then work in pairs and compare your sentences.

1 Before this lesson I didn't know…
2 When I was younger, I used to…
3 I didn't use to… (but I do now).
4 The last time I… was when…
5 I didn't spend any money when…
6 I bought… while I was…

10 Prepare notes about a trip you have taken that was memorable in some way. Use these questions to help you plan what you are going to say.

- Where did you go? Did you use to go to the same destination regularly, or was this the first time?
- How did you travel?
- When did you make the trip?
- Who did you go with?
- What memorable things happened? What were you doing when they happened?
- How did you feel about the trip in general?

11 CHOOSE Choose one of the following activities.

1 Work in pairs. Tell your stories to each other. Ask each other questions to find out more.
2 Present your story to the class.
3 Write your story. Read each other's stories and choose your favorite.

> ❝ If you think that adventure is dangerous, try routine. It's deadly. ❞

DANIELE QUERCIA

Read about Daniele Quercia and get ready to watch his TED Talk. ▶ 2.0

AUTHENTIC LISTENING SKILLS

Understanding accents

When you travel abroad or listen to people on TV and the internet, you will hear foreign and regional accents in English. It's helpful to practice listening to different accents so you can enjoy listening to people from all over the world.

1 Listen to the beginning of the TED Talk, at first said by a native English speaker and then by Daniele Quercia, a native Italian speaker. Compare the pronunciation of the underlined sounds. 🎧 12

"I <u>h</u>ave a confession to make. As a scientist and engineer, I've focus<u>ed</u> on efficiency for many years."

2 How do you say these sentences? Listen to Daniele and a native speaker to compare. 🎧 13

1 I lived in Boston and worked in Cambridge.
2 I teamed up with Luca and Rossano.
3 They also recalled how some paths smelled and sounded.

3 MY PERSPECTIVE

Which of these statements do you agree with? Why?

1 Learners should try to sound like native speakers of English.
2 Sometimes it's easier to understand other non-native speakers of English than native speakers.
3 Your foreign accent in English is an important part of your identity, so be proud of it.

WATCH

4 What do you usually see on your way to school? What can you hear? What can you smell?

5 Watch Part 1 of the talk. Answer the questions. ▶ 2.1

1 What journey helped Daniele see that travel isn't just about efficiency?
   a moving from Boston to Barcelona
   b a bicycle race he took part in
   c his commute to work

2 How was the new route different from the old one?
   a It went along Massachusetts Avenue.
   b It had less traffic.
   c It was shorter and quicker.

3 What does Daniele say about mapping apps?
   a They encourage people to explore more.
   b They give you too many choices about which way to travel.
   c They are very similar to computer games.

6 Watch Part 2 of the talk. Choose the correct option to complete each sentence. ▶ 2.2

1 Daniele changed his research to look more at how people *experience / get around* the city.
2 The red path on the map is the *shortest / most enjoyable* one.
3 They collected data by asking people to *play a game / take a test*.
4 The first map that they designed was of *Boston / London*.

TEDTALKS

5 Their research now is in developing maps based on smell, sound, and *memories / sights.*

6 Their goal is to encourage people to take *the best path / many paths* through the city.

7 VOCABULARY IN CONTEXT

a Watch the clips from the TED Talk. Choose the correct meaning of the words and phrases. ▶ 2.3

b Think of examples of the following things. Then work in pairs and compare your examples.

1 a place that's *surrounded by* nature
2 a time when you felt *shame*
3 somewhere that only has a *handful of* stores
4 a situation that makes you feel *shy*
5 a time you *teamed up with* someone

CHALLENGE

Work in pairs. Daniele asks, "What if we had a mapping tool that would return the most enjoyable routes based… on smell, sound, and memories?" Think of places near where you live that:

- have an interesting smell.
- make you think of an interesting sound.
- remind you of a memory.

Tell your partner about them.

---

8 Work in groups. Discuss the questions.

1 How does Daniele think that his mapping app will make people's lives better?

2 Daniele's London map shows routes that are short, happy, beautiful, and quiet. Which kind of route would you prefer to use to get around your city? Why?

3 Why might these people be interested in using this kind of mapping app? Give reasons for each one.

- a tourist spending a week in a new city
- a courier who delivers letters and packages quickly for companies by bicycle
- a student
- a taxi driver

4 Would you like to have this mapping app on your smartphone? Why?

9 Work in pairs. Look at a map of your town or a city that you know well. Plan two one-hour walking routes.

- Route 1. This must include as many beautiful sights and interesting places as possible.
- Route 2. This must include the places most likely to interest teenagers who are visiting the city.

10 Work in groups. Compare your routes and discuss the questions.

1 As a tourist, what tour would you enjoy most? Why?
2 What other types of (guided) tours could you offer?

2E You Can't Miss It

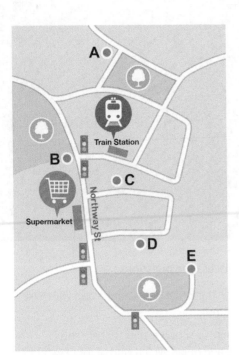

Useful language

A Asking for directions

*Excuse me. Can you tell me how to
get to…? / Do you know the
way to…?*

B Giving directions

*Go all the way up there until
you get to…*

*At the traffic lights, go straight /
turn right.*

*After 200 yards, take the first exit
off the traffic circle.*

**C Talking about landmarks
and destinations**

Go past a… on your left / right.

The train station is on your left.

**D Talking about time and
distance**

It's not very far from here.

*It's less than half a mile
from there.*

SPEAKING

1 Work in pairs. Discuss the questions.

How do you find your way when you are lost? Have you ever used a map, GPS,
or app to help you, or do you prefer to ask someone?

2 Listen to two conversations. Complete the table. 🎧 14

	Conversation 1	Conversation 2
1 Do the speakers know each other?		
2 Where do they want to get to?		
3 How are they traveling?		
4 How far is it?		
5 What will they do if they get lost?		

3 Look at the map and listen again. Match a letter from the map with each of
these places. 🎧 14

1 where the first conversation takes place   **3** the movie theater

2 the science museum   **4** Melanie's house

4 Use one word to complete the expressions. Listen again to check. 🎧 14

1 Can you _____ me? I'm trying to _____ to the museum.

2 It's a long _____ from here. About a fifteen-minute _____ .

3 Go up Northway Street for about five minutes _____ you get to the
supermarket on your left. Then take the first… no, the second _____ .

4 You can't _____ it.

5 Can you give me _____ to your house?

6 So if the station's _____ you, you'll need to turn right.

7 At the _____ of the street you'll see a movie theater in front of you.

8 _____ on Northway Street until you get to a supermarket on your right.
Just after _____ , there's a street on the left.

5 Label the sentences in Activity 4 with the correct category (A–D) from the
Useful language box.

6 Work in pairs. Ask for and give directions between places on the map.

7 Work in groups. Give directions to each other from school to destinations
around town. Listen and say what you think the destinations are.

WRITING A story

8 Work in pairs. Read the writing task below. Then tell your partner about a time
when you got lost.

Write a story that ends with the sentence: *After so many hours feeling completely
lost, I ended up just where I needed to be!*

9 Read the story on page 149. When did the writer feel uncertain?

1 talking to his cousin

2 at the bus stop

3 on the bus

4 when he got off the bus

5 on the motorcycle

6 at the boat

10 **WRITING SKILL** *just*

Match the sentences (1–5) with the meaning of *just* (a–e).

1 My cousin had just returned from an island called Koh Tao.

2 An old man pointed to a bus that was just about to leave.

3 I was just falling asleep when the driver shouted, "Koh Tao!"

4 I couldn't see the sea, just a quiet road.

5 I ended up just where I needed to be!

a only

b recently

c exactly

d almost

e very soon (*with be about to*)

11 You are going to write a story about a trip that ends with one of these three sentences. Choose your ending.

- That was one of the worst trips of my life.
- I hadn't expected to have such an exciting trip.
- Getting to school had never been so complicated.

12 Prepare to write your story.

1 Use the questions in the Writing strategies box to write the details of your story.

2 Think about the verb forms you will need to tell the story.

13 Write your story. When you have finished, share it with other people in the class. Whose stories sound like the best/worst experiences?

Writing strategies

Writing a story

Use a paragraph plan like this when you write a story:

Paragraph 1: Set the scene

Where does the story start?

Who is the story about?

When does the story take place?

Paragraphs 2 and 3: Main events

What happened?

How did you feel?

What happened next?

Paragraph 4: The end

What happened in the end?

How did you or other people feel?

What do you remember most about the events?

Koh Tao is a beautiful island in Thailand. Its name means "Turtle Island."

3 Active Lives

IN THIS UNIT, YOU...

- talk about the reasons for doing sports.
- read about how sports are saving Africa's lions.
- learn about runners.
- watch a TED Talk about swimming at the North Pole.
- write an opinion essay about sports.

Bike base jumping in Canyonlands National Park, Utah

3A Pushing the Limits

VOCABULARY Sports

1 Work in pairs. Look at the photo and read the caption. Why do people do sports like this? Have you ever done an "extreme sport"? Would you like to try one? Why?

2 Put these words into the correct category. Use a dictionary if necessary. How many more words can you add to each category?

bounce	~~climbing~~	coach	court	diving
field	gymnastics	karate	kick	net
opponent	pass	referee	rink	rope
sailing	spectator	the 100-meter dash	throw	track

Sports	People	Places	Equipment	Actions
climbing				

3 Write five sentences about sports using the words in Activity 2.

In tennis, you have to hit the ball to your opponent's side of the court.

4 Collocate these verbs with corresponding words and phrases.

achieve	beat	do	encourage	go
play	represent	score	train	win

1 a prize / a trophy / the gold medal
2 climbing / sailing / cycling
3 golf / tennis / an important role
4 gymnastics / yoga / your best
5 people to work as a team / children to exercise more
6 for the event / before the race / hard
7 your goal / your personal best / your ambition
8 your school / your country / the team
9 a goal / ten points
10 your opponent / the champion

5 Work in pairs. Read the statements. Which sport(s) are they about?

1 The field is where I met all my friends. And I **feel proud when I'm representing my team** in tournaments.
2 Being out on my boat **gives me a real sense of freedom**. It's always played an important role in my life.
3 When I'm going up a mountain, it's about **pushing my own limits**, not **winning trophies or breaking records**.
4 I'm doing it to **raise money** for a children's charity. I've been training for months, but I've still got a long way to go!
5 I want to **encourage** the younger players to have some fun on the court.
6 To be honest, I don't enjoy it much—it's pretty boring. I only do it to **stay healthy**.

6 MY PERSPECTIVE

Do you do any sports for the reasons in bold in Activity 5? Can you think of other reasons for doing sports?

Ashima Shiraishi on *Slashface*, a V13 bouldering problem in Hueco Tanks Historic Site, Texas

LISTENING

7 Look at the photo of a young climber, Ashima Shiraishi, and read the caption. What do you think the V scale measures?

8 Listen to a podcast about Ashima. Answer the questions. 🎧 **15**

1 Why does she enjoy climbing?
2 What has she achieved?

9 Listen again. Are these sentences *true* or *false*? How do you know? 🎧 **15**

1 Ashima started climbing when she was a teenager.
2 She has been a professional climber for a year.
3 She always uses ropes when she climbs.
4 She has climbed in several countries, including Japan and South Africa.
5 She is the only female athlete to successfully climb a V14 problem.
6 She is the youngest person to successfully climb a V15 problem.
7 She recently had an accident, but it hasn't stopped her from climbing.
8 She does her homework late in the evening because she has to train hard.

GRAMMAR Simple past and present perfect

10 Read the excerpts from the podcast in the Grammar box. Underline the verbs in the simple past and circle the verb in the present perfect.

Simple past and present perfect (1)

a Ashima **has traveled** to many countries looking for more and more difficult climbs.
b In 2014, she **went** to South Africa and **completed** the "Golden Shadow" problem.

11 Answer the questions about the sentences in the Grammar box.

1 Is it clear when Ashima traveled to *many countries*? Is it important here?
2 Do we know when she went to South Africa? Is it important here?
3 Which timeline illustrates sentence a? Which timeline illustrates sentence b?

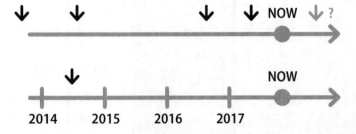

Simple past and present perfect (2)

a *Ashima discovered climbing at the age of six, and she's* **loved** *it ever since.*

b *She* **has traveled** *to many countries in her young life, looking for more and more difficult climbs.*

c *She's just* **achieved** *an even more amazing record.*

d *Earlier this year, Ashima* **climbed** *"Horizon," a V15 climb in Japan.*

e *Shortly after that, she fell and injured her back, but she* **has recovered** *and is now climbing again.*

Check page 132 for more information and practice.

12 Match the sentences in the Grammar box (a–e) above with the rules (1–5).

Simple past

The simple past is used to talk about:

1 completed actions in the past. The time is often stated, e.g., *last week*, *yesterday*, *in 2017*, etc.

Present perfect

The present perfect is used to talk about:

2 actions which started in the past and continue to the present. We often use *for* and *since* to say how long the action has continued.

3 actions in the past which are connected to a present situation.

4 past experiences, when the exact time isn't stated. Any time expression is connected to the present, e.g., *until now*, *never*, *in my life*.

5 recent actions when the exact time isn't stated. We often use *just* to emphasize that it happened very recently.

13 Choose the correct options to complete the article.

Speed climbing is a race against the clock. Climbing as a sport (1) *was / has been* around for a long time, but competition speed climbing (2) *became / has become* popular only a few years ago. Competitors try to climb a fifteen-meter wall (about 49 feet) as quickly as they can. When they reach the top, they must hit a button to stop the clock.

When the sport (3) *started / has started*, climbers (4) *used / have used* walls with different heights and holds but, since 2007, all the walls (5) *were / have been* exactly the same. The men's world record holder is Danyl Boldyrev, who (6) *broke / has broken* the record with a time of 5.6 seconds in 2014.

Competitive climbing (7) *wasn't / hasn't been* in the last Olympic Games, but the organizers of the Games (8) *just accepted / have just accepted* it as a sport for the 2020 Tokyo Olympics.

14 Put the verbs in the correct form of the simple past or present perfect to complete the conversations.

1 A (you / play) tennis recently?
  B No. I (injure) my arm in March, and I (not / play) any sports since then.
  A That's a shame. When I (see) you in the competition last year, you (be) really good.

2 A What sports (you / do) when you were younger?
  B Many different ones—soccer, volleyball, swimming. I (always / love) sports.
  A So what do you do now?
  B (I / just / start) mountain biking. That's my latest interest.

3 A (you / ever / win) a medal or a trophy?
  B Yes, several times. I (play) baseball for several years, and my team is very good.
  A Wow! I didn't know that.

4 A (you / ever / do) karate?
  B No, but I'd love to. A friend (try) it last year, and he (enjoy) it.
  A It's not something that (ever / interest) me.

5 A (you / watch) any games yet this year?
  B No, I haven't. But my dad (go) to all of them.

15 Work in pairs. Talk about your own experiences with sports. Use the questions in Activity 14 to help you, and continue the conversation.

3B Conservation through Sports

A Maasai warrior competes in the high jump event during the Maasai Olympics at the Sidai Oleng Wildlife Sanctuary, Kenya.

Can sports protect AFRICA'S LIONS?

VOCABULARY BUILDING Phrasal verbs

1 Underline the phrasal verb and its synonym.

1 More and more people are <u>taking up</u> capoeira. People often <u>start doing</u> it after seeing it on the street.
2 If you don't want to participate now, you can just watch, and join in another time.
3 Even professional athletes warm up before running. Our bodies need time to prepare for sports.
4 I wanted to keep up with the main group of runners, but it was impossible to stay with them.
5 Surprisingly, he's knocked out the second-best world athlete and could beat the world champion in the final!
6 On Sunday, Brazil takes on Germany. Can the Brazilians challenge the Germans for a place in the quarterfinals?
7 I gave up tennis in 2015. I had to stop playing because of a hand injury.
8 I don't exercise much during the week, but I work out at the gym on Sundays.

2 Complete the questions with the correct form of a phrasal verb from Activity 1.

1 Do you like to _____ sports, or do you prefer to be a spectator? Why?
2 Has your team ever _____ a better team?
3 If you could _____ a sport, what would you try? Why?
4 What sports have you _____ ? Why did you stop?
5 What's the best way to _____ before running?
6 Do you ever go to a gym to _____ ? Do you enjoy it?

3 Work in pairs. Ask and answer the questions in Activity 2.

READING

4 Read the article. Why were the Maasai Olympics started?

5 Complete the paragraphs with the topic sentences (a–f).

A **topic sentence** summarizes the main idea of the paragraph. Topic sentences are usually the first sentence of the paragraph.

a The African Wildlife Foundation got together with Maasai leaders to come up with a plan.
b The Games are not just for the men, however.
c One of Africa's most famous animals needs protection.
d Maasai tribes have been hunting lions as trophies for hundreds of years.
e Have the Games been a successful way to help conservation efforts in Kenya and Tanzania?
f Preparations for the next Games have been heating up, and everyone involved is getting excited.

16 **1** _____ . In the 1940s, there were an estimated 450,000 lions across Africa, but since then numbers have decreased dramatically, to around 20,000 today. Reasons include a loss of habitat as the human population has grown, and the trade in lion body parts. However, another threat to the lions may soon be a thing of the past.

2 _____ . In Maasai culture, killing lions has been an important tradition among the men because it shows their physical strength and skill. The Maasai also hunt lions when the lions kill their cows. Unfortunately, this has brought the lion population to dangerously low levels. Conservationists have believed for some time that the number of lion killings can be reduced without destroying the Maasai culture. But how?

3 _____ . The idea was to replace lion hunting with a sports event. The Maasai Olympics were born, and _manyattas_, or villages, from across the region were invited to join in. Since 2012, they have held three Maasai Olympics. Young men take part in six running, throwing, and jumping events, which all reflect Maasai culture. For example, the javelin competition is similar to the traditional skill of throwing a spear*, and the high jump is similar to Maasai dancing.

4 _____ . Including women in the events is very important because the women can influence the men's behavior. If the women are more aware of lion conservation, they can discourage the men from hunting. At the 2014 Games, there were two running events for women and the winners received the same prizes as the men.

5 _____ . The coaches in each _manyatta_ have already chosen their athletes for the team, and they are training hard. The competitors take their preparation very seriously. Every day they warm up before exercising in groups. Although the final is over a year away, the Games have already started, as _manyattas_ take on one another in friendly competitions before the main event.

6 _____ . A survey among Maasai men shows that attitudes have changed. Although nineteen percent of the people asked haven't even heard of the Maasai Olympics, the majority of them say that the Games have made them less interested in killing lions. And even though trophy hunting still goes on, they see sports as an effective alternative. As one of the athletes said, "We used to celebrate lion hunting, but this program has shown us a better celebration."

spear _a long, sharp stick you throw as a weapon_

6 Read the article again. Choose the correct option to complete these sentences.

1 Lion populations have become smaller because:
  a the animals have less space to live in the wild.
  b of a number of reasons.
  c the Maasai have hunted them too much.

2 Hunting:
  a is the biggest danger to the lions.
  b is how Maasai men show how brave they are.
  c has been a part of Maasai culture for a long time.

3 All of the events in the competition:
  a involve throwing.
  b are like traditional Maasai activities.
  c include all the villages.

4 Women are involved in the competition:
  a as much as the men.
  b because they asked to compete.
  c to help in the goal of reducing lion hunting.

5 The _manyattas_:
  a haven't chosen their athletes yet.
  b get all the hopeful athletes to train.
  c have already started competing.

6 The Maasai Olympics:
  a are changing the way people think.
  b have stopped the Maasai from hunting lions.
  c are less interesting to the Maasai than killing lions.

CRITICAL THINKING   A balanced view

It is important to give both sides of an argument, even if the writer wants to persuade readers that one opinion is correct. Including points that support the opposite argument shows that the writer has thought about them and makes the argument more persuasive.

7 Does the writer give a balanced view of the Maasai Games? Underline sentences that support your answer.

8 Work in pairs. Read the statements (1–5). Do you agree or disagree? Why? Try to present a balanced view.

  1 People can learn important life skills by playing sports.
  2 Sports always help people feel better about themselves.
  3 Sports are a good way to help people who don't have much money or education to achieve their ambitions.
  4 Sports aren't about winning. They're about participating and doing your best.
  5 Athletes earn too much money.

9 Work in groups. Discuss the statements in Activity 8.

Kenyan Eliud Kipchoge competes in the 2016 Rio Olympics marathon.

3C Marathon Men and Women

GRAMMAR Present perfect and present perfect continuous

1 Read the sentences in the Grammar box. Underline examples of the present perfect. Circle examples of the present perfect continuous.

Present perfect and present perfect continuous

a *Maasai tribes* **have been hunting** *lions as trophies for hundreds of years.*

b *Since the 1940s, numbers* **have decreased** *dramatically, to around 20,000 today.*

c *Preparations for the next Games* **have been heating up**, *and everyone involved is getting excited.*

d *The coaches in each manyatta* **have** *already* **chosen** *their athletes for the team.*

e **Have** *the Games* **been** *a successful way to help conservation efforts in Kenya and Tanzania?*

Check page 132 for more information and practice.

2 Match the sentences in the Grammar box with the rules (1–5).

The present perfect:

1 emphasizes the fact that an action is complete.
Sentence _____

2 emphasizes the present result of the action, i.e., *How many? / How much? / How often?*
Sentence _____

3 is used with stative verbs, e.g., *want, know, believe, be.*
Sentence _____

The present perfect continuous:

4 emphasizes the fact that an action is incomplete.
Sentence _____

5 emphasizes the duration of an action, i.e., *How long?*
Sentence _____

3 Choose the correct options to complete the paragraph about Kenyan marathon runners.

Kenyans know how to run fast. Kenyan men (1) *have run / have been running* seven of the ten fastest marathons in history. It's a similar story for the women: Jemima Sumgong has finally (2) *given / been giving* Kenya its first Olympic gold in the marathon, and Kenyan women hold more of the records than anyone else. So how long has the title of world long-distance champions (3) *belonged / been belonging* to Kenya? Interestingly, although the country (4) *has sent / has been sending* athletes to competitions, such as the Olympics, since 1956, it (5) *hasn't won / hasn't been winning* races for all of that time. So what have they (6) *done / been doing* more recently to make them so good? Well, about 40 years ago, training camps started in small towns in the mountains, like Iten, and they (7) *have become / have been becoming* major centers for sports. Since then, this area (8) *has created / has been creating* more world champions than anywhere else in the world.

4 Complete the questions about Catherine Ndereba.

RUNNER PROFILE

CATHERINE NDEREBA

Many people believe that Catherine Ndereba, or "Catherine the Great," is the greatest female marathon runner ever.

1 how long / Catherine / run?
She started when she was just a girl.

2 she / always / love running?
Yes, she has had a passion for it since she was in school.

3 how many marathons / she / win?
Many! She won the Boston Marathon four times between 2000 and 2005.

4 she / win / any Olympic medals?
Yes. She's never won gold, but she came second in the marathon in 2004 and 2008.

5 what / she / do / recently?
Since retiring in 2014, she's been helping to train young Kenyan runners.

6 how far / she / run / this week?
Only about 50 kilometers (31 miles)—much less than when she was competing.

5 Complete the interview with these time expressions. Then listen and check your answers. 🎧 **17**

already	ever	for	just
never	since	since	yet

A José, you've (1) _____ arrived here in Kenya, haven't you?

B Yes, I've only been here (2) _____ four days.

A Have you (3) _____ been to Kenya before? Why have you come?

B I've (4) _____ been here before. I've loved running (5) _____ I was a boy, and I've been competing for a couple of years. But I'm not improving. I haven't won any races (6) _____ this year.

A And you're hoping that training here will help?

B Exactly. A running friend of mine has (7) _____ been here twice to train and he's been a lot faster (8) _____ then.

6 PRONUNCIATION *For*

a Listen to the sentences (a–c). Notice how *for* is pronounced. 🎧 **18**

   a Catherine has been competing for 21 years.
   b I've only been here for four days.
   c I've been competing for a couple of years.

b Practice saying these sentences. Pay attention to the pronunciation of *for*. Then listen and check. 🎧 **19**
   1 I've only been here for a week.
   2 You've been playing that game for too long.
   3 He's been getting ready to go out for 40 minutes.
   4 We've had this car for over ten years.
   5 I've been learning English for a long time.

7 CHOOSE

Choose one of the following activities.

1 Work in pairs. Interview each other about sports and hobbies that you enjoy. Use the questions below and any others you can think of.
   1 What is one hobby or sport you enjoy?
   2 How long have you been doing it?
   3 Have you taken part in any competitions?
   4 Have you been training for any competitions recently?
   5 What are the secrets to doing your sport or hobby well?

2 Write about your sport or hobby for a class blog. Use the questions above to give you ideas.

3 Find out about an athlete you admire and write a short profile about him or her.

3D How I Swam the North Pole

" ...the paradox is that you're in freezing cold water, but actually you're on fire. "

LEWIS PUGH

Read about Lewis Pugh and get ready to watch his TED Talk. ▶ **3.0**

AUTHENTIC LISTENING SKILLS

Signposts

Signposts are words and expressions that speakers use to help the listener understand where the argument is going: what they are going to say next or what they have just said. For example: *I'm going to tell you about…*, *The main thing is…*, *First of all…*, *Let's finish by looking at…*.

1 Read the Authentic Listening Skills box. Then listen to these excerpts from the TED Talk. Underline the signposts. 🎧 **20**

1 Today I want to talk to you about swimming across the North Pole, across the most northern place in the whole world.
2 And the message was very clear: climate change is for real, and we need to do something about it. And we need to do something about it right now.
3 But the most important thing was to train my mind to prepare myself for what was going to happen.

2 Listen to four more excerpts from the talk. Complete each signpost with one word. 🎧 **21**

1 I'd just like to end by just _____ this: it took me four months…
2 And I say to them, I think we need to do three _____ . The first…
3 The _____ thing we need to do is…
4 But the most _____ thing we must do is…

WATCH

3 Work in pairs. Discuss the questions.

1 Does it take you a long time to get into the ocean or a swimming pool?
2 Do you prefer swimming in indoor swimming pools, lakes, or the ocean? Why?
3 Would you describe yourself as a confident or strong swimmer? What's the farthest you've ever swum?

4 Watch Part 1 of the talk. Match the numbers (1–8) with the reasons we hear about them (a–h). ▶ **3.1**

1	23%	5	-1.7°
2	27°	6	hundreds
3	5°	7	1
4	0°	8	5

a the number of people in Lewis's team who went with him to the North Pole
b the number of times Lewis had imagined swimming across the North Pole
c the number of years Lewis trained for the swim
d the amount of Arctic sea ice that melted in the two years before the swim
e the temperature of an indoor swimming pool
f the temperature of water when it freezes
g the temperature of the sea at the North Pole
h the temperature of the sea when the Titanic sank

5 Watch Part 2 of the talk. It describes Lewis's practice swim. Are these sentences *true* or *false*? How do you know? ▶ 3.2

1 He felt cold in the water.
2 He got out of the water after five minutes.
3 His fingers were bigger than normal when he got out of the water.
4 He was less worried about swimming for twenty minutes after doing the practice swim.
5 David was confident that Lewis could do the swim.

6 Watch Part 3 of the talk. Choose the correct option to complete each sentence. ▶ 3.3

1 Lewis believes that we need to *break the problem of climate change into smaller parts / look at climate change as one problem*.
2 Even children in poor countries *have an effect on climate change / understand climate change*.
3 Lewis *tells / asks* us what decisions we need to make to create a sustainable world.

7 VOCABULARY IN CONTEXT

a Watch the clips from the TED Talk. Choose the correct meaning of the words and phrases. ▶ 3.4

b Think of an example of these things. Then compare your examples in pairs.
 • somewhere you can swim in *fresh water*
 • a time you wore a special *costume* or suit
 • someone who can *barely* swim
 • a time you had a *swollen* ankle or wrist
 • something you *believe in* strongly

8 Read the comments. Which are in favor of Lewis Pugh's swim? Which are against it?*

1 "Lewis Pugh was very lucky that he didn't die. Nothing is worth risking your life like that."
2 "Swimming at the North Pole was a powerful way of showing people the effect of climate change."
3 "The effects of climate change in the Arctic were already very well known before he did his swim."
4 "The journey to the North Pole was long and expensive, and probably wasn't good for the environment. Wasn't there an easier way to raise awareness?"
5 "The personal story of his training and his fears and difficulties make the message about climate change more memorable and real."

*These comments were created for this activity.

9 Work in pairs. Discuss the comments. Which do you agree with most? Why?

10 Work in pairs. Discuss the questions.

1 What do you think we can do about climate change?
2 What do you already do about climate change?

CHALLENGE

Work in groups. Choose another important issue. Use these questions to plan a sporting event to raise awareness of it.

1 What issue is important to you as a group?
2 What sport will you use to raise awareness?
3 Where will you hold the event?
4 How will you advertise it?

3E School Sports

WRITING An opinion essay

1 Work in pairs. Discuss the questions.

1 How many hours a week do you play sports in school?
2 Does a break for sports help you focus on other subjects?
3 Are sports mandatory for high school students in your country?
4 Would you like to do more or fewer sports in school? Why?

2 Read the essay topic below. Which questions (1–5) do you have to answer?

"Gym should be a mandatory subject at school, with the same importance as other subjects like Math and English." Do you agree or disagree with this statement?

1 How many countries have mandatory sports in school?
2 Are sports as important as Math and English?
3 What kind of sports do most students enjoy?
4 Do schools have enough space for students to play sports?
5 Why are sports and exercise important for young people?

3 Read the essay on page 150. Are the questions you selected in Activity 2 answered?

4 Work in pairs. Read the essay again. Discuss the questions.

1 What reasons does the writer give to support the argument? Underline them.
2 What arguments does the writer give with the opposite view? Circle them.
3 Which points do you agree with most and least?
4 Can you think of any other arguments for or against the writer's opinion?

5 **WRITING SKILL** Giving your opinion

a Read the statements. What do you think? Use the Useful language box and make notes about your opinions on two or three of the statements.

1 The government should stop people from doing dangerous sports like boxing.
2 There are more disadvantages than advantages for a country when it holds international sporting events like the Olympic Games.
3 There are good reasons why some professional athletes make more money than doctors, teachers, and nurses.
4 It is better to encourage children to practice noncompetitive sports (e.g., yoga) than to play competitive sports.
5 The world of sports is a better place these days because of all the money that has come into it from business and advertising.
6 Young people often see professional athletes as heroes. Some people think that those athletes have a responsibility to be good role models.

b **MY PERSPECTIVE**

Work in groups. Compare your opinions about the statements in Activity 5a.

Useful language

Giving your opinion

Personally, I think that…
I strongly believe that…
I do not think that…
Of course,…
There is no question that…
I would say that…
It's true that…
In my opinion,…
In my view,…

---

6 Choose one of the statements in Activity 5a and write an essay giving your opinion. Think about the questions you must answer. Make sure each paragraph has a topic sentence. Write about 150 words.

Paragraph 1 Introduce the topic by describing the situation and clearly stating your opinion.

Paragraph 2 Give at least two points that support your opinion.

Paragraph 3 Give one or two points against your opinion.

Paragraph 4 Summarize the main points and give your opinion again.

7 Read another student's essay. Is his or her opinion clear? Do you agree with it?

SPEAKING

8 Listen to a conversation between three friends. Which statement from Activity 5a are they discussing? 🎧 **22**

9 Listen again. Which of the expressions in the Useful language box do you hear? 🎧 **22**

10 Read about a competition. Which three sports would you like your school to win? Why?

Your school has entered a competition to win modern equipment and new facilities for **three** sports. Winners can develop existing sports at the school, or choose equipment for new sports. The school with the best argument for its choice of sports will win. Each school can only send one proposal.

11 Work in pairs. Discuss your choice of sports with your partner. Decide on three sports you would like to propose and the reasons why.

12 Work with another pair. Decide on the three sports you would all like to propose. Present your proposal to the class.

Useful language
Agreeing
I totally agree with you.
That's true.
That's a good point.
He's right about that.
He's got a good point.
You're not wrong there.
Disagreeing
Yes, but…
I'm not sure I agree.
Maybe, but…
I agree up to a point, but…
I see what you're saying, but…
I understand what you mean, it's just…

4 Food

IN THIS UNIT, YOU...

- talk about food and cooking.
- read about Filipino street food.
- learn why you might start eating insects.
- watch a TED Talk about becoming a weekday vegetarian.
- write a social media update.

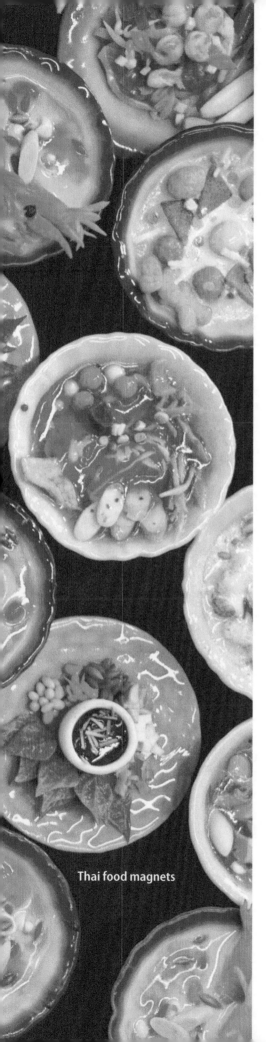

Thai food magnets

4A Learning to Cook

VOCABULARY Describing food

1 In pairs, find a dish or food in the photo, or suggest one that:

1 looks **delicious**.
2 you think probably tastes **disgusting**.
3 looks like **junk food**.
4 is very **unhealthy**.
5 contains lots of **vitamins**.
6 would make good **fast food**.
7 is made from **raw** ingredients.
8 is highly **processed** food.
9 has a **well-balanced** mixture of ingredients.
10 is often **steamed**.
11 would be suitable for **a vegetarian.**
12 contains **wheat.**

2 Find a word in bold in Activity 1 that is an opposite of:

1 natural.   3 a meat-eater.   5 cooked.
2 fried.   4 delicious.

3 What's the difference between:

1 *fresh* vegetables and *raw* vegetables?
2 *fast* food and *junk* food?
3 *cooked* food and *processed* food?
4 *boiled* vegetables and *steamed* vegetables?
5 a *strong* flavor and a *spicy* flavor?

4 Think of an example for each category below. Then compare your ideas with a partner. How similar were your answers?

I love having a hamburger and French fries sometimes. I probably have that once or twice a month.

1 a type of junk food you think is delicious
2 an ingredient that contains lots of vitamin C
3 food from your country that people from other countries might find disgusting
4 a dish that contains raw meat or fish
5 a type of processed food that is popular in your country
6 a well-balanced meal that you know how to cook
7 a type of fast food that is suitable for vegetarians
8 something containing wheat that you'd enjoy right now

5 MY PERSPECTIVE

1 Which of these "bad habits" annoy you most? Which are the most unacceptable where you live?
   • talking with your mouth full
   • being a noisy eater
   • never offering to do the dishes
   • not finishing your main course, but eating dessert
   • talking about your healthy diet all the time
   • eating while you're shopping in the supermarket

2 Are there any other bad habits that annoy you?

A robot created by Moley Robotics cooks crab soup.

LISTENING

6 Listen to a podcast about food. Do the two speakers agree about cooking in schools? 🎧 23

7 Listen again. Which speaker, Terry (T) or Mali (M): 🎧 23

1 is going to cook after the show?
2 will do the dishes today?
3 says that the secret to being a good cook is to start young?
4 says students are going to have cooking classes?
5 believes that schools have more important things to focus on than cooking?
6 says that school is a good place to teach children about healthy food?
7 plans to learn to cook?
8 has a brother who cooks?

8 Work in pairs. Discuss the questions.

1 Is cooking a required school subject in your country?
2 What dishes can you cook?

GRAMMAR Future plans, intentions, and arrangements

9 Look at the Grammar box. Match the future uses (1–7) with the sentences from the Grammar box (a–g).

1 decisions that we make at the moment of speaking
2 arrangements between people
3 hopes, expectations, beliefs, and plans
4 plans and intentions
5 ideas that are only possible, not certain
6 after *if* and time expressions like *when*, *until*, *after*, and *as soon as*
7 future scheduled events

---

will, may/might, going to, present continuous, simple present

a *OK, I'll do the dishes if you want.*

b *I think children will learn some simple dishes at about eight years old.*

c *Children should learn about basic food preparation before they leave school.*

d *They may teach them about the dangers of a poor diet in those lessons, too.*

e *I've recently decided I'm going to learn one new recipe each week.*

f *My brother's showing me how to make vegetable lasagna at his house tomorrow.*

g *Next week, the podcast goes out at the same time and it's all about eating raw food.*

Check page 134 for more information and practice.

10 Match the forms (a–e) with the future uses (1–7) in Activity 9.

a *going to*
b *may/might*
c present continuous
d simple present
e *will/won't*

11 Choose the correct option.

According to a recent survey, 60% of today's 18- to 25-year-olds in Britain are leaving home without being able to cook five simple recipes.

Ana I don't want that to be me, because I think home cooking means a healthier diet, so (1) *I'm going to / I may* learn. My friend's aunt is a chef, and she's agreed to teach me. My lessons (2) *start / will start* next Thursday. She says she (3) *teaches / might teach* me to make spaghetti Bolognese, but (4) *I'll / I might* probably ask her if we can do something vegetarian because I don't like touching raw meat.

Fumio I've never cooked in my life, and I'm never (5) *cooking / going to cook*, either. (6) *I'm moving / I'll move* in with friends next week, and they're all learning to cook. I'm sure (7) *they'll practice / they're practicing* their skills on me when (8) *I'm / I will be* hungry.

Mohammed I've never thought about it, but I probably (9) *don't / won't* learn unless (10) *I'm needing / I need* to. Right now I live at home, but when I live on my own, (11) *I might / I'm going to* get more interested in cooking. It doesn't look very hard, though, so I'm sure (12) *I'm picking / I'll pick* it up fast.

12 **MY PERSPECTIVE**

Work in pairs. When you leave home, will you be more like Ana, Fumio, or Mohammed? Tell your partner why.

13 Complete the article with the best form of the verbs. Use *will*, *may*, *going to*, or the simple present.

People say that cooking is fun, but I (1) _____ (do) everything I can to not cook when I (2) _____ (leave) home. If, like me, you can't even cook an egg, you (3) _____ (probably / be) disappointed with anything you make at home. But, bad home cooking (4) _____ (disappear) in the near future. Moley Robotics has designed a kitchen robot that (5) _____ (cook) any dish in the world as well as a professional chef.

It looks like two human arms and it works by "learning" the hand and arm movements of professional chefs as they work. The company (6) _____ (record) celebrity chefs cooking fantastic meals and the arms can copy these instructions in people's homes. You will be able to start the machine before you (7) _____ (get) home by choosing what to eat from thousands of recipes on your phone. That's if you can afford it: it (8) _____ (go) on sale soon for $12,500. Despite the price, the makers think that in years to come robots (9) _____ (make) all home food. Personally, I find the idea of robot arms in my house very strange, so I think I (10) _____ (spend) my money on restaurants instead.

14 Work in pairs. Discuss the questions.

1 Do you think there will be robot chefs in the future? If so, will you use one? Why?
2 Do you think they will help us eat better?
3 How is your diet preparing you for a healthy future? What will you eat less or more of?

4B Street Food

A food stall on Mactan Island in the Philippines

WORLD FOOD BLOG

Could the best street food in the world be FILIPINO?

VOCABULARY BUILDING Compound adjectives

1 Read about compound adjectives. Then choose the correct option to complete the sentences (1–5).

> Compound adjectives are formed with two words. They often have a hyphen (-). Many compound adjectives are formed from the past or present participles of verbs.
>
> *It's better to eat **oven-baked** food that hasn't been fried in oil.* (The food has been **baked** in the **oven**.)
>
> *You'll keep coming back for more **great-tasting** lemonade.* (The lemonade **tastes great**.)

1 I fried the chicken in deep oil.
It's *deep-fried / deep-frying* chicken.

2 That salad looks good.
It's a *good-looked / good-looking* salad.

3 What's the ingredient that tastes sweet?
What's the *sweet-tasted / sweet-tasting* ingredient?

4 The tomatoes are filled with rice.
They're *rice-filled / rice-filling* tomatoes.

5 I don't think they've cooked this chicken enough.
It's *undercooked / undercooking* chicken.

2 Complete the sentences with one of these compound adjectives.

homemade	modern-looking	old-fashioned
overcooked	well-known	

1 I've eaten in so many restaurants recently. It's great to get back to some good _____ food.

2 You've never heard of *tiramisu*? It's a _____ Italian dessert.

3 We had lunch in a lovely _____ restaurant in the historic center of town.

4 The restaurant is very traditional but it has a _____ menu. I'd love to go there someday.

5 Be careful not to leave it in the oven for too long. It gets dry if it's _____ .

3 Choose a dish that is popular where you live. Write three sentences to describe it using compound adjectives.

Churros are sweet-tasting, deep-fried things that we eat for breakfast in Spain.

24 Walk down the street in most big cities and you'll find a Middle Eastern grill selling kebabs and falafel. Without a doubt, you'll also find a restaurant selling burgers or Mexican tacos. If you look for spicy
5 food, there's a good chance you'll find Indian or Thai food. You might even find Vietnamese curry for takeout. But you probably won't find food from the Philippines. That's strange, because Filipinos make the best street food in the world.

10 One reason Filipino food is so good is that there's so much variety! You only have to look at the country's rich history to see why. The Philippines have been influenced by Chinese, Malay, Arab, and Spanish cultures, to name a few. Filipinos took these influences
15 and mixed them in their own way. A popular street breakfast illustrates this very well: take some Chinese rice porridge*, mix in some chocolate (the Spanish introduced cocoa to the islands), then add some 100 percent Filipino salted fish. That's *champorado* with *tuyo*,
20 and it'll wake you up! So, Filipino food is a wonderful mix of many countries' ingredients and styles.

You'll recognize many dishes for this reason. *Lumpia*, for example, are delicious spring rolls, very similar to the ones on a Chinese menu. However, there are
25 a few characteristics of Filipino cuisine that make it unique. Seafood is everywhere in this nation of 7,000 islands. *Ukoy* is a popular prawn* dish; the prawns are mixed with vegetables in egg and flour, fried until they are golden, and served with spicy vinegar. You may

30 discover that the food isn't as hot as in countries like Thailand, but it has flavorful dishes with many great-tasting ingredients in each bite. The best-known dessert of the islands is *halu halo*—it contains cooked banana, sweet beans, coconut, fruit, sweetened milk, sugar, and
35 ice. A milkshake like no other!

You'll find the best *adidas* (grilled chicken feet) in Manila at a food stall called Maong's Grill. Filipinos don't let anything go to waste and make the most delicious snacks out of every part of the animal. At
40 Maong's, for example, you can also get grilled chicken head and chicken intestine*. In many parts of the world, street food started as food for people who weren't wealthy enough to have their own kitchens, and here in the Philippines they do it best.

45 So why has the world not discovered Filipino street cuisine? Perhaps it's because some of its tastiest dishes are very unusual, so you have to be open to trying new things. But adventurous young people are exploring world food more than ever, so this is going to change,
50 and in a few years, we'll all be eating Filipino food. For now, though, the best place to experience it is still on the streets of Manila.

porridge *a soft food made with water or milk and grain (e.g., oats or rice), eaten hot for breakfast*
prawn *shrimp*
intestine *the part of an animal that processes and digests food*

READING

4 Work in pairs. Discuss the questions.

1 If you're out in the city or in your town, what do you eat? Are there many choices?
2 What are the characteristics of "street food"?

5 Read the blog. What are two characteristics of Filipino street food?

6 Match the dish (1–5) with the idea that it illustrates (a–e).

1 *champorado* with *tuyo*
2 *lumpia*
3 *ukoy*
4 *halu halo*
5 *adidas*

a Filipino food often puts many flavors together.
b Some dishes are similar to dishes from other countries.
c The cuisine shows the simple origins of street food.
d A lot of Filipino food uses local ingredients, like seafood.
e The food shows the multicultural past of the country.

7 Work in pairs. Discuss the questions.

1 Have you ever tried Filipino food? What dishes would you like to try? Which ones would you avoid?
2 The writer believes that "in a few years, we'll all be eating Filipino food." Do you agree? Why?
3 Are you an adventurous eater? What strange things have you eaten?
4 What other types of food are you interested in trying?

8 It is useful to increase your vocabulary by trying to understand new words in texts. Find words in the blog with these meanings.

1 food that you buy in a restaurant but don't eat there (paragraph 1)
2 individual components of a meal (paragraph 3)
3 animals from the ocean that we eat (paragraph 3)
4 a small meal (paragraph 4)
5 a place in the street used for selling food and other things (paragraph 4)
6 a style of cooking, such as a national style (paragraph 5)

9 What food would you use to promote your country or region? Are there any dishes you would not mention because they might not sound attractive to tourists?

A food stall sells fried insects in Bangkok, Thailand.

4C Feed the world with... bugs?

GRAMMAR Making predictions

1 Read the excerpts (a–f) in the Grammar box. Use them to complete the summary below.

> **will, may/might, going to, future continuous, future perfect**
>
> **a** By 2050, the human population **will almost certainly have grown** to nine billion
>
> **b** we **may be able to find** our protein from somewhere else
>
> **c** They think we **will run out of** food
>
> **d** we **will** all soon **be eating** insects
>
> **e** we can see that figure is **going to** rise
>
> **f** We **won't have** enough of these resources

There are more than seven billion people on the planet, and (1) _____ . (2) _____ , and experts are worried. (3) _____ . People in developed countries get most of their protein from animals like chickens and cows, but these animals need a lot of land, water, and food to live. (4) _____ as the world's population grows and more people want to eat this kind of meat. But (5) _____ . There's a chance that (6) _____ .

Check page 134 for more information and practice.

2 Activity 1 talks about a problem. How could insects be the solution?

3 How likely is it that the events in bold in the Grammar box will happen? Match the excerpts (a–f) with the probabilities (1–3).

1 certain—100% **2** probable—80 to 100% **3** possible—10 to 80%

4 Complete the rules for making predictions (1–6) with these verb forms. Then match the rules with the excerpts (a–f) in the Grammar box.

Use:

future continuous	future perfect	*going to*	*may/might*	*will* (x2)

1 _____ to make predictions when there is a clear reason in the present for the prediction. Excerpt _____

2 _____ to make predictions that we believe are true, often with verbs like *think, expect, imagine,* and *know,* adverbs like *definitely,* and expressions like *I'm sure.* Excerpt _____

3 _____ to talk about future things that are certain to happen. Excerpt _____

4 _____ if we are less certain that the prediction is true. Excerpt _____

5 the _____ to talk about an action that you know or think will be in progress at a certain point in the future. Excerpt _____

6 the _____ to talk about an action that will be finished before a particular time in the future. Excerpt _____

5 Complete the voicemail with either the future continuous or future perfect form of the verbs.

"Just wanted to let you know what we (1) _____ (do) this weekend. Remember the World Food Fair last year? We're going again! If it's like last year's, by the end of the weekend I (2) _____ (try) all sorts of strange snacks. Apparently, this year, they're promoting insects, but I (3) _____ (not eat) any ants, even if they are covered in chocolate! What about you? (4) _____ (you do) your school project? Do you think you (5) _____ (finish) before Monday morning? Good luck! I (6) _____ (not finish) mine by then!"

6 **PRONUNCIATION** Sentence stress with the future continuous and future perfect

a Listen and check your answers to Activity 5. 🎧 25

b Listen to the positive and negative sentences again. How does the stress change? 🎧 26
  1 Just wanted to let you know what we'll be doing this weekend.
  2 If it's like last year's, by the end of the weekend I'll have tried all sorts of strange snacks.
  3 I won't be eating any ants, even if they are covered in chocolate!
  4 I won't have finished mine by then!

c Work in pairs. Practice reading the voicemail.

7 Read about a possible solution. Choose the best form of each verb to complete the text.

Researcher Marcel Dicke gives several reasons why insects (1) *are going to / won't* provide us with a lot of the protein we need. First, farming insects is efficient: "Give cows ten kilograms of food and you will (2) *be getting / get* only one kilogram of beef, but locusts can give you nine kilograms of locust meat."

Second, you will (3) *be already eating / have already eaten* hundreds of meals containing insects in your life, whether you like it or not! Next time you eat processed food, you (4) *will / may* probably be eating insects. A lot of fruit gets damaged by insects, so it (5) *won't go / isn't going* to the supermarkets, but (6) *is going to / may* be used to make processed foods like tomato soup.

Third, insects are already a popular form of good, healthy food. Up to two billion people in Asia, Africa, and Latin America will (7) *be enjoying / have enjoyed* an insect recently. Even so, Dicke expects that other people will (8) *find / be finding* it hard to get used to the idea of eating insects. One possibility is that food manufacturers (9) *are going to / might* start introducing processed insect protein into their products. Dicke predicts that, by 2020, we (10) *are going to buy / will be buying* them, knowing that we are eating insects.

8 **MY PERSPECTIVE**

Work in pairs. Discuss the questions.

1 What are the advantages of eating insects?
2 Do you think you will be eating them in the future?

9 Work in groups. Create an insect recipe using the prompts.

- Our dish is going to use… (type of insect)
- It's going to be a… (type of food)
- Other ingredients will include…
- We think it will look more attractive if we…
- We'll be promoting it in… (places)
- When you eat it, make sure you…
- We're sure it will… (predictions)

10 **CHOOSE** Choose one of the following activities.

1 Work in groups. Have a food invention competition. Persuade other groups to buy your dish from Activity 9.
2 Write the recipe and instructions for your dish in Activity 9.
3 Find out how people around the world eat insects. Give a short presentation.

Crispy, fried insects

4D Why I'm a Weekday Vegetarian

" If all of us ate half as much meat, it would be like half of us were vegetarians. "

GRAHAM HILL

Read about Graham Hill and get ready to watch his TED Talk. ▶ 4.0

AUTHENTIC LISTENING SKILLS

Pausing

When people are speaking to an audience, they often pause to break their sentences up into short sections, or chunks. This makes it easier for listeners to follow. Speakers often pause:

- at the end of sentences.
- where there is a comma or other punctuation.
- to separate adverbial phrases (e.g., expressions about time or place).
- before an important word or phrase.
- between the subject of a sentence and its verb when the subject is long.

1 Listen to the beginning of the TED Talk. Mark the pauses. 🎧 27

About a year ago, | I asked myself a question: "Knowing what I know, why am I not a vegetarian?"

2 Mark where you think Graham will pause in the next two sentences. Then listen to check. 🎧 28

After all, I'm one of the green guys: I grew up with hippie parents in a log cabin. I started a site called TreeHugger—I care about this stuff.

WATCH

3 Work in pairs. Make a list of reasons that somebody might be a vegetarian (e.g., "It's good for your health.").

4 Watch Part 1 of the talk. Put the problems with eating meat in the order that Graham mentions them. Which problem <u>doesn't</u> he mention? ▶ 4.1

a It is bad for the planet.
b The animals suffer in poor conditions.
c It is expensive.
d It is unhealthy.
e People are eating more and more meat.

5 Complete the facts about eating meat. Then watch Part 1 again and check your answers. ▶ 4.1

1 If you eat one _____ every day, it can increase the possibility of dying by a third.
2 We keep _____ animals for meat each year in factory-farm conditions.
3 Meat causes more emissions than all _____ .
4 Beef production uses 100 times more _____ than most vegetables do.
5 We are eating _____ meat as in the 1950s.

6 Watch Part 2. Choose the correct option. ▶ 4.2

1 Why does Graham say to the audience: "Imagine your last hamburger"?
  a He wants them to see what a difficult decision becoming a vegetarian is.
  b He wants to help the audience become vegetarian.
  c He wants them to feel sorry for him.

2 Which of these rules is part of Graham's solution?
  a Only eat fish on the weekend.
  b Don't eat meat on Saturdays and Sundays.
  c Reduce the amount of meat you eat by 70 percent.

3 Which part of Graham's solution is he happiest about?
   a He's not creating so much pollution.
   b He has more money.   **c** He's healthier.

7 Work in pairs. Graham says that "we as a society are eating twice as much meat as we did in the '50s." How has diet changed in your country in the last 100 years?

8 **VOCABULARY IN CONTEXT**

   a Watch the clips from the TED Talk. Choose the correct meaning of the words and phrases. ▶ 4.3

   b Answer the questions. Compare answers in pairs.
      1 Do you do any hobbies where there is a *risk* of hurting yourself?
      2 What is the *combined* age of your family?
      3 Do you ever want to do things that are *in conflict with* what you should be doing? What?
      4 Have you ever *come up with* a way of making money? What?
      5 Have you ever done any *damage* to another person's possessions?

CRITICAL THINKING Persuading

There are many ways that speakers can use to persuade their listeners to do things. They can:
a describe personal experiences that others can relate to.
b make it sound achievable.
c offer choice and flexibility.
d point out the personal benefits of doing it.
e ask themselves and the audience questions.
f ask listeners to imagine a situation.

9 How does Graham try to persuade his audience? Match the excerpts with techniques (a–f) in the Critical Thinking box. Each excerpt may use more than one technique.

   1 Knowing what I know, why am I not a vegetarian?
   2 Any of these angles should have been enough to convince me to go vegetarian. Yet, there I was—chk, chk, chk—tucking into a big old steak.
   3 Imagine your last hamburger.
   4 I'd commit to doing it later, and not surprisingly, later never came. Sound familiar?
   5 I've been doing it for the last year, and it's great. It's called Weekday Veg.
   6 On the weekend, your choice. Simple. If you want to take it to the next level…
   7 It's okay to break it here and there.
   8 Best of all, I'm healthier, I know that I'm going to live longer, and I've even lost a little weight.

10 Work in pairs. Discuss the questions.

   1 Which of Graham's reasons for becoming a weekday vegetarian are the most convincing?
   2 Would you consider becoming a weekday vegetarian (if you aren't already)? How easy or difficult do you think it would be? Why?
   3 If you are a vegetarian, do you think part-time vegetarianism is a good thing?

CHALLENGE

Do a survey. Find out what other people in the class think about becoming a weekday vegetarian.

4E Future Plans

SPEAKING

Useful language

Talking about hopes and goals

I expect to…
I think I might…
I'd really like to…
I'm aiming to have… by next month.
I'm interested in -ing.
I'm looking forward to -ing.
I'm thinking about / of -ing.
In the long / short term, I'm going to / hoping to / planning to…

1 Listen to three people talking about something they would like to change in their life. Which speaker, João, Emily, or Kei, is not happy about: 🎧 **29**

a money?   **b** their home life?   **c** their diet?

2 Listen again. Which of the expressions in the Useful language box do you hear? 🎧 **29**

3 Work in pairs. Use expressions from the Useful language box to discuss some of your hopes and goals.

4 Look at these instructions for helping other people achieve their goals. What goals from Activity 3 could a classmate help you with?

1 Ask them to describe the problem as they see it. Ask what they want to change. Make sure they say exactly what their goal is, (e.g., not *eat less chocolate*, but *eat no more than one bar of chocolate a day*).

2 Ask them what is stopping them from achieving their goal.

3 Ask them to set a time limit for their goal. How long do they need to achieve their goal?

4 Together, talk about what they will do to achieve their goal. Ask them to list the advantages of achieving their goal and to commit to them.

5 Work in pairs. Follow the instructions and take turns helping each other to achieve the goals you identified in Activity 4.

- You want to eat more healthily. (What do you want to cut down on?)
- You think you and your family should eat more organic food, but your parents say it's expensive.
- You want to give up a bad habit, (e.g., biting your nails, drinking soft drinks).
- You don't get along with someone and want to have a better relationship.
- You want to travel (where to?) but need to save money for the trip. You find it hard to save money.

La Boqueria food market, Barcelona, Spain

WRITING A social media update

6 Work in pairs. Look at the types of trips and discuss the questions.

a biking vacation	a cooking vacation	a photography expedition
a school trip	a volunteering trip	

1 What activities would you expect to do on these trips?
2 Which trip would you prefer to go on? Why?

7 Read the social media update on page 150. Which of these activities has Lali already done? Which is she hoping to do? Which is she going to do?

1 **get to** Leh *already done*
2 **quickly visit** the Red Fort
3 **walk around** Delhi streets
4 **travel slowly** between Delhi and Leh
5 learn to cook **nice** food
6 go **walking**
7 **talk to** people for a project
8 **see** a festival

8 WRITING SKILL Interesting language

a Read the update on page 150 again. Find words that Lali uses instead of the words in bold in Activity 7. Why does she use these words?

b Find the words in the update that Lali uses instead of these words.

1 big (line 2)
2 hot (line 3)
3 cooler (line 4)
4 tiring (line 5)
5 very (line 6)

9 Choose one of the trips below, or a trip you would like to take one day, and plan a social media update.

- a trip to a region in your country with its own special local cuisine
- a visit to the house of a friend or relative where you tried a new dish
- a trip abroad when you ate some interesting food

10 Write your social media update. Use phrases from the Useful language box. Make it interesting to read.

- Is it a vacation, expedition, school trip, or some other type of trip?
- What have you already done?
- What are you going to do? What else are you hoping to do or see?

11 Read your classmates' updates. Whose trips sound the most interesting? Whose food sounds the most delicious?

Useful language

Writing a social media update
We finally… after…
What a beautiful place / long journey!
It's such a / an adjective + noun (noisy city, huge country).
The food was so + adjective (tasty, spicy, fresh, etc.).
The weather's wonderful / boiling / freezing.
I'm hoping to…
I want to… while I'm here.
We might… if there's time.

5 Work

IN THIS UNIT, YOU...

- talk about jobs and describe working life.
- read about a real-life superpower.
- learn about jobs that no longer exist.
- watch a TED Talk about finding the best person for a job.
- write a job application letter.

A painter works on a colorful underpass in Munich, Germany.

5A New Ways of Working

VOCABULARY Describing work

1 What skills, abilities, and personal qualities do people need to work successfully in the 21st century? Is it more than just qualifications?

2 Work in pairs. Think of a job:

1 that is popular, so the job market is **competitive**.
2 in which you need to be **flexible** (able to adapt to changing situations).
3 that's **well paid** (you get a good salary).
4 **in the** construction **industry**.
5 where employees **work long hours** (50 hours a week or more).
6 that you would find very **stressful**.
7 that has good **career prospects**.
8 in which you would be **in charge of** many people (responsible for them).
9 that is physically **demanding**, so you need to be healthy.
10 that needs **creative** people with new ideas and new ways of doing things.

3 Use the words and phrases in bold in Activity 2 to complete the paragraph.

A survey about the reasons people leave their jobs shows some surprising results. You might think that people want more money, so they move to jobs that are (1) _____ or prefer an easy life, but in fact this is not always the case. Many employees are happy to (2) _____ in (3) _____ jobs, where they are (4) _____ large teams, working with important clients. In return, they want exciting (5) _____ in their chosen (6) _____ . Work only becomes (7) _____ if employers refuse to listen to their workers' needs or don't trust them with responsibility. For example, employees with a long commute may want more (8) _____ working hours. The lesson for business? To keep good employees, you need to trust them and listen to them.

4 Put the lines in order, 1–9. The first and last lines have been done for you.

a I've always wanted to **work in**   *1*
b **charge of** the boys' football teams. It wasn't a very **well-paid**
c **for** organizing a football tournament. Since that job, I've never been **out**
d **work** at the sports center, where I was **in**
e **job** as a coach. I'm currently **working**
f **job,** but it was very satisfying—I was **responsible**
g **of work.** Now I have got **a full-time**
h the sports industry. I got qualified as a personal trainer and got **part-time**
i **on** a fitness program for one of my clients who is a professional athlete.   *9*

5 Work in pairs. Discuss the difference between these terms.

1 *part-time* and *temporary* work
2 to work *in* something and to work *on* something
3 to have a *full-time job* and to *work long hours*

6 MY PERSPECTIVE

Write about the career path you would like to take. Work in pairs and compare your plans. Who has the clearest idea of what they want to do?

I'm not sure what industry I'd like to work in yet, but I'm looking for a well-paid job that tests my abilities…

LISTENING

7 Work in pairs. Imagine you are a company manager. Which of these ideas would make your employees most productive? Put them in order with 1 as the best idea.

a Give employees a share of the company.
b Give everyone a day every month to volunteer for a charity.
c Let workers choose their work hours.
d Let everyone decide if they want to work from home or in the office.
e Let each person decide when to take vacations.

8 Listen to a podcast about the world of work. Which of the ideas in Activity 7 are mentioned? Which employer uses them, Hamdi Ulukaya or Jenny Biggam?
🎧 30

9 Listen again. Complete each excerpt with the missing verb. 🎧 30

1 Ulukaya started the business a few years ago, and it has ___gone on___ to become a multibillion-dollar company.
2 Does he just _____ to be nice, or is this actually good management?
3 He _____ feeling grateful to his workers for helping him start the business.
4 Do you think he might _____ giving so much of the company away?

5 Jenny Biggam decided to _____ treating her workers like children.
6 They are _____ to make coming to work a happier experience.
7 What kind of boss would you like? Don't _____ to call in and tell us!

GRAMMAR Verb patterns: verb + -ing or infinitive with to

10 Look at the completed sentences in Activity 9. Are the verbs you wrote followed by -ing or the infinitive?

Verb patterns: verb + -ing or infinitive with to

a *Do you think other companies will **go on treating** their workers the same?*
b *__Making__ work enjoyable **means creating** a more productive company.*
c *Some managers **remember to show** their employees how much they appreciate their work.*
d *I **regret to inform** you that we can't afford to employ you anymore. I'm so sorry.*
e *I **stopped to buy** a coffee on the way to work.*
f *If it's taking so long to get to the office, **try working** from home for a few days.*
g *Hamdi Ulukaya will never **forget making** his first million dollars.*

Check page 136 for more information and practice.

11 Work in pairs. Look at the verbs in bold in the Grammar box. Compare them with the sentences in Activity 9. Discuss how their meanings change.

go on + *infinitive with* to *means "to do something after doing something else"*

go on + *-ing means "to continue"*

12 Complete the paragraph with the correct form of the verbs.

Sometimes being a good boss means (1) _____ (give up) important personal things. I remember (2) _____ (hear) about a company that lost a lot of money. If they wanted the company to go on (3) _____ (do) business, they had to stop (4) _____ (employ) some of the workers. But the director of the company didn't want to say to some of his employees, "I regret (5) _____ (tell) you that we have to let you go." He wanted (6) _____ (keep) everyone employed and motivated. So, he tried (7) _____ (talk) to the workers. Together, they decided to reduce their salaries and to give up paid vacations. He didn't forget (8) _____ (include) himself in the cuts. In fact, he remembered (9) _____ (lead) by example and took the biggest salary cut of all. The company went on (10) _____ (survive) the bad times and is now doing very well.

13 Complete the topics with the correct form of the verbs. Choose three or four of the topics and make notes about them. Discuss your notes in pairs.

 1 something you meant _____ (do) this morning
 2 a mistake you regret _____ (make)
 3 the job you'll go on _____ (do) in the future
 4 an item of clothing you've tried _____ (wear)
 5 a bad habit you've stopped _____ (do)
 6 something you never remember _____ (do), which annoys your family
 7 a person you'll never forget _____ (meet)
 8 something you forgot _____ (do) which meant _____ (do) a lot more work later
 9 a day you remember _____ (enjoy) when you were a very young child
 10 a sport or game you tried _____ (do) but found too hard

14 MY PERSPECTIVE

Work in pairs. Discuss the questions.

 1 What do the companies described in this lesson have in common?
 2 Which company would you prefer to work for? Why?
 3 What hopes do you have about the places you will work at in the future?

A worker checks her smartphone sitting on a swing in the offices of PT Tokopedia in Indonesia.

5B An Unusual Job

VOCABULARY BUILDING Ways of seeing

1 Read the sentences (1–7). Underline a verb related to seeing. Then match the verbs with their definitions (a–g).

1 The police <u>spotted</u> him leaving the parking lot in a van. *f*
2 She stole from three stores and they caught her on camera.
3 He only glanced at the woman but he knew who she was immediately.
4 I waved at her but I don't think she noticed me because she didn't stop to say hello.
5 The person in the photo was identified as Adam Smith.
6 Officers observed people leaving and entering the building entrance throughout the night.
7 I recognized an old friend at the train station, even though I haven't seen her for years.

a became aware of someone or something
b looked quickly at someone or something
c saw someone and was able to say who they were
d knew who the person was because you had seen them before
e saw someone doing something wrong
f saw someone or something because you were looking for them
g watched someone or something carefully in order to learn information

2 Rewrite the sentences, replacing all the words in bold with the correct form of one verb from Activity 1.

1 I didn't **know it was** Christophe at first—he's grown a beard since the last time I saw him.
2 I only need to **look** at a phone number **briefly** and I can remember it.
3 How many of these people can you **put a name to**?
4 I looked for you at the park but I didn't **see** you. Where were you?
5 If my parents **see** me playing games when I should be doing homework, they take my laptop away.
6 He learned the job by **watching and studying** what the other staff members did.
7 I **saw** that the window was open when I heard a loud noise outside.

READING

3 Work in pairs. Discuss the questions.

1 Do you find it easy to recognize people you have only met once?
2 How good are you at remembering names?
3 Can you recognize people from their voice?

4 Read the article. Complete the descriptions of super-recognizers.

1 To be a super-recognizer, you must be very good at _____ .
2 Super-recognizers work mostly _____ .

5 Read the article again. Are the sentences *true* or *false*?

1 The article mentions two problems with CCTV.
2 One answer to these problems is to install more cameras.
3 Super-recognizers don't need to look at a face for long in order to identify it.
4 The police use super-recognizers to prevent violent situations from developing.
5 If you are good at recognizing faces, you will probably have a good general memory.
6 To become a super-recognizer, you need years of training.

6 Work in pairs. Discuss the questions.

1 Would you like to be a super-recognizer? Why?
2 Do you think it is possible to develop your skills at recognizing faces, or is it something that you can't change?

CRITICAL THINKING Exaggerating

Sometimes writers exaggerate (describe things so that they seem a lot better / worse / more important than they really are) to make their point. It's important to be able to recognize when the author is exaggerating and when they are stating facts. For example, to say that there were lots of people at a party, you might say that there were *hundreds* of people, when in fact, there were not that many.

7 Work in groups. Which of these excerpts from the article are probably exaggerating facts? Why does the writer do this in each case?

1 You are being watched.
2 Many large cities have thousands of security cameras.
3 …people with the amazing ability to remember thousands of faces.
4 Collins was able to identify a total of 190 troublemakers.
5 Collins admits he can't even remember a shopping list.
6 …if you're looking for a job where you are allowed to watch TV all day…

8 Work in pairs. Discuss the questions.

1 Do you think the job name "super-recognizer" is an exaggeration? Why?
2 Think about a job you would like to do. Write three sentences to exaggerate it. Tell your partner. Whose job sounds most interesting?

A Real-Life, Crime-Fighting Superpower!

🎧 31 You are being watched.

Next time you're in a busy city center, look up. The chances are there will be a CCTV * camera somewhere nearby. Many large cities have thousands of security cameras: on
5 buildings, next to roads, even in public buses and trains. They are supposed to prevent crime, but there is a problem. No matter how many cameras are in place to catch people breaking the law, criminals can't always be identified. For one thing, the police can only put a name to a face if they
10 have a file on that person. Also, even if the criminal is known to the police, the CCTV image is often of such a poor quality that it is impossible to recognize them.

Impossible for most people, that is, but not if you're a "super-recognizer." These are people with the amazing
15 ability to remember thousands of faces and pick them out from a crowded street, even if they only see them for a moment. At soccer games, for example, the police must spot troublemakers immediately, before they start fighting, and this means acting fast. The 152 super-recognizers employed
20 by the London police can do this, and they get results.

The police didn't need to worry, for example, when there was trouble in the streets in 2011. Officers sat in CCTV control centers, observing the scenes on TV and picking out known criminals for their colleagues on the ground. Just one
25 member of the team, Gary Collins, was able to identify a total of 190 troublemakers! The police later arrested many of them; others weren't allowed to go back on the streets.

You might think that with a memory this good, super-recognizers must be good at remembering lots of things,
30 but Collins admits he can't even remember a shopping list. "I have to write that down," he says. Scientists believe that the ability to recognize faces is different from other kinds of memory, and uses a special part of the brain. Damage to that area of the brain can cause "face blindness," where
35 people can't recognize faces at all. Having said that, most of us are really good at recognizing faces. We are even able to identify people we know from the back of their heads and from the way they walk, something computers are unlikely to do in the near future. However, we can't all do it as well
40 as professionals like Gary Collins, who do it better than 99 percent of the population.

You might also be in the top one percent and not even know it. So, if you're looking for a job where you are allowed to watch TV all day, you should find out whether you're a
45 super-recognizer and join the police!

CCTV *closed-circuit television—a camera system used for watching activity in some places*

5C Job Evolution

GRAMMAR Present and past modals

1 Work in pairs. Discuss the questions.

1 The concept of super-recognizers did not exist a few years ago. Make a list of new jobs that were not around until very recently.
2 What jobs from the past no longer exist, or are disappearing? Make another list.
3 Look at your lists. What do you think "job evolution" means?

2 Look at the sentences in the Grammar box. Which sentence describes:

1 obligation?
2 no obligation?
3 permission?
4 prohibition?
5 ability or possibility?
6 no ability or possibility?
7 advice?
8 deduction or speculation?

Present and past modals

a At soccer games, the police **must** spot troublemakers immediately.

b Gary Collins **was able to** identify 190 troublemakers.

c If you're looking for a job where you **are allowed to** watch TV all day...

d ...you **should** find out whether you're a super-recognizer.

e ...others **weren't allowed to** go back on the streets.

f "Face blindness"... where people **can't** recognize faces at all.

g The police **didn't need to** worry when there was trouble in the streets.

h With a memory this good, super-recognizers **must** be good at remembering lots of things.

Check page 136 for more information and practice.

3 What sentences in the Grammar box refer to the present? Which refer to the past?

4 Complete the table with the words in bold from the sentences that refer to the present.

Meaning	Present
obligation	have to, (1) _____ , need to
no obligation	don't have to, don't need to
permission	can, (2) _____
prohibition	must not, can't, isn't / aren't allowed to
ability or possibility	can, is / are able to
no ability or possibility	(3) _____ , isn't / aren't able to
advice	(4) _____ , ought to
deduction or speculation	(5) _____ , may, might, can't

5 Match these past forms with a meaning from the table in Activity 4.

didn't have to   managed to   needed to   weren't able to

6 Complete the paragraphs about jobs that no longer exist.

can	can't	couldn't	don't have to
had to	have to	needed	shouldn't

They say that the world is changing faster now than at any time in history. We (1) _____ do things that were unimaginable just a few years ago. Twenty years ago, you (2) _____ send photos from your phone, for example, and you (3) _____ carry a map before GPS existed. These changes affect everything. Smartphones mean people (4) _____ buy cameras anymore, so camera companies (5) _____ survive and employees (6) _____ find new jobs. Technology is changing the way we live, but also the way we work.

Many professions are changing or disappearing entirely due to technology, but you (7) _____ think that job evolution is a recent thing. Many old jobs you have probably never heard of (8) _____ to make way for new ones because of advances in technology.

7 Work in pairs. Look at the photos. What jobs do you think these people are doing?

8 Read the article to find out what the jobs are. Then choose the correct options to complete the sentences.

Here are two jobs from the past we have forgotten existed:

Icemen and icewomen (1) *had to / weren't allowed to* deliver heavy blocks of ice to wealthy families who (2) *are able to / could* afford to buy it to keep their food cold. This was before every home had a fridge. If you (3) *didn't need to / couldn't* buy ice, you (4) *had to / didn't manage to* find another way to keep your food fresh.

In the UK, if you (5) *must / needed to* wake up early, you (6) *could / ought to* pay a knocker-up. Their job was to wake people up by tapping on bedroom windows with a long stick. They (7) *didn't manage to / weren't allowed to* leave until they were sure their customers were awake. But why is it that the knocker-up (8) *couldn't / didn't have to* be awakened?

9 Complete the paragraphs with one word in each blank. Contractions count as one word.

Until very recently, there were many jobs you (1) _____ do, that we're all (2) _____ to do nowadays thanks to computers. Travel agents still exist of course, but there (3) _____ be many people who still book their vacations the old-fashioned way. The internet means we (4) _____ pay a professional to book our airline tickets or hotels.

Is it possible that some very common jobs may soon disappear? Companies like Google have shown that driverless vehicles (5) _____ work, but at the moment the law says that automated cars and buses aren't (6) _____ to drive on most public roads. However, if technology can make them safe, they (7) _____ be allowed on the roads. In fact, some people think that we (8) _____ to replace all drivers, for safety reasons. Perhaps one day we will look back and wonder how we (9) _____ to drive safely without robots at the wheel!

10 CHOOSE Choose one of the following activities.

1 Work in groups to play a game. Think of a job. Let the other people in the group take turns asking ten *yes/no* questions to guess the job.

A *Do you need to travel long distances?*
B *Yes.*
A *Are you a pilot?*
B *No, but I do have to work in an airplane.*

2 Work in pairs. Together, choose a job. Then, on your own, write as many sentences as you can in two minutes about things that you have to do in this job. Compare lists. Score one point for each obligation that you both wrote. Score two points for obligations that your partner doesn't have. The winner is the player with the most points.

3 Find out about another job that has disappeared. Write a paragraph about it.

5D Why the Best Hire Might Not Have the Perfect Resume

" I want to urge you to interview the Scrapper. "

REGINA HARTLEY

Read about Regina Hartley and get ready to watch her TED Talk. ▶ **5.0**

AUTHENTIC LISTENING SKILLS

Understanding contrasts

We often compare and contrast ideas when we are explaining things. When you listen, try to identify these contrasts. Speakers often show that you are about to hear contrasting ideas by:

- using words like *but; however; not x, y; in spite of this; on the other hand*, etc.
- repeating structures, replacing some words with their opposites.

1 Read the Authentic Listening Skills box. Then listen and complete these excerpts. Which contrasting technique does Regina use? 🎧 **32**

1 A series of odd jobs _____ indicate inconsistency, lack of focus, unpredictability. Or, it _____ signal a committed struggle against obstacles.

2 Graduating from an elite university takes a lot of hard work and sacrifice. _____ if your whole life has been engineered toward success, how will you handle the tough times?

2 Listen to two more sentences from the talk. Complete the sentences, then practice reading them with intonation that shows the contrasts. 🎧 **33**

1 If your whole life has been engineered toward success, how will you handle the tough times? … But on the flip side, what happens when _____ ?

2 They don't think they are who they are in spite of adversity, they _____ .

WATCH

3 Which of these reasons do you think are important for choosing candidates for a job? Put them in order from most to least important.

a their personality
b their qualifications
c their work experience
d how many jobs they have had in the past
e references from other employers
f the university they attended
g a sense of humor

4 Watch Part 1 of the talk. Regina describes two types of candidates, A and B. Do these expressions belong to A, B, or both? ▶ **5.1**

1 destined for success
2 had to fight
3 Ivy League
4 job hopping
5 odd jobs
6 perfect résumé
7 qualified
8 state school
9 "the Scrapper"
10 "the Silver Spoon"

5 Work in pairs. Would you hire the Scrapper or the Silver Spoon? Why?

6 Watch Part 2 of the talk. Choose the best option. ▶ 5.2

Regina has learned that a resume with lots of jobs on it doesn't always show a person who is not (1) *focused / well educated*. She believes that the Scrapper should have (2) *success / an interview*. For example, Steve Jobs (founder of Apple) (3) *had / didn't have* a good resume. He (4) *didn't finish / finished* college, had (5) *a few / many* different jobs, spent time abroad, and had dyslexia.

7 Watch Part 3 of the talk. Choose the options that are <u>not</u> true according to Regina. ▶ 5.3

1 Dyslexia, a learning difficulty that makes it hard to read and spell,
   a affected 35 percent of the entrepreneurs in one study.
   b was a problem that held entrepreneurs back.
   c meant entrepreneurs were better at listening and paying attention.

2 Scrappers
   a often don't feel that they are in control of their own lives.
   b are not scared by business challenges because they have dealt with much harder things.
   c can cope by seeing the funny side of difficult situations.

3 Regina
   a used to drive the president's assistant to work every day.
   b had a colleague in her first job who gave her good advice.
   c once worked as a singing waitress.

8 **VOCABULARY IN CONTEXT**

a Watch the clips from the TED Talk. Choose the correct meaning of the words and phrases. ▶ 5.4

b Think of an example for each of these things. Then work in pairs and compare your examples.

- a technical *term* used in a sport or hobby that you do
- an *assignment* that a teacher gave you that you enjoyed doing
- a situation that *turned out* better than you expected
- a skill that many people find tough but you think is a *piece of cake*
- a friend or family member who you know you can always *count on*

CHALLENGE

Regina says that successful entrepreneurs "don't think they are who they are in spite of adversity, they know they are who they are because of adversity." Work in groups and discuss the questions.

1 Have you ever experienced adversity?

2 Has adversity helped you become who you are?

3 Do you know anyone who has had to deal with adversity in their life?

5E Going for the Job

SANTA CRUZ FRUITS—summer workers needed in the Colchagua Valley

Would you like to work outdoors as part of our friendly team? Are you a hard-working person who wants to stay fit? Join this family-run fruit farm during our busy summer season. Good pay, and free fruit every day!

Part-time waiters at AquaParks

Popular water park looking for enthusiastic staff to work at our restaurant. No waiter experience necessary, but applicants must be polite and well dressed. Must speak English. Hours 11:30am to 4:00pm, Tuesday to Sunday. Openings now until September. Free entry to water park for family and friends.

Personal care assistant

50-year-old wheelchair user looking for a reliable caregiver during the summer while regular provider is on vacation. The right person will be happy to help with household tasks, such as cleaning and cooking, as well as grocery shopping, etc. Must be relaxed and happy and have a sense of humor. About five hours' work daily, with plenty of free time.

SPEAKING

1. Look at the photo. In some countries, students have part-time jobs like this while they are in school, and some work during vacations. Is this the same in your country?

2. Work in pairs. Look at the job ads on the left. Which job would you prefer? Why? What other types of jobs could you do to make money?

3. Listen to a job interview. Which job in Activity 2 is the interview for? Would you give Roberta the job? Why? 🎧 34

4. Listen again. Which expressions in the Useful language box do you hear? What does Roberta say after each one? 🎧 34

5. **PRONUNCIATION** Showing confidence

These are some tips to sound confident in conversation:
- Speak slowly.
- Avoid using filler phrases such as "I mean" and "well."
- Use an even tone of voice so your statements do not sound like questions.

a. Listen to the sentences. Do the speakers sound confident or insecure? What makes the speakers sound insecure? 🎧 35
   1 I'm very good at handling multiple projects.
   2 I'm kind of good at handling multiple projects.
   3 The graph shows a decrease in book sales.
   4 The graph shows a decrease in book sales.

6. Work in pairs. Take turns interviewing each other for one of the jobs advertised in Activity 2. Use the phrases in the Useful language box and these questions.

- Can I ask you why you're interested in this job?
- What experience do you have that could be useful in the job?
- What personal skills do you have that you think would help you?
- Is there anything you want to ask me?

WRITING A cover letter

7 Read the cover letter on page 151. Which information (1–7) does Aya include?

1 details of when she is available to work
2 experience she has that is relevant to the job
3 her interests
4 personal qualities she thinks are relevant to the job
5 her reasons for wanting the job
6 her reason for writing the letter
7 her academic degrees

8 WRITING SKILL Hedging

> When you talk about your own positive qualities, it is important not to sound arrogant.

a Find sentences in Aya's letter that give us the information below. How are the sentences in the letter different?
  1 I am perfectly qualified for the job.
  2 I have a lot of experience.
  3 I am an awesome cook.
  4 I get along with everyone.
  5 I am really smart, so I'm a fast learner.

b Rewrite these sentences to sound less arrogant.
  1 My Chinese is perfect and I have a good level of Japanese.
  2 I am an amazing driver.
  3 My grade point average was impressive.
  4 I had a lot of responsibility in my last job. I was basically in charge.
  5 I am an extremely creative thinker.

9 Write a cover letter for one of the other jobs in Activity 2 or a job of your choice. Follow the organization and writing conventions of the letter on page 151.

10 Work in a group with students who applied for the same job. Read the other students' letters. Who is the best candidate?

Useful language

Talking about skills and personality
I'd say I was very…
I wouldn't say that I was…
I'm willing to…
I'm usually very good at…
I like to think I'm not afraid to…
I know I can sometimes…
I've had a lot of experience…
I'm working on…

Being positive about the job
I've always wanted to…
I think this job would give me…

Asking about the job
What does the job involve?
I was just wondering if I would have to… ?
Are we allowed to… ?

SUBJECT / OBJECT QUESTIONS

Wh- questions start with a question word (e.g., *What, Where, Who, When, How*). The question word sometimes asks about the subject and sometimes it asks about the object.

In **object questions**, the question word asks about the object of the verb. Use the auxiliary verb *do/does* in simple present and simple past questions (*am/were*, etc. in continuous tenses; *have/has*, etc. in perfect tenses). The auxiliary verb goes before the subject.

Which movie *do you want to see? I want to see* **Jason Bourne**. (*Which movie* asks about the object.)

Who *have you spoken to? I've spoken to* **Diane**. (*Who* asks about the object.)

Don't use a question word in *Yes/No* questions.
Did you call Diane? Yes, I did.

Some verbs have two objects (e.g., *tell, give, invite*). Questions can be asked about both objects.
Gurpreet gave Anita a present.
Who did Gurpreet give a present to? (Anita)
What did Gurpreet give Anita? (a present)

In **subject questions**, the question word asks about the subject. Don't use the auxiliary verb (*do/does*) in simple present and simple past questions.

Who *likes this game? I like it.* (*Who* asks about the subject.)

Which video *made you laugh the most?* **The one with the cats** *made me laugh the most.* (*Which video* asks about the subject.)

Not ~~Who does like the game?~~   ~~Which video did make…?~~

In questions in other tenses, always use the auxiliary verb (e.g., *has, will, am*).
Who **is** *making all that noise?*
Which movies **have** *made the most money?*

▶ Activities 1 and 2

TALKING ABOUT THE PRESENT

To talk about the present, you can use the simple present, the present continuous, and the present perfect. (Some people think of the present perfect as a past tense, but it always has a connection to the present, so it is really a present tense.)

The simple present is used:
- to talk about things that are always or generally true (e.g., scientific facts).

Some planets **have** *many moons. Jupiter* **has** *at least 67!*

- to describe habits and routines (often with words like *sometimes* and *never*).

I **don't** *normally* **go** *out during the week, but sometimes I* **go** *to the movies on Saturdays.*

- with stative verbs (verbs of feeling, thinking, owning, and sensing) (e.g., *enjoy, think, belong, seem*).

I **don't believe** *that you stayed home all weekend.*

The present continuous is used:
- to talk about temporary actions happening at or around the present time, or at the time of speaking/writing.

What's that man **doing**? *He's* **looking** *for something.*

I'm **reading** *a really interesting book about technology right now.*

- to talk about changing situations.

The world **is getting** *warmer at a very fast rate.*

- with *always* to describe actions that happen often (and perhaps annoy the speaker).

He's **always telling** *lies about me. Don't listen to him!*

The present perfect is used:
- to describe actions that started in the past and continue in the present.

Natsuki and I **have been** *friends since we were young.*

To make negatives and questions in the simple present, use the auxiliary verb *do/does* + infinitive.

She **doesn't** *often* **cry** *in public.*

Why **do** *you* **enjoy** *making cakes and cookies?*

To make affirmatives, negatives, and questions in the present continuous, use the auxiliary verb *is/am/are* + *-ing*.

He's **talking** *to his friends online, so he* **isn't listening** *to me.*

I'm **not studying** *very hard right now.*

Why **are** *you always* **stealing** *my pens?*

To make affirmatives, negatives, and questions in the present perfect, use the auxiliary verb *have/has* + past participle.

They've only **known** *each other for two weeks.*

She **hasn't been** *very happy recently.*

How long **have** *you* **lived** *in Istanbul?*

▶ Activities 3–7

1 Are the questions correct? If not, correct the mistake.

1 Where does Henri work? (He works in Paris.)
2 What Ingrid does? (She's a pilot.)
3 Which bus does go downtown? (Bus number 12.)
4 Who saw the show yesterday? (We all saw it.)
5 What you were doing when the concert started? (We were stuck in traffic.)
6 Who loved Lina in the story? (She loved Antonio.)

2 Write subject and object questions about these sentences.

1 Tariq dropped his phone.
  a What _did Tariq drop_ ?
  b Who _dropped his phone_ ?
2 The children enjoy their math classes.
  a Who _____ ?
  b Which classes _____ ?
3 Evgeny watched three movies yesterday.
  a What _____ do yesterday?
  b How many _____ ?
4 Most of the class likes the new teacher.
  a Who _____ ? (subject)
  b Who _____ ? (object)
5 Karina has lost her purse.
  a What _____ ?
  b Who _____ ?
6 Kei told Naomi the secret.
  a What _____ Naomi?
  b Who _____ the secret to?

3 Choose the best option to complete the conversations.

1 A How often *do you go / are you going* camping?
  B Not that often, but we *plan / are planning* a trip soon.
2 A *Do you come? / Are you coming?* Hurry up!
  B Wait! *I need / I'm needing* to send my brother a text.
3 A I *normally take / have normally taken* the bus, but this week the bus drivers *don't work / aren't working*, so I *ride / I'm riding* my bike instead.
  B My mom *always takes / is always taking* me in the car.
4 A How long *are you having / have you had* a cell phone?
  B It's not mine. *I borrow / I'm borrowing* it from my sister.
5 A *You always play / You're always playing* computer games. You should go outside more!
  B *I'm finishing / I finish* my game now, and then I'll go out.
6 A Can you help me? *I'm looking / I've looked* for my hat. I *don't see / haven't seen* it since Saturday.
  B Sorry, *I don't know / I'm not knowing* where it is and *I'm doing / I've done* my homework right now. Can I help you look later?

4 Complete the sentences about changing situations with the correct form of these verbs.

become	eat	get	go up	use

1 Teenagers in many parts of the world _____ fatter because they _____ too much.
2 The temperature of the planet _____ year by year.
3 More and more people _____ text messaging as a way to communicate.
4 Riding a bike _____ popular in cities again because driving is slow and expensive.

5 Write questions with *How long*. Use the simple present or present perfect. Ask a classmate the questions.

1 know your best friend?
2 be your commute to school?
3 be at this school?
4 this lesson last?
5 be able to swim?
6 know how to speak English?
7 live in your house?

6 Match the two parts of the sentences.

1 I've enjoyed drawing and painting
2 I do some drawing or painting
3 I go to art class
4 I've been in the class
5 I'm painting a picture of a forest
6 In fact, I'm doing a lot of painting
7 But of course I'm not drawing anything

a for about two years. I've learned a lot since I started going.
b my whole life.
c almost every day, even if it's only a quick drawing.
d right now; I'm studying English!
e these days. More than ever!
f this week.
g twice a week.

7 Complete the conversation with the simple present, present continuous, and present perfect forms of the verbs.

A What jobs / your parents / do?
B Well, my mom is a doctor, but my dad / not / work / right now. He / study / to be a computer programmer.
A Oh, really? Why's that?
B He / be / a restaurant manager for most of his life, but he wants to do something different.
A And / he / like / computers?
B Oh, yes, he / always / play / with computers at home. My computer / never / work / because my dad / think / he can "improve" it!
A Oh, no! Well, I / hope / he learns how to fix your computer in this class!

ADJECTIVES ENDING IN -ED AND -ING

Many adjectives ending in -ed and -ing (participial adjectives) are formed from verbs. Many participial adjectives describe feelings.

*The Aztec culture **excites** a lot of visitors.* (verb)

*We went on **exciting** excursions from Mexico City.* (adjective)

*I was **excited** about visiting the Aztec pyramids.* (adjective)

Use -ing adjectives to describe what makes you feel an emotion (e.g., **exciting** excursions; The excursions make us feel this way.)

Use -ed adjectives to describe how you feel (e.g., *I **was excited**;* That's how I felt.)

▶ Activities 1 and 2

NARRATIVE FORMS

To tell stories or talk about actions in the past, use the simple past, past continuous, and past perfect.

Simple past

The simple past is used:

* to describe completed actions and situations in the past.

*I **bought** a ticket to Athens last week.*

* if actions happen one after another.

*When the food **arrived**, they **sat down** and **started** to eat.*

* to describe repeated past actions.

*When I was younger, I **walked** to school every day.*

The simple past is formed by adding -ed to the infinitive.

pack ⟶ *pack**ed***
hope ⟶ *hop**ed*** (add only -d if the infinitive ends in e)
stop ⟶ *stop**ped*** (double the final consonant if the infinitive ends in a consonant + vowel + consonant)
study ⟶ *stud**ied*** (change the y to i if the infinitive ends in a consonant + y)

Many common verbs are irregular.

go ⟶ ***went***   *get* ⟶ ***got***   *catch* ⟶ ***caught***

For questions and negative forms in the simple past, use *did/didn't* with the infinitive.

***Did** you **visit** the Guggenheim Museum when you were in New York?*

*It's strange that we **didn't meet** when we lived in Tokyo.*

The verb *be* is the only verb that doesn't use *did/didn't*.

***Was** it a scary trip?*   *I **wasn't** scared.*

For a list of irregular verbs, see page 148.

Past continuous

The past continuous is used:

* to give background information or to describe a situation when other things happen.

*Some people **were** already **dancing** when we arrived at the party.*

* to describe an incomplete action when another action happened.

*The train **left** while they **were buying** coffee.*

The actions are often connected with *when, while,* or *as.*

*She was checking her bag **when** she realized that her pen was missing.*

The past continuous is formed with *was/were* + present participle (-ing form).

*While I **was unpacking**, Joanna went to the reception to ask for a map.*

Past perfect

The past perfect is used to emphasize that one past action finished before another past action. The actions are often connected with *after, before,* and *already.*

*She **had** already **been** to Peru and didn't want to go back.*

The past perfect is formed with *had* + past participle. *Had* is often pronounced /d/ and written as a contraction, *'d.*

*I didn't get to the concert on time because I**'d missed** my train.*

used to

Use *used to* + infinitive to talk about situations, habits, and routines that were true in the past but are not true anymore. Don't use *used to* to talk about single actions.

*They **used to have** a house in Bucharest.* (situation)

*She **used to eat** meat.* (habit)

*We **used to see** them every Sunday.* (routine)

The simple past can be used to talk about these actions when the situation is clear:

*They **had** a house in Bucharest.* (It's clear that they don't have a house there now.)

~~*She ate meat.*~~ (It is not clear whether this happened once or many times, or whether she has stopped eating meat.)

Form negatives and questions using *did/didn't use to* + infinitive.

*The voyage to America **didn't use to be** as safe as it is today.*

***Did** you **use to live** in an apartment?*

▶ Activities 3–6

1 Choose the correct option to complete the sentences.

1 If you get *bored / boring* reading on the train, try listening to audiobooks instead.

2 A *surprised / surprising* number of students spend more than two hours a day getting to and from school.

3 Were you *worried / worrying* about traveling alone on the train late at night?

4 Bolivia's cable cars look *frightened / frightening*, but many commuters say they feel more *relaxed / relaxing* after their trip.

5 The trip to the museum was *interested / interesting*, but I was very *tired / tiring* by the end of the day.

6 I understand when I'm in class, but when I'm doing my homework I get *confused / confusing*.

7 I didn't enjoy that at all! The taxi was driving too fast. It was *terrified / terrifying*!

8 Phew! Those stairs are *exhausted / exhausting*. They should put an elevator in your building.

2 Are the sentences correct? If not, correct the mistake.

1 Don't be worried. It's not an embarrassed photo of you at all. You look great!

2 Simon enjoyed watching horror movies, but he didn't like feeling frightening.

3 The activity is complicated and I'm not surprised that you feel confused.

4 Everyone told her the movie was great, but she was boring after the first ten minutes.

5 If you want to feel relaxing while you explore Canada's west coast, consider a cruise.

6 The news is shocking, isn't it?

7 Our vacation was fun, even though the weather was depressed.

8 You must be feeling disappointed with that result. What went wrong?

3 Match sentences 1–3 with a–c, and sentences 4–6 with d–f.

1 When the police **searched** the train, the man **got off**.

2 When the police **searched** the train, the man **was getting off**.

3 When the police **searched** the train, the man **had gotten off**.

a The man got off before the police started searching the train.

b The man got off at the same time as the police started searching the train.

c The man got off after the police started searching the train.

4 Everyone **had left** when she got home.

5 Everyone **left** when she got home.

6 Everyone **was leaving** when she got home.

d Everyone left after she got home.

e Everyone left before she got home.

f Everyone left at the same time as she got home.

4 Choose the correct option to complete the sentences. Sometimes both options are possible.

1 Where did you *go / use to go* last weekend?

2 When you were a child, *did you have / did you use to have* a bicycle?

3 I *talked / used to talk* to him after school every day.

4 We didn't *move / use to move* from Toronto to Vancouver until 2015.

5 As a family, we *didn't go / didn't use to go* to the movies unless it was somebody's birthday.

6 My father *smoked / used to smoke*.

5 Correct the mistake in each sentence.

1 Who was teaching you to ride a bike?

2 He ran out of money while he traveled in Germany.

3 Had you seen Gareth yesterday?

4 When I arrived in class, the exam already started.

5 Did you used to walk to school?

6 First I missed the bus, then I had lost my train ticket!

6 Complete the second sentence so that it means the same as the first sentence. Use between two and four words, including the word in bold.

1 John checked that no one was in the house, then he slowly opened the door. **until**
John didn't open the door _____ that no one was in the house.

2 We spent every holiday with my grandparents when we were little, but we don't these days. **to**
We _____ every holiday with my grandparents when we were little.

3 Everyone started to eat dinner before I got home. They still hadn't finished when I arrived. **eating**
When I got home, everyone _____ dinner.

4 Marcos met a friend in Budapest before he went to Japan. **already**
When Marcos went to Japan he _____ a friend in Budapest.

5 We got on the bus in the middle of an argument among all the passengers. **argue**
When we got on the bus, all the passengers _____ .

6 She didn't bring her passport, so she couldn't get on the flight. **brought**
She couldn't get on the flight because she _____ her passport.

SIMPLE PAST AND PRESENT PERFECT

The simple past is used for completed past actions in the past, often with expressions of completed time (*last week, yesterday*).

*Australia **beat** Fiji on Sunday in the World Cup.*

The present perfect is used to talk about:
- actions that started in the past and continue to the present.

*Teams **have played** modern ice hockey for almost 150 years.*
(This continues today.)

- actions in the past which are connected to a present situation.

*He's **been** sick this week, so he's not going to practice.*
(He still doesn't feel well.)

- past experiences when the exact time isn't stated.

*If they choose Lee, it's because he's **played** more matches than Kal.*
(He played more matches at any point in the past until now.)

- recent actions.

*You haven't missed anything. They've just **started**.*
*The game's already **finished**—you missed it!*
*I **haven't seen** her score yet, but she's looking very good.*

There are many cases where either the simple present or the present perfect can be used without much change in meaning.

*The game just **started**. (simple past)*
*The game **has** just started. (present perfect)*

The first example expresses that the start of the game is in the past; the second expresses that this is a recent event and connects it to the present. Both sentences are correct, with a slight difference in the intended meaning.

The present perfect is formed with *has/have* + past participle. *Has* and *have* are often contracted to *'s/'ve*.

*She's **improved** her swimming style.*

Go has two past participle forms: *been* and *gone*. Use *been* to say someone went to a place and came back. Use *gone* to say that the person is still in that place.

*He's **been** to China. (And now he's back home.)*
*He's **gone** to China. (He's still in China.)*

For a list of irregular past participles, see page 148.

▶ Activities 1 and 2

PRESENT PERFECT AND PRESENT PERFECT CONTINUOUS

These tenses both describe actions that started or finished in the past but have a connection to the present. However, they emphasize different things.

Present perfect	Present perfect continuous
• emphasizes the fact that an action is finished. *William **has practiced** enough today. He's coming off the court.*	• emphasizes the fact that an action is unfinished. *Jo's **been practicing** all day. She won't stop until late.*
• emphasizes the present result of the action (i.e., *How many/much/often?*). *We've **played** five times. I've **won** two games and lost three.*	• emphasizes the action itself. *The girls **have been training** hard.*
• is used with stative verbs (e.g., *want, know, believe, be*). *I've **wanted** to try his racket ever since he bought it.*	• emphasizes the duration of an action. *They've **been playing** together for a couple of years.*

The present perfect continuous is formed with *has/have* + *been* + present participle.

A *Has Chloe **been practicing**?*
B *Yes, she **has**. She's **been resting**, but will start again soon.*

Questions with *How long* are often formed with the present perfect continuous.

*How long **has** she **been competing** professionally?*

Time expressions

For and *since* are used with the present perfect and present perfect continuous to say how long an action has been going on.

*They've been swimming **for** an hour. (for + period of time)*
*He's played golf **since** the age of ten. (since + point in time)*

Use *ever* and *never* + the present perfect to say *at any/no time in the past*.

*He's **never** been snowboarding. Have you **ever** tried it?*

Use *already* and *just* + the present perfect to say that an action is complete.

*We've **already** played three games this morning. (past action)*
*I've **just** come back from work. (I came back very recently.)*

Yet is used in questions and negatives to ask if an action is complete, and to say it isn't.

*Has the team won **yet**?*
*We haven't played any games **yet**.*

▶ Activities 3–6

1 Complete the paragraph with the simple past or present perfect form of the verbs.

I (1) _____ (always love) the ocean, ever since I was a girl, so when a friend (2) _____ (invite) me to go sailing with her last summer, I was very excited. I (3) _____ (go) on boat trips many times in my life, but my first day sailing (4) _____ (be) very scary. There was a lot of wind and the boat almost (5) _____ (tip over)! However, I (6) _____ (not give up) that day, and now I love it. Since then, I (7) _____ (spend) almost every weekend at the sailing club or on the water. In fact, I (8) _____ (just buy) a small boat. I (9) _____ (not take) anyone sailing with me yet, but I (10) _____ (take) the boat out on my own on Wednesday for a short trip and it was great. I (11) _____ (not see) my friend for a while because she (12) _____ (go) to New Zealand to sail professionally!

2 Correct the mistake in each sentence.

1 We have had three games yesterday.
2 She hasn't tried yet rollerblading, but I'm sure she will.
3 The team competed in the tournament for more than 30 years. In fact, this year will be their 33rd year!
4 Oh, no! You hurt your arm. It looks really sore.
5 **A** Where's Tariq?
  B He's been to the locker room to get ready.
6 José and I have played together since three years.
7 They hasn't won many matches so far this year.
8 I've met him since 2014.

3 Choose the best option to complete the sentences.

1 Two races have already *taken* / *been taking* place this morning, but it's *rained* / *been raining* since 2pm, so nothing is happening right now.
2 *I've hurt* / *I've been hurting* my leg, so I *haven't wanted* / *haven't been wanting* to compete in the last month.
3 Although she *has known* / *has been knowing* how to play chess since she was a little girl, she's only just *started* / *been starting* to play seriously.
4 **A** How far have you *swum* / *been swimming*?
  B Well, *I've swum* / *I've been swimming* for 45 minutes, so about one mile, I think.
5 The coach *hasn't chosen* / *hasn't been choosing* me for the team yet, but *I've trained* / *I've been training* all year!
6 **A** How many times has your team *been winning* / *won* the cup?
  B None, but they have a chance this year. They've *been playing* / *played* really well recently.
7 He's *been reading* / *read* books since he was five. He's *been finishing* / *finished* hundreds.

4 Use the prompts to complete the conversations. Use the present perfect or present perfect continuous.

1 **A** How long / you / play / hockey?
  B Six years. In that time, I / play / for three different teams.
  A And / your teams / win / any tournaments?
  B We / not / win / any big trophies, but we won the local tournament last month.
2 **A** Where / you / be?
  B I / work out / at the gym.
  A You / not / take / a shower yet, that's for sure! You smell terrible!
  B Give me a chance! I / only / be / home / five minutes.
3 **A** Who's that player with the ball? He / play / well so far.
  B That's Gareth Bale. You must have heard of him! He / play / for Madrid all season.
  A Of course I / hear / of him! But I didn't know what he looked like.

5 Write *How long/many/much* questions in response to these comments. Use the simple past, present perfect, or present perfect continuous.

1 I can't believe Serena Williams has won another Grand Slam!
  _____ ? (Grand Slams / she / win)
2 The club is spending so much money on new players these days.
  _____ ? (it / spend / so far)
3 Darya isn't doing tai chi anymore. She left the club a few weeks ago.
  _____ ? (she / be / a member)
4 I met my oldest friend when we played volleyball on vacation together.
  _____ ? (you / know / each other)
5 I'm not enjoying riding my bike anymore. I'm thinking about selling it.
  _____ ? (you / bike)
6 This new tennis racket was expensive.
  _____ ? (it / cost)

6 Put the words in parentheses in the correct place in the sentences.

1 Have you run a marathon? (ever)
2 He bought some new sneakers. (just)
3 They've won before. (never)
4 Has she played for the team? (yet)
5 We've met a famous person. (never)
6 I haven't had time to wash my football cleats. They're very dirty! (yet)
7 I've done some exercise today. (already)
8 Did you arrive? Get your swimsuit on! (just)

FUTURE PLANS, INTENTIONS, AND ARRANGEMENTS

Present continuous and *going to*

Both the present continuous and *going to* can be used to talk about future plans. They often have the same meaning.

Are you having lunch with your uncle tomorrow?

*I**'m going to have*** lunch with my uncle tomorrow.

The present continuous is more commonly used to talk about things the speaker has already decided to do and made arrangements for, involving other people.

*We**'re eating** at Coco's. The table is booked for 7pm.*

Going to is more commonly used to talk about plans and intentions the speaker definitely plans to do, but which are not firm arrangements yet.

*I**'m not going to have** the soup. I don't like spicy food.*

Going to is used to talk about intentions when there is no clear time given. The present continuous cannot be used here.

*I**'m going to read** that book.* (= I plan to read it in the future.)

~~*I'm reading that book.*~~ (= I'm reading it at the moment.)

will

Will is used:

- to talk about decisions made at the moment of speaking. These are often offers to help or promises.

*You're going to the supermarket? I**'ll give** you a ride.*

*I **won't say** anything about it to him, I promise.*

- when you haven't made any plans, but you are thinking about hopes, expectations, beliefs, and plans. *Will* is often used with words and expressions like *I think, I'm sure, probably, possibly, maybe,* or *perhaps*.

*I haven't decided who I'll invite. I**'ll probably ask** Sanjay.*

may/might

Another way to talk about plans and intentions that aren't firm decisions yet is to use *may* or *might*.

*She **may** ask Sanjay.* (= It's possible that she will ask him.)

*I **might** stay in tonight. It depends on what's on TV.* (= It's possible that I will stay in.)

Use *may* and *might* with *possibly*. Use *will* with *probably*.

Simple present

The simple present is used:

- for events in the future which are on timetables or schedules.

*The restaurant **opens** at six o'clock.*

- after time expressions with *when, until, after, as soon as, if,* and *unless*. *Will* is used in the main clause.

***When** you **speak** to Hanif next week, will you say hi for me?*

▶ Activities 1–4

MAKING PREDICTIONS

Will or *going to* is often used to make predictions.

will

Will is used for future events that are certain to happen.

*Dinner **will be** ready in ten minutes.*

Will is often used with *think, expect, imagine,* and *know,* and expressions like *I'm sure. Will* is usually contracted to *'ll*.

*I **imagine** he**'ll want** a big dinner. He didn't eat lunch.*

If the sentence is negative, *not* usually goes with the first verb.

*I **don't think** she'll eat it.* (Not ~~I think she won't eat it.~~)

going to

Going to is often used when there is a clear reason in the present for the prediction.

*This food is very hot. You**'re going to burn** your mouth. Be careful!*

may/might

May or *might* can be used if the speaker is less certain that a prediction is true.

*It **might** rain. If it does, we can eat indoors.*

Future continuous and future perfect

The future continuous is used to talk about an action that the speaker knows or thinks will be in progress at a certain point in the future. The future continuous is formed with *will + be + -ing*.

***Will** restaurants **be serving** insects as sweet or savory dishes?*

The future perfect is used to talk about an action that the speaker knows or thinks will be finished before a given time in the future. The future perfect is formed with *will + have +* past participle.

*I **won't have finished** this work before 10pm.*

▶ Activities 5 and 6

1 Choose the best option to complete the sentences.

1 I haven't written much of the essay yet, but I'm *working / going to work* on it soon.
2 What time *does the plane / is the plane going to* take off?
3 Those bags look heavy. *I'm going to / I'll* help you carry them to the car.
4 *I'll / I'm going to* make a sandwich. Do you want one?
5 What *will you / are you going to* wear to the party?
6 I'll have a pizza. What *might you / are you going to* have?
7 *I spend / I'm spending* a few days with a friend after I *visit / will visit* my grandparents.
8 I don't know what to do. I have to study, but I *might / will* go to the park instead.

2 Complete the sentences using the pairs of verbs in the correct form.

call + give	find out + text	get + arrive
get + not be	understand + talk	

1 I imagine the audience _____ very excited when he _____ at the stadium in an hour.
2 Until Dad _____ home with the groceries, there _____ any lunch.
3 He _____ the situation better after you _____ to him.
4 When you _____ what's happening, _____ you _____ me? You can't call me at work.
5 I _____ you as soon as they _____ me the results.

3 Complete the offers and decisions using the correct form of these verbs.

be	call	~~carry~~	cook	help	make

1 A These grocery bags are heavy.
   B I *'ll carry* _____ them for you.
2 A Could you help me clean the kitchen in about an hour?
   B I'm sorry, I can't. I _____ Beril with her computer then.
3 A Make sure you get to the restaurant on time.
   B I _____ late, I promise.
4 A Where's Agata? She said she'd be here ten minutes ago.
   B I _____ her.
5 A I'm not going to have time to cook dinner today.
   B You told me that yesterday. I told you, I _____ . I bought some fish this morning.
6 A This coffee tastes horrible!
   B Oh, no! I put salt in it, not sugar! Sorry! I _____ some more.

4 Use the prompts to write the questions or answers.

1 Q: _____ ? (what / do / weekend)
   A: I'm getting my hair cut and going to a party.
2 Q: Can you let me know what the doctor says?
   A: OK. _____ . (I / text / you / after / speak / to her)
3 Q: _____ ? (you / see / anyone / this evening)
   A: Yes, Judit is meeting me after basketball.
4 Q: Could you try not to wake Olivia? She's sleeping.
   A: _____ . (I / not / make / a sound)
5 Q: So, _____ ? (you / think / you / go back / to that restaurant)
   A: I don't know. The food wasn't that good, but the atmosphere was great.
6 Q: Could you please ask Seong-ja if she's coming on the trip?
   A: Sorry, _____ (I / not / see / her) until Tuesday, when we're having coffee.

5 Complete the sentences with the future continuous or future perfect form of the verbs.

1 Good evening, everybody. We _____ (eat) in about twenty minutes, so you have time to get a drink.
2 This time next week, I _____ (receive) my culinary diploma. I'm excited, but sad the program is ending.
3 Marc will stay in your bedroom. But don't worry—he _____ (not stay) long. Just a few days.
4 By the time you get this note, I _____ (go), so if you need anything from the store, call me.
5 At the speed he's running, he _____ (not cross) the finish line before it gets dark!
6 We've decided to go to the burger place this evening. _____ (you join) us?

6 Complete the conversation with the best form of the verbs.

A I'm taking my brother to the park. Do you want to come?
B What are you going to do there?
A I'm not sure. I imagine Victor (1) _____ (want) to go rollerblading.
B In that case, I (2) _____ (definitely come). (3) _____ (you leave) in the next five minutes?
A Victor has to get ready and put his rollerblades on. I think we (4) _____ (be) ready in about ten minutes.
B Oh! I just remembered. Carrie's going to call me, so I (5) _____ (not be) able to come with you.
A Should we just meet at the park?
B Good idea. I (6) _____ (see) you at the park gate. Tell Victor that when he sees me, I (7) _____ (wear) my rollerblades, too.

VERB + -ING OR INFINITIVE WITH TO

forget + -ing is used to talk about memories
*I'll never **forget receiving** my first job offer. I was so excited!*

forget + infinitive with *to* indicates things you need to do
*Don't **forget to send** me a text when you arrive.*

go on + -ing talks about an action that is in progress
*They **went on talking** after the meeting had finished.*

go on + infinitive with *to* talks about doing one thing after doing something else
*After college, she **went on to become** a lawyer.*

mean + -ing talks about the consequence of an action
*I can't be late again! It would **mean losing** my job!*

mean + infinitive with *to* talks about intentions or plans
*Sorry, I **meant to call** you earlier.*

regret + -ing talks about things you are sorry you did
*I **regret not taking** that job. I hate this job!*

regret + infinitive with *to* introduces something bad
*I **regret to say** that you didn't get the job.*

remember + -ing talks about memories
*I clearly **remember leaving** the letter on your desk.*

remember + infinitive with *to* talks about things you need to do
*Did you **remember to buy** some stamps?*

stop + -ing talks about an action ending
*The camera **stopped working** after I dropped it.*

stop + infinitive with *to* gives the reason for ending an action
*They **stopped to look** at the view.*

try + -ing talks about ways of solving problems, or experiments
*Isn't it working? Have you **tried restarting** it?*

try + infinitive with *to* talks about things that are difficult to do
*She **tried to fix it**, but it was impossible.*

▶ Activity 1

PRESENT AND PAST MODALS

must/shouldn't

In terms of meaning, *have to* and *must* are usually interchangeable to express obligation. However, *have to* is much more common in American English (which makes *must* sound a bit stronger). Use *have to* or *must* + infinitive for obligations. Use *have to* in questions.

*I **must call** my brother to congratulate him on his new job.*
*Do you **have to do** that now?*

In the past, use *had to*, not *must*.
*I **had to walk** to work because the buses weren't running.*

Use *can't* + infinitive to talk about things that are prohibited. You can also use *not allowed to*.
*You **can't ask** questions until the end of the presentation.*

Use *couldn't* or *wasn't/weren't allowed to* for prohibition in the past.
*I **couldn't wear** jeans yesterday because I had an interview.*
*I **wasn't allowed to** touch my sister's computer.*

Use *don't/didn't have to*, *don't/didn't need to* to say that something is not obligatory or necessary. Do not use *must*.
*I **didn't have to wear** a uniform in my last job.*
*You **don't need to worry** about it. Everything will be fine.*

Use *must* to express deductions (things that you think are true based on evidence you have).
*She **must be** the boss. She's wearing a suit.*

can/can't/could

Use *can/can't* or *be able to* to say whether something is possible, or someone is able to do something.
*Robots **can serve** food, but they **can't eat**.*

Use *can/can't* or *be allowed to* to talk about permission.
*They **can** start and finish work when they want.*
***Were** you **allowed to take** three weeks off?*

Use *could* or *was/were able to* for possibility or ability in the past. Use *could* for general ability. For a single event, use *was/were able to / managed to*.
*My computer stopped working, but I **was able to save** my work. I **couldn't** finish the document though.*

Can't (but not *can*) is also used to talk about deductions.
*It **can't be** lunchtime already. I've only just had breakfast.*

should/shouldn't

Should and *shouldn't* are used to talk about advice.
***Should** I wear a suit to the interview?*

Ought to is also used for advice. It is less common, and sounds more formal, in American English.
*You **ought to** see a career counselor.*

▶ Activities 2–5

1 Complete the sentences with the pairs of verbs. Change the form of the verb where necessary.

forget + arrive	forget + pay	go on + chat
go on + win	mean + hurt	mean + miss
regret + do	regret + inform	remember + put
remember + set	stop + do	stop + look
try + open	~~try + talk~~	

1 I know she's angry, but you haven't even *tried talking* to her yet. I'm sure she'd listen.

2 He _____ the door, but the key got stuck in the lock.

3 I _____ my cell phone charger in my bag, but it isn't there now.

4 Can you _____ your alarm for 7:30 tomorrow morning, please?

5 The team started doing poorly, but they _____ the game.

6 It was late, but they _____ into the night.

7 Can you _____ that? It's really annoying!

8 I _____ in the window of the new store on Main Street.

9 We _____ you that we are unable to accept your application.

10 It was a stupid thing to do, but I don't _____ it because it was so much fun.

11 Oh, no! I think I _____ for my drink! I'll have to go back to the café right away.

12 I'll never _____ on the island. It was so beautiful!

13 I could go back home to get an umbrella, but that would _____ my train.

14 I didn't _____ you. It was an accident.

2 Choose the correct option to complete the sentences.

1 Do I *must / have to* answer this email?

2 Employees in most companies *are allowed to / don't need to* choose when to take vacation.

3 I didn't get the job, but I *could / managed to* find a better one.

4 I have a good typing speed now, but I *couldn't / shouldn't* type very well when I started.

5 My boss says I *should / have to* go to the conference.

6 Receptionists *can't often / don't often have to* work after the office closes.

7 The old stars of silent movies *didn't need to / shouldn't* have good voices.

8 We *can't / aren't allowed to* talk to our colleagues. The boss thinks we're wasting time!

3 Complete the sentences with *must* or *can't*.

1 A It's eight o'clock. Is Paco still at work?
B Yes. He _____ love his job!

2 A Oh, no! The printer's broken again!
B It _____ be. It was working ten minutes ago.

3 A Oh, that's your phone.
B It _____ be Shona—she said she would call.

4 A You know that Kristina's leaving?
B Really? That _____ be true. She told me she likes her job.

4 Complete the second sentence so that it means the same as the first sentence. Use a form of *can, have to,* or *must.*

1 A few years ago, wearing a suit was obligatory in the office.
A few years ago, you _____ in the office.

2 I really think it is important for me to eat less sugar.
I really _____ less sugar.

3 They weren't allowed to take breaks during work hours.
They _____ during work hours.

4 Is it obligatory to wear a helmet when you ride a bicycle in your country?
_____ when you ride a bicycle in your country?

5 It isn't possible to use the printer because there isn't any paper.
You _____ because there isn't any paper.

6 It wasn't necessary for him to buy a new phone.
He _____ a new phone.

7 Smoking was permitted in the building until last year.
You _____ in the building until last year.

8 The manager says that it is necessary to arrive at the store half an hour before it opens.
We _____ at the store half an hour before it opens.

9 Eating and drinking are prohibited in the library.
You _____ in the library.

5 Correct the mistake in each sentence.

1 When I was younger, I didn't have to touch my parents' computer.

2 When do we must tell the teacher if we can't go on the school trip?

3 We shouldn't complete the project until next week, so we've got lots of time.

4 When you finish your lunch you must not to do the dishes. I'll do them later.

5 Working with criminals must not be an easy job for police officers.

IRREGULAR VERBS

INFINITIVE	SIMPLE PAST	PAST PARTICIPLE
beat	beat	beaten
become	became	become
bend	bent	bent
bet	bet	bet
bite	bit	bitten
blow	blew	blown
break	broke	broken
bring	brought	brought
broadcast	broadcast	broadcast
build	built	built
burn	burned/burnt	burned/burnt
burst	burst	burst
cost	cost	cost
cut	cut	cut
deal	dealt	dealt
dig	dug	dug
dream	dreamed/dreamt	dreamed/dreamt
fall	fell	fallen
feed	fed	fed
fight	fought	fought
forget	forgot	forgotten
forgive	forgave	forgiven
freeze	froze	frozen
hide	hid	hidden
hit	hit	hit
hold	held	held
hurt	hurt	hurt
keep	kept	kept
kneel	kneeled/knelt	kneeled/knelt
lay	laid	laid
lead	led	led
lend	lent	lent
let	let	let
lie	lay	lain
light	lit	lit
lose	lost	lost
mean	meant	meant
misunderstand	misunderstood	misunderstood
must	had to	had to
ring	rang	rung

INFINITIVE	SIMPLE PAST	PAST PARTICIPLE
rise	rose	risen
sell	sold	sold
set	set	set
shake	shook	shaken
shine	shone	shone
shoot	shot	shot
shrink	shrank	shrunk
shut	shut	shut
sink	sank	sunk
slide	slid	slid
spend	spent	spent
split	split	split
spread	spread	spread
stand	stood	stood
steal	stole	stolen
stick	stuck	stuck
strike	struck	struck
swear	swore	sworn
tear	tore	torn
throw	threw	thrown
upset	upset	upset
wake	woke	woken
win	won	won

UNIT 1 A review

In the first paragraph, explain the basic storyline and introduce the main characters.

Breathe is Sarah Crossan's second novel, written in 2012. The main characters are three teenagers with different abilities. It is set in a terrible future, a world with very little oxygen, so most of the animals and humans are dead. The survivors live in cities protected by roofs. The three friends have to leave the safety of their city to find a mysterious place called The Grove. What I really loved was the plot, which is full of action and mystery. It is an exciting book, and I couldn't put it down.

Include any basic information about the book or movie, such as the title, author or director, and date of publication or release.

Try to include at least two or three reasons for reading the book or watching the movie. You should also include points against it. If you are recommending it, make sure there are more positive points than negative ones.

Another thing that I really liked was the way the story is told by the three main characters. This means you get to see the same events in different ways. Alina is strong and angry, Bea is smart but also the bravest, and Quinn is smart and funny. They all have qualities that you can understand.

Make sure you express your personal reaction to the book or movie.

One thing that lets the book down is the sudden change in Alina's personality. Half way through the novel, she becomes kinder and more loving, but I didn't understand why.

I would really recommend *Breathe*. It reminds us that a lot of the things that we need—trees, water, air—may not be here forever. We need to protect our planet. But what makes it really worth reading is its vision of the future.

In your final paragraph, give a clear recommendation, either positive or negative.

UNIT 2 A story

Set the scene in the first paragraph, with background information such as when and where the story takes place.

Three years ago, I went to Thailand. I wanted to visit a beautiful island. My cousin had just returned from an island called Koh Tao, and told me I could catch a bus and a boat there.

Use narrative tenses (simple past, past continuous, past perfect) to show how the different actions relate to each other.

Use adverbs to comment on the story.

Use longer sentences to describe or explain the situation.

Unfortunately, no one spoke English at the bus stop, and the destinations were written in Thai, so I didn't understand anything. Eventually, an old man pointed to a bus that was just about to leave. I got on the bus.

During the long trip, I looked out of the window. I was just falling asleep when the driver shouted "Koh Tao!" I got out and looked around. I couldn't see water, just a quiet road. A man on a motorcycle came over. "Koh Tao?," I asked. He just pointed to his bike. I didn't have any choice. I got on the bike.

Use shorter sentences to describe the action and move the story along.

He drove fast. When he stopped, I saw a boat. A sign said "Koh Tao ferry." After so many hours feeling completely lost, I ended up just where I needed to be!

If the story needs to start or end with a given sentence, it should fit logically with the rest of the story.

UNIT 3 An opinion essay

In an opinion essay, make sure you state your opinion clearly in the first paragraph.

Don't forget to include one or two points against your opinion. They show that you have considered both sides of the argument, so they make your argument stronger.

State your opinion again in the final paragraph, but say it in a different way from the way you said it in the first paragraph.

The amount of time that children spend playing sports at school has decreased in many countries. These days, students are spending more time in the classroom working on subjects like math and English. Of course, these subjects are important, but I do not think it is a good idea to take time away from sports.

Sports have many benefits. First, many of us enjoy playing them. Personally, the day when we play sports is the day I enjoy most. Some students do not enjoy academic subjects, but they like sports and PE class, and this may encourage them to enjoy school more. Second, there is no question that young people are spending too much time in front of screens. People aren't doing enough exercise in their free time, so schools should help. Finally, sports are good for the brain as well as the body, in my opinion. If I have just done exercise, I have more energy for learning.

However, it's true that children have a lot to study these days, so if they're spending time at school playing sports, they have to do more work at home. Also, there are other important subjects such as art and music. Should we give them time, too?

Overall, I would say that sports are as important as any other school subject. In fact, schools should prepare students for healthy lives as well as future jobs. I strongly believe that making sports a required subject would help achieve this goal.

In the second paragraph, write at least three points that support your opinion.

Use connectors like First, Also, and Finally to structure your argument.

Using questions can make a point more interesting or powerful.

UNIT 4 A social media update

You can leave out the subject (*We finally reached*) in some sentences in informal social media posts. This makes it sound as if you are writing it during the trip, like a diary entry or a postcard.

Exclamations (*What a…!, It's so…!*) help the reader understand the writer's emotions.

Finally reached Leh last night after three incredible days in Delhi! We rushed around the Red Fort (not much time, and it's huge!), then wandered through the streets of the old city. What a beautiful place! It was boiling though, so we're all happy to feel the fresher weather of the Himalayas. The train to Leh crawled along, but at least we were able to rest. Delhi is exhausting!

My host family are super friendly and welcoming. Last night, they cooked a vegetable curry with delicious little dumplings called *momos*. Over the next week, we'll be learning how to make a few tasty local dishes.
We'll have to buy the ingredients ourselves from local markets. But tomorrow we're hoping to go hiking in the hills if the weather's good. And I'm also planning to interview some of the people in town for my culture project. I think there will be plenty of time for that—we're here for two weeks.
Next week there's the Ladakh Festival. I'm looking forward to it!

Use descriptive vocabulary to make the writing more interesting.

Emotionally powerful words make the writing more interesting, too.

Talk about recent events.

Also talk about future plans and hopes.

UNIT 5 A cover letter

Begin formal letters with *To Whom It May Concern* or *Dear Sir or Madam* if you don't know the name of the person, and *Dear Mr./ Mrs. Smith* if you know the name.

Always begin formal letters by giving your reason for writing.

Do not use contractions in formal letters: *I am*, not *I'm*.

Don't forget to include practical information about your availability, etc.

This phrase is used to ask for a reply in formal letters.

Keep paragraphs short. Include a paragraph describing any relevant experience, skills, or qualifications you may have. Use a separate paragraph for personal qualities.

End formal letters with a polite and professional salutation, like *Yours Sincerely*, *Sincerely yours*, or *Best regards*.

1-3-5 Kamiosaki
Shinagawa-ku, Tokyo 141-0021
Japan

Re: Application for summer work   May 25, 2018

To Whom It May Concern:

I am writing to apply for the job advertised on summerwork.com. I believe I am a good candidate for the job.

While I have not worked as a caregiver before, I have a lot of experience helping my father, who uses a wheelchair, get in and out of the car. What is more, I am not a bad cook and would be happy to clean the house.

I am a friendly person who gets along well with people. I am hard-working and enthusiastic, and I am sure that I would bring these qualities to the job. I would say I am a fast learner.

I finish school on June 22, and would be able to start then. I can continue until September 5.

I look forward to hearing from you soon.

Sincerely,
Aya Fujito

WORD LISTS

UNIT 1

ability (n)	/əˈbɪlɪti/
action (n)	/ˈækʃən/
affection (n)	/əˈfɛkʃən/
argument (n)	/ˈɑrgjəmənt/
attack (n/v)	/əˈtæk/
automatically (adv)	/ˌɔtəˈmætɪkli/
brave (adj)	/breɪv/
breathe (v)	/brið/
chance (n)	/tʃæns/
character (n)	/ˈkærɪktər/
characteristic (n)	/ˌkærɪktəˈrɪstɪk/
come down (phr v)	/ˌkʌm ˈdaʊn/
come out (phr v)	/ˌkʌm ˈaʊt/
comedy (n)	/ˈkɒmɪdi/
common (adj)	/ˈkɒmən/
communicate (v)	/kəˈmjunɪˌkeɪt/
confused (adj)	/kənˈfjuzd/
confusion (n)	/kənˈfjuʒən/
connect (v)	/kəˈnɛkt/
conservation (n)	/ˌkɒnsərˈveɪʃən/
control (n)	/kənˈtroʊl/
curiosity (n)	/ˌkjʊriˈɒsɪti/
cut down (phr v)	/ˈkʌt ˈdaʊn/
definitely (adv)	/ˈdɛfənɪtli/
delighted (adj)	/dɪˈlaɪtɪd/
depressed (adj)	/dɪˈprɛst/
depression (n)	/dɪˈprɛʃən/
disappointed (adj)	/ˌdɪsəˈpɔɪntɪd/
disappointment (n)	/ˌdɪsəˈpɔɪntmənt/
effect (n)	/ɪˈfɛkt/
embarrassed (adj)	/ɛmˈbærəst/
embarrassing (adj)	/ɛmˈbærəsɪŋ/
embarrassment (n)	/ɛmˈbærəsmənt/
emotion (n)	/ɪˈmoʊʃən/
end up (phr v)	/ˈɛnd ˈʌp/
enjoyment (n)	/ɛnˈdʒɔɪmənt/
estimate (v)	/ˈɛstəˌmeɪt/
event (n)	/ɪˈvɛnt/
excitement (n)	/ɪkˈsaɪtmənt/
exhausted (adj)	/ɪgˈzɔstɪd/
exhaustion (n)	/ɪgˈzɔstʃən/
exist (v)	/ɪgˈzɪst/
expect (v)	/ɪkˈspɛkt/
expedition (n)	/ˌɛkspəˈdɪʃən/
experience (n)	/ɪkˈspɪəriəns/
express (v)	/ɪkˈsprɛs/
friendliness (n)	/ˈfrɛndlinɪs/
gender (n)	/ˈdʒɛndər/
get out of (phr v)	/ˌgɛt ˈaʊt əv/
get to do something (phr)	/ˈgɛt tə ˈdu ˌsʌmθɪŋ/
happiness (n)	/ˈhæpinɪs/
hide (v)	/haɪd/
homesick (adj)	/ˈhoʊmˌsɪk/
host (n)	/hoʊst/
human (adj/n)	/ˈhjumən/
hurt (v)	/hɜrt/
increase (v)	/ɪnˈkris/
joy (n)	/dʒɔɪ/
loneliness (n)	/ˈloʊnlinɪs/
lonely (adj)	/ˈloʊnli/
memorable (adj)	/ˈmɛmərəbəl/
muscle (n)	/ˈmʌsəl/
mysterious (adj)	/mɪˈstɪəriəs/
mystery (n)	/ˈmɪstəri/
nearby (adj)	/ˈnɪərˈbaɪ/
nervous (adj)	/ˈnɜrvəs/
nervousness (n)	/ˈnɜrvəsnɪs/
novel (n)	/ˈnɒvəl/
operator (n)	/ˈɒpəˌreɪtər/
oxygen (n)	/ˈɒksɪdʒən/
personality (n)	/ˌpɜrsəˈnælɪti/
photograph (v)	/ˈfoʊtəˌgræf/
planet (n)	/ˈplænɪt/
plot (n)	/plɒt/
positive (adj)	/ˈpɒzɪtɪv/
powerful (adj)	/ˈpaʊərfəl/
protect (v)	/prəˈtɛkt/
protected (adj)	/prəˈtɛktɪd/
publish (v)	/ˈpʌblɪʃ/
quality (n)	/ˈkwɒlɪti/
rainforest (n)	/ˈreɪnˌfɔrɪst/
reader (n)	/ˈridər/
recognize (v)	/ˈrɛkəgˌnaɪz/
recommend (v)	/ˌrɛkəˈmɛnd/
regularly (adv)	/ˈrɛgjələrli/
relationship (n)	/rɪˈleɪʃənˌʃɪp/
relaxed (adj)	/rɪˈlækst/
remind (v)	/rɪˈmaɪnd/
research (n)	/ˈrisɜrtʃ/
respond (v)	/rɪˈspɒnd/
sadness (n)	/ˈsædnɪs/
safety (n)	/ˈseɪfti/
scared (adj)	/skɛərd/
scientist (n)	/ˈsaɪəntɪst/
seriously (adv)	/ˈsɪəriəsli/
service (n)	/ˈsɜrvɪs/
situation (n)	/ˌsɪtʃuˈeɪʃən/
skill (n)	/skɪl/
smart (adj)	/smɑrt/
smile (n/v)	/smaɪl/
social (adj)	/ˈsoʊʃəl/
speed (n)	/spid/
stressed (adj)	/strɛst/
sudden (adj)	/ˈsʌdən/
suggest (v)	/səˈdʒɛst/
survivor (n)	/sərˈvaɪvər/
teenage (adj)	/ˈtinˌeɪdʒ/
vision (n)	/ˈvɪʒən/
voice (n)	/vɔɪs/
warn (v)	/wɔrn/
whether (conj)	/ˈhwɛðər/
worth (adj)	/wɜrθ/
wrinkle (n)	/ˈrɪŋkəl/

UNIT 2

a handful of (n)	/ə ˈhændfʊl əv/
abandon (v)	/əˈbændən/
amusement park (n)	/əˈmjuzmənt ˌpɑrk/
avid (adj)	/ˈævɪd/
backpack (v)	/ˈbækˌpæk/
be supposed to (phr)	/ˌbi səˈpoʊzd tə/
blog (n)	/blɒg/
cable (n)	/ˈkeɪbəl/
choice (n)	/tʃɔɪs/
commute (v)	/kəˈmjut/

completely (adv)	/kəmˈplitli/
consider (v)	/kənˈsɪdər/
construction site (n)	/kənˈstrʌkʃən ˌsaɪt/
cruise (n)	/kruz/
destination (n)	/ˌdɛstəˈneɪʃən/
don't get me wrong (phr)	/ˈdoʊnt ˌgɛt mi ˈrɒŋ/
energetic (adj)	/ˌɛnərˈdʒɛtɪk/
eventually (adv)	/ɪˈvɛntʃuəli/
excursion (n)	/ɪkˈskɜrʒən/
exhausting (adj)	/ɪgˈzɔstɪŋ/
ferry (n)	/ˈfɛri/
frightened (adj)	/ˈfraɪtənd/
frozen (adj)	/ˈfroʊzən/
get to (phr v)	/ˈgɛt tu/
get to know (phr)	/ˈgɛt tə ˈnoʊ/
get up (phr v)	/ˈgɛt ˈʌp/
ghost (n)	/goʊst/
go down (phr v)	/ˈgoʊ ˈdaʊn/
go up (phr v)	/ˌgoʊ ˈʌp/
ground (n)	/graʊnd/
height (n)	/haɪt/
icy (adj)	/ˈaɪsi/
identify (v)	/aɪˈdɛntəˌfaɪ/
industrial (adj)	/ɪnˈdʌstriəl/
injury (n)	/ˈɪndʒəri/
look around (phr v)	/ˈlʊk əˈraʊnd/
look up (phr v)	/ˈlʊk ˈʌp/
manage (v)	/ˈmænɪdʒ/
normally (adv)	/ˈnɔrməli/
option (n)	/ˈɒpʃən/
plan (v)	/plæn/
public transportation (n)	/ˈpʌblɪk ˌtrænspərˈteɪʃən/
region (n)	/ˈridʒən/
resident (n)	/ˈrɛzɪdənt/
risk (n)	/rɪsk/
rooftop (n)	/ˈrufˌtɒp/
rope (n)	/roʊp/
route (n)	/rut/
shy (adj)	/ʃaɪ/
sight (n)	/saɪt/
skyscraper (n)	/ˈskaɪˌskreɪpər/
slide (n)	/slaɪd/
standard (adj)	/ˈstændərd/
story (n)	/ˈstɔri/
subway (n)	/ˈsʌbˌweɪ/
subway station (n)	/ˈsʌbweɪ ˌsteɪʃən/
surrounded by (trees) (phr)	/səˈraʊndɪd ˌbaɪ (ˈtriz)/
taste (n)	/teɪst/
team up with (phr v)	/ˈtim ˈʌp ˌwɪð/
terrifying (adj)	/ˈtɛrəˌfaɪɪŋ/
tower (n)	/ˈtaʊər/
train track (n)	/ˈtreɪn ˌtræk/
tunnel (n)	/ˈtʌnəl/
typical (adj)	/ˈtɪpɪkəl/
urban exploration (n)	/ˈɜrbən ˌɛkspləˈreɪʃən/
viewpoint (n)	/ˈvjuˌpɔɪnt/
voyage (n)	/ˈvɔɪɪdʒ/
willing (adj)	/ˈwɪlɪŋ/

UNIT 3

academic (adj)	/ˌækəˈdɛmɪk/
achieve something (phr)	/əˈtʃiv ˌsʌmθɪŋ/
alternative (adj)	/ɔlˈtɜrnətɪv/
although (conj)	/ɔlˈðoʊ/
among (prep)	/əˈmʌŋ/
amount (n)	/əˈmaʊnt/
architect (n)	/ˈɑrkɪˌtɛkt/
athlete (n)	/ˈæθlit/
attitude (n)	/ˈætɪˌtud/
aware (adj)	/əˈwɛər/
barely (adv)	/ˈbɛərli/
beat someone (phr)	/ˈbit ˌsʌmwʌn/
behavior (n)	/bɪˈheɪvjər/
benefit (n)	/ˈbɛnəfɪt/
bounce (v)	/baʊns/
break a record (phr)	/ˈbreɪk ə ˈrɛkərd/
celebrate (v)	/ˈsɛləˌbreɪt/
celebration (n)	/ˌsɛləˈbreɪʃən/
compare (v)	/kəmˈpɛər/
compete (v)	/kəmˈpit/
competitor (n)	/kəmˈpɛtɪtər/
costume (n)	/ˈkɒstum/
court (n)	/kɔrt/
culture (n)	/ˈkʌltʃər/
dangerously (adv)	/ˈdeɪndʒərəsli/
decrease (v)	/dɪˈkris/
destroy (v)	/dɪˈstrɔɪ/
difficulty (n)	/ˈdɪfɪˌkʌlti/
discourage (v)	/dɪsˈkʌrɪdʒ/
diving (n)	/ˈdaɪvɪŋ/
do something (phr)	/ˈdu ˌsʌmθɪŋ/
do your best (phr)	/ˈdu jər ˈbɛst/
dramatically (adv)	/drəˈmætɪkli/
effective (adj)	/ɪˈfɛktɪv/
encourage someone to do something (phr)	/ɪnˈkɜrɪdʒ ˌsʌmwʌn tə ˈdu ˌsʌmθɪŋ/
energy (n)	/ˈɛnərdʒi/
estimated (adj)	/ˈɛstəˌmeɪtɪd/
feel proud (phr)	/ˈfil ˈpraʊd/
field (n)	/fild/
fresh water (n)	/ˈfrɛʃ ˈwɔtər/
give someone a sense of (phr)	/ˈgɪv ˌsʌmwʌn ə ˈsɛns əv/
give up (phr v)	/ˈgɪv ˈʌp/
go on (phr v)	/ˈgoʊ ˈɒn/
gym (n)	/dʒɪm/
gymnastics (n)	/dʒɪmˈnæstɪks/
habitat (n)	/ˈhæbɪˌtæt/
hero (n)	/ˈhɪəroʊ/
hunt (v)	/hʌnt/
hunting (n)	/ˈhʌntɪŋ/
I believe in you (phr)	/ˌaɪ bɪˈliv ɪn ˈju/
impossible (adj)	/ɪmˈpɒsəbəl/
incredibly (adv)	/ɪnˈkrɛdəbli/
influence (v)	/ˈɪnfluəns/
join in (phr v)	/ˈdʒɔɪn ˈɪn/
karate (n)	/kəˈrɑti/
keep up (phr v)	/ˈkip ˈʌp/
killing (n)	/ˈkɪlɪŋ/
knock out (phr v)	/ˈnɒk ˈaʊt/
limit (n)	/ˈlɪmɪt/
loss (n)	/lɔs/
majority (n)	/məˈdʒɔrɪti/

make sense (phr)	/ˈmeɪk ˈsɛns/
mandatory (adj)	/ˈmændəˌtɔri/
marathon (n)	/ˈmærəˌθɒn/
measure (v)	/ˈmɛʒər/
opponent (n)	/əˈpoʊnənt/
overall (adv)	/ˈoʊvərˈɔl/
percent (n)	/pərˈsɛnt/
personally (adv)	/ˈpɜrsənəli/
physical (adj)	/ˈfɪzɪkəl/
play an important role (phr)	/ˈpleɪ ən ɪmˈpɔrtənt ˈroʊl/
population (n)	/ˌpɒpjəˈleɪʃən/
preparation (n)	/ˌprɛpəˈreɪʃən/
professional (adj)	/prəˈfɛʃənəl/
push one's limits (phr)	/ˈpʊʃ ˈwʌnz ˈlɪmɪts/
raise money (phr)	/ˈreɪz ˈmʌni/
recover (v)	/rɪˈkʌvər/
reduce (v)	/rɪˈdus/
referee (n)	/ˌrɛfəˈri/
reflect (v)	/rɪˈflɛkt/
replace (v)	/rɪˈpleɪs/
represent someone (phr)	/ˌrɛprɪˈzɛnt ˌsʌmwʌn/
rink (n)	/rɪŋk/
salary (n)	/ˈsæləri/
score a goal (phr)	/ˈskɔr ə ˈgoʊl/
score points (phr)	/ˈskɔr ˈpɔɪnts/
shadow (n)	/ˈʃædoʊ/
shortly (adv)	/ˈʃɔrtli/
similar (adj)	/ˈsɪmələr/
solve (v)	/sɒlv/
spectator (n)	/ˈspɛkteɪtər/
sprint (n)	/sprɪnt/
stay healthy (phr)	/ˈsteɪ ˈhɛlθi/
strength (n)	/strɛŋθ/
strongly (adv)	/ˈstrɒŋli/
survey (n)	/ˈsɜrveɪ/
swollen (adj)	/ˈswoʊlən/
take on (phr v)	/ˈteɪk ˈɒn/
take part (phr v)	/ˈteɪk ˈpɑrt/
take up (phr v)	/ˈteɪk ˈʌp/
talented (adj)	/ˈtæləntɪd/
though (adv)	/ðoʊ/
threat (n)	/θrɛt/
track (n)	/træk/
trade (n)	/treɪd/
tradition (n)	/trəˈdɪʃən/
traditional (adj)	/trəˈdɪʃənəl/
train for an event (phr)	/ˈtreɪn fər ən ɪˈvɛnt/
train hard (phr)	/ˈtreɪn ˈhɑrd/
trophy (n)	/ˈtroʊfi/
warm up (phr v)	/ˈwɔrm ˈʌp/
weapon (n)	/ˈwɛpən/
work out (phr v)	/ˈwɜrk ˈaʊt/

UNIT 4

aim (v)	/eɪm/
basic (adj)	/ˈbeɪsɪk/
coconut (n)	/ˈkoʊkəˌnʌt/
combined (adj)	/kəmˈbaɪnd/
concentrate (v)	/ˈkɒnsənˌtreɪt/
contain (v)	/kənˈteɪn/
crawl (v)	/krɔl/
damage (n)	/ˈdæmɪdʒ/

deal (n)	/dil/
deep-fried (adj)	/ˈdipˈfraɪd/
delicious (adj)	/dɪˈlɪʃəs/
diet (n)	/ˈdaɪət/
disgusting (adj)	/dɪsˈgʌstɪŋ/
distinguish (v)	/dɪˈstɪŋgwɪʃ/
doubt (n)	/daʊt/
eastern (adj)	/ˈistərn/
environment (n)	/ɛnˈvaɪrənmənt/
explore (v)	/ɪkˈsplɔr/
farming (n)	/ˈfɑrmɪŋ/
festival (n)	/ˈfɛstəvəl/
flour (n)	/flaʊər/
good-looking (adj)	/ˈgʊd ˈlʊkɪŋ/
government (n)	/ˈgʌvərnmənt/
grill (n)	/grɪl/
guess (v)	/gɛs/
hike (v)	/haɪk/
homemade (adj)	/ˈhoʊmˈmeɪd/
honest (adj)	/ˈɒnɪst/
hope to (v)	/ˈhoʊp tə/
huge (adj)	/hjudʒ/
illustrate (v)	/ˈɪləˌstreɪt/
in conflict with (phr)	/ˌɪn ˈkɒnflɪkt ˌwɪð/
incredible (adj)	/ɪnˈkrɛdəbəl/
ingredient (n)	/ɪnˈgridiənt/
interview (v)	/ˈɪntərˌvju/
introduce (v)	/ˌɪntrəˈdus/
junk food (n)	/ˈdʒʌŋk ˌfud/
local (adj)	/ˈloʊkəl/
long term (n)	/ˈlɒŋ ˈtɜrm/
look forward to (phr v)	/ˈlʊk ˈfɔrwərd tu/
meat-eater (n)	/ˈmitˌitər/
modern-looking (adj)	/ˈmɒdərnˌlʊkɪŋ/
move out (phr v)	/ˈmuv ˈaʊt/
nation (n)	/ˈneɪʃən/
natural (adj)	/ˈnætʃərəl/
old-fashioned (adj)	/ˈoʊldˈfæʃənd/
plenty (pron)	/ˈplɛnti/
prawn (n)	/prɔn/
process (n)	/ˈprɒsɛs/
processed (adj)	/ˈprɒsɛst/
raw (adj)	/rɔ/
reach (v)	/ritʃ/
recently (adv)	/ˈrisəntli/
recipe (n)	/ˈrɛsəpi/
rice-filled (adj)	/ˈraɪsˌfɪld/
rise (v)	/raɪz/
roll (n)	/roʊl/
rush (v)	/rʌʃ/
secret (n)	/ˈsikrɪt/
spicy (adj)	/ˈspaɪsi/
stall (n)	/stɔl/
steamed (adj)	/stimd/
stick with (phr v)	/ˈstɪk ˌwɪð/
style (n)	/staɪl/
sweet-tasting (adj)	/ˈswitˌteɪstɪŋ/
tasty (adj)	/ˈteɪsti/
think of (phr v)	/ˈθɪŋk əv/
undercooked (adj)	/ˌʌndərˈkʊkt/
unhealthy (adj)	/ʌnˈhɛlθi/
vegetarian (n)	/ˌvɛdʒɪˈtɛəriən/
vinegar (n)	/ˈvɪnɪgər/
vitamin (n)	/ˈvaɪtəmɪn/
wander (v)	/ˈwɒndər/
waste (v)	/weɪst/

wealthy (adj)	/ˈwɛlθi/		mean to (phr v)	/ˈmin tu/
weight (n)	/weɪt/		media (n)	/ˈmidiə/
welcoming (adj)	/ˈwɛlkəmɪŋ/		observe (v)	/əbˈzɜrv/
well-balanced (adj)	/ˈwɛlˈbælənst/		officer (n)	/ˈɔfɪsər/
well-known (adj)	/ˈwɛlˈnoʊn/		out of work (phr)	/ˈaʊt əv ˈwɜrk/
wheat (n)	/hwit/		own (v)	/oʊn/

UNIT 5

			particularly (adv)	/pərˈtɪkjələrli/
			part-time work (phr)	/ˈpɑrtˌtaɪm ˈwɜrk/
			personal (adj)	/ˈpɜrsənəl/
act (v)	/ækt/		physically (adv)	/ˈfɪzɪkli/
admit (v)	/ədˈmɪt/		piece of cake (phr)	/ˈpis əv ˈkeɪk/
advertise (v)	/ˈædvərˌtaɪz/		prevent (v)	/prɪˈvɛnt/
agency (n)	/ˈeɪdʒənsi/		productive (adj)	/prəˈdʌktɪv/
application (n)	/ˌæplɪˈkeɪʃən/		professional (n)	/prəˈfɛʃənəl/
apply (v)	/əˈplaɪ/		public (adj)	/ˈpʌblɪk/
appreciate (v)	/əˈpriʃiˌeɪt/		regret (v)	/rɪˈgrɛt/
appreciated (adj)	/əˈpriʃiˌeɪtɪd/		result (n)	/rɪˈzʌlt/
arrest (v)	/əˈrɛst/		scene (n)	/sin/
assignment (n)	/əˈsaɪnmənt/		security (n)	/sɪˈkjʊrɪti/
basically (adv)	/ˈbeɪsɪkli/		sir (n)	/sɜr/
be allowed to (phr)	/ˈbi əˈlaʊd tu/		spot (v)	/spɒt/
be responsible for (phr)	/ˈbi rɪˈspɒnsəbəl fɔr/		stressful (adj)	/ˈstrɛsfəl/
billion (n)	/ˈbɪljən/		system (n)	/ˈsɪstəm/
break the law (phr)	/ˈbreɪk ðə ˈlɔ/		temporary (adj)	/ˈtɛmpəˌrɛri/
calm (adj)	/kɑm/		total (n)	/ˈtoʊtəl/
candidate (n)	/ˈkændɪˌdeɪt/		tough (adj)	/tʌf/
career prospects (phr)	/kəˈrɪər ˌprɒspɛkts/		treat (v)	/trit/
catering (n)	/ˈkeɪtərɪŋ/		trouble (n)	/ˈtrʌbəl/
cause (v)	/kɔz/		trust (v)	/trʌst/
challenging (adj)	/ˈtʃælɪndʒɪŋ/		turn out (phr v)	/ˈtɜrn ˈaʊt/
come to (phr v)	/ˈkʌm tu/		valuable (adj)	/ˈvæljuəbəl/
committed (adj)	/kəˈmɪtɪd/		welcomed (adj)	/ˈwɛlkəmd/
competitive (adj)	/kəmˈpɛtətɪv/		well-paid (adj)	/ˈwɛl ˈpeɪd/
condition (n)	/kənˈdɪʃən/		wheelchair (n)	/ˈhwilˌtʃɛər/
continue (v)	/kənˈtɪnju/		wonder (v)	/ˈwʌndər/
control (n/v)	/kənˈtroʊl/		work in (phr v)	/ˈwɜrk ˌɪn/
count on (phr v)	/ˈkaʊnt ˌɒn/		work on (phr v)	/ˈwɜrk ˌɒn/
create (v)	/kriˈeɪt/			
creative (adj)	/kriˈeɪtɪv/			
crime (n)	/kraɪm/			
criminal (n)	/ˈkrɪmɪnəl/			
deal with (phr v)	/ˈdil ˌwɪð/			
demanding (adj)	/dɪˈmændɪŋ/			
employed (adj)	/ɛmˈplɔɪd/			
employee (n)	/ɛmˈplɔɪi/			
employer (n)	/ɛmˈplɔɪər/			
enthusiastic (adj)	/ɪnˌθuziˈæstɪk/			
faithfully (adv)	/ˈfeɪθfəli/			
fault (n)	/fɔlt/			
fighting (n)	/ˈfaɪtɪŋ/			
flexible (adj)	/ˈflɛksəbəl/			
full-time job (phr)	/ˈfʊlˌtaɪm ˈdʒɒb/			
give away (phr v)	/ˈgɪv əˈweɪ/			
glance (v)	/glæns/			
go back (phr v)	/ˈgoʊ ˈbæk/			
grateful (adj)	/ˈgreɪtfəl/			
hear from (phr v)	/ˈhɪər frəm/			
image (n)	/ˈɪmɪdʒ/			
in charge of (phr)	/ˌɪn ˈtʃɑrdʒ əv/			
in the industry (phr)	/ˈɪn ði ˈɪndəstri/			
intensive (adj)	/ɪnˈtɛnsɪv/			
involve (v)	/ɪnˈvɒlv/			
learner (n)	/ˈlɜrnər/			
madam (n)	/ˈmædəm/			
management (n)	/ˈmænɪdʒmənt/			

PERSPECTIVES

2

Workbook

**NATIONAL
GEOGRAPHIC**
L E A R N I N G

Australia · Brazil · Mexico · Singapore · United Kingdom · United States

NATIONAL GEOGRAPHIC
L E A R N I N G

Perspectives 2

Publisher: Sherrise Roehr

Executive Editor: Sarah Kenney

Assistant Editor: Becky Long

Media Researcher: Leila Hishmeh

Senior Technology Product Manager:
 Lauren Krolick

Director of Global Marketing: Ian Martin

Sr. Director, ELT & World Languages:
 Michael Burggren

Production Manager: Daisy Sosa

Senior Print Buyer: Mary Beth Hennebury

Composition: Lumina Datamatics, Inc.

Cover/Text Design: Brenda Carmichael

Art Director: Brenda Carmichael

Cover Image: ©JR-art.net/Redux Pictures

© 2018 National Geographic Learning, a part of Cengage Learning

ALL RIGHTS RESERVED. No part of this work covered by the copyright herein may be reproduced or distributed in any form or by any means, except as permitted by U.S. copyright law, without the prior written permission of the copyright owner.

"National Geographic", "National Geographic Society" and the Yellow Border Design are registered trademarks of the National Geographic Society
® Marcas Registradas

For product information and technology assistance, contact us at
Cengage Learning Customer & Sales Support, cengage.com/contact
For permission to use material from this text or product,
submit all requests online at **cengage.com/permissions**
Further permissions questions can be emailed to
permissionrequest@cengage.com

Perspectives 2 Workbook

ISBN: 978-1-337-29729-5

National Geographic Learning
20 Channel Center Street
Boston, MA 02210
USA

National Geographic Learning, a Cengage Learning Company, has a mission to bring the world to the classroom and the classroom to life. With our English language programs, students learn about their world by experiencing it. Through our partnerships with National Geographic and TED Talks, they develop the language and skills they need to be successful global citizens and leaders.

Locate your local office at **international.cengage.com/region**

Visit National Geographic Learning online at **NGL.Cengage.com/ELT**
Visit our corporate website at **www.cengage.com**

Printed in the United States of America
Print Number: 02   Print Year: 2021

1A Show Your Emotions

VOCABULARY Describing emotions

1 **Review** Unscramble the letters to make adjectives about emotions.

1 d r i a f a   _ _ _ _ _ d
2 y a p n u h p   _ n _ _ p _ _
3 g r a y n   _ _ g _ _
4 t u p e s   u _ _ _ _
5 r o d e b   _ _ r _ _
6 d o r w e i r   w _ _ _ _ _ _
7 y a p h p   _ _ _ _ y
8 x e i d e t c   _ _ c _ _ _ d

2 **Review** Complete the sentences with the adjectives from Activity 1.

1 Anja was really _____ when she heard that the dog had died.
2 Have you always been _____ of spiders?
3 Max told me he's _____ about failing the test.
4 He hated the school and had a very _____ childhood.
5 We're so _____ that you can come to the wedding!
6 The trip sounds amazing—are you getting _____ about it?
7 I think he was really _____ with her for not offering to help.
8 Were you as _____ as I was during that movie? I almost fell asleep!

3 **Review** Listen and choose the correct emotions. 🎧 1

1 angry   afraid   worried
2 excited   bored   happy
3 bored   worried   upset
4 afraid   excited   worried
5 worried   upset   angry
6 relaxed   afraid   unhappy

4 Read the sentences (1–8) and match the words in bold with their definitions (a–h).

1 When it's very dark he sometimes gets **scared**. _____
2 I was very **confused** when he started speaking in German. _____
3 You must be **delighted** that you won! _____
4 I was so **embarrassed** when Jack started to sing. _____
5 Living here can be really **lonely** at times. _____
6 Please don't be **annoyed**—I'm sorry I forgot. _____
7 I always feel **nervous** before job interviews. _____
8 She was **relaxed** and enjoying the sunshine. _____

a not able to understand
b afraid
c feeling happy and calm
d unhappy because you are not with other people
e angry or impatient
f worried
g ashamed or shy
h very happy

5 Match the adjectives with similar meanings.

1 embarrassed   a afraid
2 delighted   b angry
3 scared   c worried
4 annoyed   d ashamed
5 anxious   e happy

6 Choose the correct options to complete the sentences.

1 I'm worried *about / for / with* failing the exam.
2 She was embarrassed *with / by / of* Richard's silly comments.
3 Jamal seems very nervous *with / by / about* the interview.
4 There's no need to get annoyed *of / to / with* Jasmine—she was only trying to help.
5 Are you feeling anxious *over / about / of* your driving test?
6 He was ashamed *by / for / of* his bad grade on the test.
7 Don't be scared *for / of / with* Jason—he's really nice when you get to know him.
8 I'm confused *of / by / from* your text. Can you call me?

7 Put the words in the correct order to make sentences.

1 My / makes / feel / me / stressed / job / .

_____

2 scared / you / Are / heights / of / very / ?

_____

3 lonely / be / your / on / own / Living / can / .

_____

4 was / She / her / score / with / delighted / test / .

_____

5 about / I'm / the meaning / this / of / confused / word / .

_____

6 came / very / We're / that / happy / you / .

_____

7 have / nothing / of / ashamed / to be / They / .

_____

8 worried / moving / I'm / a / about / to / city / new / .

_____

8 Choose the correct adjectives to complete the sentences.

1 I'm often really *nervous / embarrassed* at the start of a test, but after I've answered a couple of questions, I begin to feel more *excited / relaxed*.

2 We were so *excited / stressed* when we heard the news! You must be absolutely *ashamed /delighted*.

3 **A** So was Mike *annoyed / pleased* with Eve for being so late?

   B Yes, and Eve was really *bored / upset* when he shouted at her.

4 With her family far away, Amy often feels a bit *scared / lonely* during the holidays, so she's really *grateful / relaxed* that you invited her.

5 Sorry, I'm *delighted / embarrassed* to admit this, but I'm *confused / worried* about what this sentence means.

6 Rosa's working late—she's feeling really *stressed / pleased* about getting everything finished on time and is *nervous / lonely* about doing the presentation.

9 Complete the sentences so they are true for you.

1 I got really angry when _____.

2 I sometimes get confused about _____.

3 _____ always makes me feel stressed.

4 One thing I'm happy about is _____.

5 I felt so embarrassed when _____.

6 The time I feel most relaxed is _____.

10 **Extension** Complete the sentences with these words. There are two adjectives you don't need.

cheerful	disappointed	grateful	impatient
jealous	proud	scared	selfish

1 I'm very _____ of Ava's new phone—it's so much better than mine.

2 You shouldn't be so _____ with him when he makes a mess—he's only four.

3 We're extremely _____ to you for being so generous.

4 I'm really _____ with my grade—I only got a B.

5 Javier has been incredibly successful, but we're very _____ of all our children.

6 Pete never helps out with the chores. It's really _____ of him.

11 **Extension** Choose the adjective that <u>can't</u> be followed by the preposition.

1 *proud / jealous / cheerful* + **of**

2 *impatient / selfish / disappointed* + **with**

3 *lonely / worried / nervous* + **about**

4 *upset / ashamed / scared* + **of**

5 *annoyed / angry / embarrassed* + **with**

6 *excited / proud / happy* + **about**

12 **Extension** Are these adjectives positive or negative? Complete the chart.

angry	ashamed	bored	cheerful
confused	excited	friendly	grateful
happy	impatient	lonely	relaxed
scared	selfish	upset	worried

Positive	Negative

PRONUNCIATION -ed adjectives

13 Listen to each adjective and choose the correct pronunciation of -ed. 🎧 2

1	annoyed	/t/	/d/	/ɪd/
2	stressed	/t/	/d/	/ɪd/
3	relaxed	/t/	/d/	/ɪd/
4	delighted	/t/	/d/	/ɪd/
5	bored	/t/	/d/	/ɪd/
6	excited	/t/	/d/	/ɪd/
7	scared	/t/	/d/	/ɪd/

14 Choose the correct options. Then listen and check your answers. 🎧 3

1 Yes, I was terrified.
  a Were you scared of him?
  b Were you annoyed with him?
  c Were you ashamed of him?

2 Yes, he was. He thought she'd had an accident.
  a Was he worried about her?
  b Was he scared of her?
  c Was he bored by her?

3 Yes, she is. The test is worth 50% of her grade.
  a Is she annoyed with him?
  b Is she disappointed with them?
  c Is she stressed about it?

4 Yes, they are. They can't wait!
  a Are they confused about it?
  b Are they excited about it?
  c Are they scared by it?

5 Yes, it helps me sleep.
  a Does that make you feel relaxed?
  b Does that make you feel stressed?
  c Does that make you feel scared?

LISTENING

15 Do you have a funny habit? Think of something about yourself that only a close friend or family member might know.

Soccer player Wayne Rooney turns on a vacuum cleaner to help him fall asleep.
Author Stephen King eats a slice of cheesecake before writing.
Actress Jennifer Aniston touches the outside of a plane before getting on.

16 Listen and choose the correct answers. 🎧 4

1 In the show *Tell Me Straight*…
  a Charlie talks to celebrities.
  b Charlie talks to people who know celebrities well.
  c Charlie talks to people who know a lot of celebrities.

2 Why does Sandra Rind eat a carrot?
  a Because it makes her feel relaxed.
  b Because she's hungry before she goes on stage.
  c Because it's good for her voice.

3 Bruce Collins sometimes finds it difficult…
  a to count to 100.
  b to fall asleep.
  c to know the difference between left and right.

4 Which celebrity sang in a car?
  a Jamie Cawley.
  b Gerri Pennington.
  c Ralph Powell.

5 Who told a secret about Gerri Pennington?
  a Her driving instructor.
  b Her best friend.
  c Her boyfriend.

6 Charlie thinks that…
  a everyone has a few secrets.
  b the celebrities feel very embarrassed.
  c Fred is going to tell her a secret.

17 Listen again and complete the sentences. 🎧 4

1 Fred is surprised to hear that a soccer player is _____ of spiders.

2 Ralph Powell was _____ that he passed his test.

3 Sandra Rind feels very _____ before she goes on stage.

4 Eating a carrot helps Sandra to be more _____.

5 If he says the wrong numbers, Bruce Collins feels _____ and he becomes more _____.

6 Gerri Pennington writes *left* and *right* on her hands so that she isn't _____.

7 Charlie is _____ to the celebrities and hopes they aren't too _____.

18 Think about what you heard about the celebrities and decide who said the things below. There is one name you don't need.

| Bruce Collins | Gerri Pennington | Jamie Cawley |
| Ralph Powell | Sandra Rind | |

1 "Yes, I've finally done it! No more lessons!"

_____

2 "Sorry, did you mean this side of the street, or the other side?" _____

_____

3 "One hundred, ninety-nine, ninety-eight…"

_____

4 "Camp in the forest? No way! Not with all those insects!"

_____

GRAMMAR   Subject / object questions

19 Match the questions (1–6) with the answers (a–f).

1 Who brought the chocolate cake? _____
2 How much does Gary earn? _____
3 Why was Priya so angry? _____
4 Who earns the most? _____
5 Who was angry? _____
6 What did she bring? _____

a Gary does; he earns about $90,000.
b Priya. She was angry because Duane was late.
c Gary earns about $90,000, I think.
d Anna brought it. She made it herself.
e Priya was angry because Duane was late.
f Anna brought a chocolate cake.

20 Correct the mistakes in the questions. Each question contains one mistake.

1 What TV shows do make you angry?
2 Who you talk to when you are confused?
3 Who does laughs most in your family?
4 Why they feel excited?
5 How many people do think this is wrong?
6 Whose cake does taste the best?

21 Put the words in the correct order to make questions.

1 look / why / angry / so / Jo / does / ?

_____

2 food / did / eat / how much / they / ?

_____

3 a / has / bike / flat tire / whose / ?

_____

4 what / them / did / Pepé / say / to / ?

_____

5 swimming / go / do / how often / you / ?

_____

6 people / came / how many / the / party / to / ?

_____

22 Read the answers and complete the questions.

1 A How much money _____?
B They collected more than $500.
2 A Who _____?
B Lena gave us the flowers.
3 A How often _____?
B She cries every once in a while.
4 A What _____?
B Work makes me feel stressed.
5 A Why _____?
B I listen to music to help me relax.
6 A How many _____?
B He invited twenty people.

23 Write answers that are true for you.

1 What is your favorite type of movie?

_____

2 How often do you go out to eat?

_____

3 How many English classes have you taken?

_____

4 When is your mother's birthday?

_____

5 How many times have you seen your favorite movie?

_____

1B Fake It until You Feel It

VOCABULARY BUILDING Suffixes

1 How are nouns formed from these adjectives? Complete the chart.

confused	depressed	disappointed	embarrassed
excited	exhausted	friendly	happy
lonely	nervous	sad	selfish

+ment	+ness	+ion

2 Complete each sentence with a noun formed from the adjective in parentheses.

1 Your _____happiness_____ is what's most important. (happy)

2 Not being picked for the team was a big _____. (disappointed)

3 There seems to be some _____ about the result. (confused)

4 Having to wait only added to the _____. (excited)

5 It's with great _____ that we announce the death of Anna Jackson. (sad)

6 John has always suffered from _____. (depressed)

7 She could see the _____ on his face. (embarrassed)

READING

3 Read the text. What is the World Happiness Report?

a A description of how to make the world happier.

b A comparison of levels of happiness in different countries.

c A list of the 156 happiest places on Earth.

4 Look at the words in bold in the text and match them with their definitions.

benchmark	consistently	corruption	evaluation
imaginary	life expectancy	rank	stark

1 in a way that does not change _____

2 not real _____

3 a level used as a standard when comparing other things _____

4 the length of time that a person is likely to live _____

5 obvious in an unpleasant way _____

6 to put something into a position on a list according to importance, success, size, etc. _____

7 dishonest or illegal behavior _____

8 the act of deciding how good or bad something is _____

5 Read the statements. Are the sentences true (T), false (F), or is the information not given (NG)?

1 The World Happiness Report is only read by governments. _____

2 In the survey, people are asked to decide how happy their lives are. _____

3 Dystopia is an imaginary country where people are extremely happy. _____

4 Children are not included in the survey. _____

5 Some people think that the number of people surveyed is too small. _____

6 The World Happiness Report doesn't consider economic factors. _____

7 In Iceland and Denmark, people don't pay for medical treatment. _____

8 People live longer in Madagascar than in Togo. _____

6 Match the statements and countries.

Australia	Denmark	Iceland
Madagascar	Switzerland	United States

1 Most of its citizens know more than one language. _____

2 It's ranked 13th in the 2016 World Happiness Report. _____

3 Higher education is free here. _____

4 It's an island and one of the world's unhappiest countries. _____

5 Its citizens live nine years longer than the global average. _____

6 It usually has pleasant weather. _____

The World Happiness Report

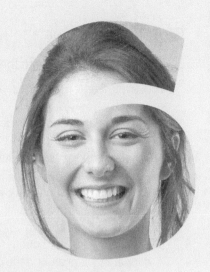

🎧 **5** The World Happiness Report is a survey of happiness in different countries published by the United Nations. First produced in 2012, it **ranks** 156 countries by their happiness levels. The report is attracting increasing interest because many governments are now using happiness data to develop policies that support people more effectively.

In the survey, which is available to the public on the World Happiness Report website, leading experts in fields such as economics, psychology, health, and statistics describe how measurements of happiness can be used to assess the progress of a country. The report reviews the state of happiness in the world today and explains national variations. For example, in 2016, Denmark was the world's happiest country, with the US ranked 13th, and the United Kingdom 23rd. The island country of Madagascar, with a ranking of 148, is among the world's unhappiest nations.

So, how do researchers decide on these rankings? They are, in fact, based on answers to a life **evaluation** question called "The Cantril Ladder." People are asked to think of a ladder, in which the best possible life for them is ranked 10, and the worst 0, and decide where their current life is on this 0 to 10 scale. Their answers are then adjusted based on six other factors: levels of GDP (Gross Domestic Product, the value of goods and services that a country produces in a year), **life expectancy**, generosity, social support, freedom, and **corruption**. The results are compared to those of Dystopia, an **imaginary** country that has the world's least happy people. Dystopia is the lowest

benchmark of happiness, so that all other countries will be higher than it in relation to those six factors.

One criticism of the report is that it only examines two to three thousand people per country, but researchers believe this is a large enough sample. They also think the report is helpful because, unlike many other world surveys, it doesn't only look at economic factors.

Why, then, is Denmark the world's happiest country? One thing is its life expectancy of 80 years, when the global average is only 71. It also has free health care and an excellent welfare system, which means that wealth is spread fairly across the population. Another country in the top ten is Australia, with its beaches and **consistently** warm temperatures. Melbourne has even been named the best city in the world to live in, because of low crime levels, good climate, medical care, and public transportation. The country of Iceland came in third, offering its citizens low taxes, free higher education, and free health care. It is also rated as the most peaceful nation on Earth. Switzerland, where the majority of citizens understand French, German, and English, is currently in second place, enjoying healthy public finances, low taxes, an average life expectancy of nearly 83, and beautiful scenery connected by efficient railroads. By **stark** contrast, African countries are among the least happy nations in the world, many affected by civil war and extreme poverty. The country of Togo, ranked in 155th place, has a life expectancy of just 58.

1C Do you always...?

GRAMMAR Talking about the present

1 Match the rules (1–7) with the sentences (a–g).

1 Use the simple present to talk about things that are generally true. _____
2 Use the present perfect to describe actions that started in the past and continue to the present. _____
3 Use the simple present to describe habits and routines. _____
4 Use the present continuous with *always* to describe actions that happen often and may cause an emotional response in the speaker. _____
5 Use the present continuous to talk about actions happening at or around the present time. _____
6 Use the simple present with stative verbs, e.g., *enjoy*, *agree*, *think*. _____
7 Use the present continuous to talk about changing situations. _____

a We're sending cards less often these days.
b Riku is speaking to another customer at the moment.
c Karen and I have known each other for over 30 years.
d I definitely agree with your decision.
e Niamh is always making silly comments.
f She goes to a karate class on Tuesdays.
g Planets closer to the sun have shorter years than Earth.

2 Are the verbs in bold correct or incorrect? Correct those that are incorrect.

1 Water **is freezing** at 32 degrees Fahrenheit.
2 The phone **rings**. Can you answer it?
3 If it's not raining, she usually **walks** to work.
4 I'm bored. I **am wanting** to watch TV.
5 A It's 6 o'clock already. We need to go.
   B Sorry, Freya, **I've come.**
6 Koala bears **sleep** for more than twenty hours a day.
7 Ahmed's often confused. He's always **asking** questions.
8 I **feed** the cat while Jade and Lee are on vacation this month.

3 Choose the correct options to complete the sentences.

1 Chris usually *reads / is reading* before going to sleep.
2 I often *am enjoying / enjoy* a cup of tea at bedtime.
3 *We're shopping / We've shopped* online for two hours.
4 Beth is so angry all the time. *She's always shouting / She shouts.*
5 The sun *doesn't set / isn't setting* in Iceland in June.
6 Some people *think / are thinking* this is a good idea.
7 They *never go / are never going* to bed before midnight.
8 *I laugh / I'm laughing* because he told me a joke.

4 Put the words in the correct order to make sentences and questions.

1 bakes / Blanca / every / bread / day / .
_____

2 long / how / you / have / truth / known / the / ?
_____

3 Jack / always / to / me / asking / help / him / is / .
_____

4 right / now / feeling / are / how / you / ?
_____

5 the / internet / changing / the / communicate / we / way / is / .
_____

6 moon / the / at / per hour / ten / miles / rotates / .
_____

7 become / recently / life / very / has / difficult / .
_____

8 usually / to / TV / I / watch / relax / .
_____

5 Complete the conversations using *always* + the present continuous form of the verbs in parentheses.

1 A There's a problem with my car again.
   B No way! _____ . (break down)
2 A Sarah finds it difficult to get up in the morning.
   B I'm not surprised. She _____ to bed late. (go)
3 A Amy was really angry with her parents.
   B I don't blame her. _____ . (interfere)
4 A Kira wants to borrow $20.
   B Typical! _____ for money. (ask)
5 A I can't read the menu without my glasses.
   B Where are they? _____ to bring them. (forget)
6 A It's going to be another long night at the office.
   B Really? _____ late. (work)
7 A Li has a stomach bug and can't come out tonight.
   B Poor Li! _____ sick. (feel)
8 A Dean is the worst roommate. He never helps with the cleaning.
   B Maybe you should move. _____ about him. (complain)

6 Complete the text with the simple present, present continuous, or present perfect form of the verb in parentheses.

Kenji and I **(1)** _____ (share) an apartment for about a year. He **(2)** _____ (enjoy) exercise and every morning he **(3)** _____ (run) around the park. He **(4)** _____ (always ask) me to go with him, but I really **(5)** _____ (not like) getting up early, so sometimes I **(6)** _____ (swim) in the local pool after work. In the evenings, I usually just **(7)** _____ (watch) TV, but Kenji is the sort of person who **(8)** _____ (read) a book or **(9)** _____ (do) a crossword puzzle. Right now, he **(10)** _____ (cook) a meal for the two of us and **(11)** _____ (listen) to the radio. He **(12)** _____ (find) it very difficult to relax, so he often **(13)** _____ (clean) the kitchen after dinner, too. That's great for me, though, since I **(14)** _____ (always be) very lazy.

7 Choose the correct options. Then listen and check your answers. 🎧 6

1 Do you know Jason?
   a Yes, we're knowing him for a couple of years.
   b Yes, we've known him for a couple of years.

2 Are you ready yet?
   a Almost, I just come.
   b Almost, I'm coming now.

3 Is Simon angry about it?
   a No, he agrees with my decision.
   b No, he's agreeing with my decision.

4 What does she do on the weekends?
   a She's usually gone shopping.
   b She usually goes shopping.

5 Is Alex with you?
   a No, he's playing tennis with a friend.
   b No, he plays tennis with a friend.

6 Does Alice have a part-time job?
   a Yes, she works in a café.
   b Yes, she's worked in a café.

7 Is Erica still living in Spain?
   a No, she lives in Portugal now.
   b No, she's lived in Portugal now.

8 When do you go to the gym?
   a I go before work.
   b I am going before work.

1D This app knows how you feel—from the look on your face.

TEDTALKS

AUTHENTIC LISTENING SKILLS

1 Listen to Part 1 of the TED Talk and underline the words that are stressed. 🎧 **7**

At Cambridge, thousands of miles away from home, I realized I was spending more hours with my laptop than I did with any other human.

2 Listen and complete the excerpt with the words you hear. Listen and check—are these content words stressed? 🎧 **8**

I was _____, I was _____, and on some days I was actually _____, but all I had to communicate these _____ was this.

WATCH ▶

3 Look at the words and choose the correct emoji.

1 confused   ☺ ☹ ☺
2 angry   ☺ ☺ ☹
3 embarrassed ☺ ☹ ☺
4 scared   ☹ ☺ ☺
5 delighted ☺ ☹ ☺

4 Choose the correct options to complete the sentences.

1 Rana says that our emotions influence…
   a what we learn.
   b how we shop.
   c everything about our lives.

2 Fifteen years ago, Rana…
   a got married.
   b went to live in England.
   c became a computer scientist.

3 Rana was frustrated because…
   a her laptop couldn't understand her feelings.
   b she spent a lot of time alone.
   c she felt homesick.

4 Action unit 12 is…
   a a facial muscle.   **b** a smile.   **c** an emotion.

5 A smirk and a smile…
   a look the same, but mean different things.
   b look different, but mean similar things.
   c look similar, but mean different things.

6 A computer learns to recognize expressions by…
   a looking at thousands of pictures.
   b learning about the characteristics of a face.
   c storing information about emotions.

5 Match the paraphrases in bold with the words from Part 3 of the TED Talk. Then watch and check your answers.

down the line	especially close to my heart
fighting a losing battle	golden opportunity
tracked your mood	visually impaired
want to share	

Where is this data used today? I **would like to tell you about (1)** _____ some examples that are **very important to me (2)** _____.
Emotion-enabled wearable glasses can help individuals who are **not able to see very well (3)** _____ read the faces of others…

What if your wristwatch **knew how you were feeling (4)** _____, or your car sensed that you're tired, or perhaps your fridge knows that you're stressed…

I think in five years **from now (5)** _____, all our devices are going to have an emotion chip…

As more and more of our lives become digital, we are **failing when (6)** _____ trying to curb our usage of devices in order to reclaim our emotions.

And by humanizing technology, we have this **important chance (7)** _____ to reimagine how we connect with machines…

VOCABULARY IN CONTEXT

6 Complete the sentences with these words.

characteristics	curiosity	gender
homesick	joy	wrinkles

1 There are several _____ of a leader.
2 There were tears of _____ in her eyes as she held her grandson for the first time.
3 Talking to my parents on the phone makes me feel a little _____ .
4 Despite his age, he was very good-looking, with just a few _____ around his eyes.
5 **A** Why do you want to know?
   B Oh, just for my own _____ .
6 The competition is open to everyone, regardless of age or _____ .

1E The Feel-Good Factor

SPEAKING

1 Read and complete the conversation. Then listen and check your answers. 🎧 9

Tom I just saw *Scarlet's Destiny*.

Paul Oh, I haven't heard of that. **(1)** _____ of movie is it?

Tom It's a sci-fi movie. It has great special effects.

Paul **(2)** _____ come out?

Tom It was released about a week ago, I think.

Paul **(3)** _____ in it? Any well-known actors?

Tom Well, there's Jake Pomfroy, and Sara Linnett—she's really beautiful…

Paul I'm not sure I know who that is. **(4)** _____ she been in?

Tom She was in that movie with Matt Grieve about Mars.

Paul Oh, yes, I remember the one. So, **(5)** _____?

Tom It's about a woman who gets more intelligent every time she sleeps.

Paul Sounds interesting. **(6)** _____ set?

Tom In London, in 2070. I really loved the plot—a little weird, but fascinating.

Paul Oh, OK. So, **(7)** _____ it?

Tom Yeah, I would. There were some pretty good scenes in it and the ending was amazing.

Paul I'll give it a try!

2 Listen to the questions in Activity 1 and underline the words that are stressed. Then listen again and practice. 🎧 10

3 Put the words in the correct order to make questions. Then match the questions with the answers (a–g).

1 did / come / when / out / it / ? ___

_____

2 it / directed / who / ? ___

_____

3 it / so / about / what's / ? ___

_____

4 like / the / what's / acting / ? ___

_____

5 recommend / would / it / you / ? ___

_____

6 set / it / where's / ? ___

_____

7 kind / what / movie / it / of / is / ? ___

_____

a An action adventure.
b In New York.
c Some characters aren't well acted.
d It's about a battle to save the Earth.
e I'm not sure—it's not the best movie I've seen recently.
f Jack Peterson.
g Last month.

4 Choose three of these movie genres and give your own answers to the questions in Activity 3 on a separate sheet of paper.

| comedy | drama | horror | musical | sci-fi | thriller |

5 Read the review and listen to the conversation that follows it. Then answer the question below. 🎧 11

Can sequels ever be a good thing? Although the quality of the second film in this superhero movie franchise is good, it's like a repeat of something that was magical the first time, but isn't quite as great anymore. *Cosmic Cops 2* has a fantastic plot and special effects, great characters, and excellent performances, but it just doesn't have the same impact as the first movie.

While they are protecting space and delivering vital top-secret supplies to a research facility, the team meets a space thief who steals the supplies and flies across the galaxy. They then chase after him. Add to this a subplot about an older officer returning to duty, and an accident that leaves the team stuck on an alien planet, and this is classic science-fiction.

Although we've seen it all before, the special effects, characters, and acting are all very high quality. The whole audience loved the movie's excitement and wonderful soundtrack.

Question: The woman expresses her opinion of the movie, *Cosmic Cops 2*. State her opinion and explain the reasons she gives for having that opinion.

WRITING A review

6 Put the parts of the movie review in the correct order.

_____ *The Pursuit of Happyness* is a **moving** film. Based on the real-life experiences of Chris Gardner, the movie explores the bond between a father and son who find themselves homeless. The two move from place to place, even spending one night in a subway bathroom. But despite such extreme hardships, Gardner continues to pursue his dream, eventually securing the job he really wants at a successful investment company.

_____ This is not a **feel-good** movie, but a real **tearjerker**, a touching portrayal of a true story. It might not be **action-packed** or make you smile, but it's a movie you won't quickly forget—definitely one to watch. Rating ****

_____ *The Pursuit of Happyness*

_____ However, though the story is very moving, it's also a bit depressing. We see Gardner face one problem after another in his struggle for financial stability. One thing I found myself wanting to know more about was what happened in the later part of Gardner's life. Although we find out he got the job, we never get to see the joy and success that come from his earlier struggles.

_____ In my opinion, it's the emotional connection between the two stars, Smith and his real-life son Jaden, that is the main strength of this movie. Jaden gives a brilliant performance as a child whose life and economic background are so very different from his own. The film is also a **thought-provoking** portrayal of homelessness and the problems faced by many in our society every day.

_____ 2006, Drama / **Biography**, 117 minutes Starring Will Smith, Jaden Smith, Thandie Newton

7 Read the review again. Does the writer like the movie?

8 Match the parts of the movie review in Activity 6 with these headings.

a recommendation	a description of the plot
what the writer didn't like	title
what the writer liked	basic information

1 _____   4 _____
2 _____   5 _____
3 _____   6 _____

9 Complete the definitions with the words in bold in the review.

1 A _____ is a sad movie or story that makes you want to cry.

2 A _____ movie makes you feel happy.

3 A _____ is a book or movie about someone's life.

4 If something is _____, it makes you think a lot about a particular subject.

5 If a movie is _____, it is full of exciting events.

6 If a film is _____, it makes you feel emotional.

10 Rewrite the sentences to add emphasis.

1 I really loved the ending.
The thing that _____
_____

2 I found the special effects a bit disappointing.
What _____
_____

3 I didn't like the soundtrack.
One thing that _____
_____

4 The portrayal of the prison wasn't very realistic.
It was _____
_____

5 I enjoyed the song and dance scenes the most.
What _____
_____

11 Write a review of the last movie you saw. Include at least one sentence that starts with *One thing I didn't like / really loved…* Answer these questions:

- What type of movie is it?
- What's it about?
- Where / When is it set?
- Who's in it?
- What was good / bad?
- Would you recommend it?

Tip box
• Include introductory sentences that give basic information about the movie.
• Provide a short description of the plot.
• Say the good and bad things about the movie.
• Give your opinion and emotional response to the movie.
• Include a sentence that tells the reader to watch it (or not).

Review

1 Read the definitions and complete the words.

1 not able to understand
c __ __ __ __ __ d

2 frightened
s __ __ __ d

3 feeling happy and calm
r __ __ __ __ __ d

4 unhappy because you are not with other people
l __ __ __ __ y

5 angry or impatient
a __ __ __ __ __ d

6 worried and unable to relax
s __ __ __ __ __ d

7 ashamed or shy
e __ __ __ __ __ __ __ d

8 very happy
d __ __ __ __ __ __ __ d

2 Choose the correct options to complete the text.

Where **(1)** *do you eat / are you eating* lunch? I usually **(2)** *have gone / go* to the café on the main plaza. **(3)** *I try / I've tried* the university cafeteria, but the food **(4)** *doesn't taste / isn't tasting* as good. I **(5)** *have preferred / prefer* to eat sandwiches at lunchtime, and the café **(6)** *is having / has* much more choice. It also **(7)** *sells / has sold* really delicious salads. However, it's much more expensive than making them yourself, so this semester **(8)** *I've started / I start* to bring my own food sometimes. **(9)** *I'm saving / I have saved* for a trip to Brazil next summer, so **(10)** *I decide / I've decided* to spend less.

3 Use the prompts to write questions in the simple past.

1 What / they / decide / do?
_____

2 How often / you / go / gym?
_____

3 Whose / daughter / play / the piano?
_____

4 How many / friends / she / invite?
_____

5 What / he / ask / Elena?
_____

6 What / make / you / feel / embarrassed?
_____

7 How many / students / pass / test?
_____

4 Complete the email with these words.

bored	confused	delighted	embarrassed
excited	interested	lonely	nervous
relaxed	worried		

Hi Amina,

Just thought I'd send you a quick message to tell you that I got the job at the tourist office! I'm absolutely
(1) _____! I've been really
(2) _____ where I'm currently working because there's not enough to do, and it also gets very
(3) _____ with no one to talk to all day.
I felt very **(4)** _____ when I went into the interview, and I was **(5)** _____ that I wouldn't do my best, but the manager was very kind. After a few minutes, I began to feel more
(6) _____ . He seemed really
(7) _____ in my past experience and although I got a bit **(8)** _____ about one of the questions, I generally gave good answers. The only bad thing was that I completely forgot his name when we were saying goodbye. I felt so
(9) _____! Anyway, never mind, it's all good and I start next month, so I'm feeling very
(10) _____ about it!
Hope to see you soon,
Mei

5 Choose the correct options. Then listen and check your answers. 🎧 12

1 What did he win in the competition?
  a He won a television. Lucky man!
  b Rami won. Lucky man!

2 Who has the largest family?
  a Paul does. He has four brothers and two sisters.
  b Paul has four brothers and two sisters.

3 What does she eat for lunch?
  a Amy usually eats a sandwich.
  b Amy does. She usually eats a sandwich.

4 How much did they collect?
  a The teachers did. They were so generous.
  b Over $5,000. They were so generous.

6 Correct the sentences. Use the simple present, present continuous, or present perfect.

1 He'll only be a minute—he just puts his coat on.

2 My cellphone alarm rings. I'll turn it off.

3 Carlos and Niko live in York since 2001.

4 I've usually run in the park on Sundays.

5 If water is freezing, it is turning to ice.

6 We're knowing Kevin for about two years.

2 Enjoy the Ride

2A Getting from A to B

VOCABULARY Travel

1 Review Choose the correct options to complete the sentences.

1 The *airport / fly* was crowded, and the line for security was really long.
2 I always enjoy *visiting / getting to* my family in Mexico during the summer.
3 Some *visits / tourists* are respectful travelers, and some are not.
4 The *plane / bus* station is in the city center—about 1,500 feet from the train station.
5 I prefer to stay in *hotels / stations* when I travel to new countries.
6 She *drives / flies* too fast, so she sometimes gets speeding tickets.
7 He's an experienced *travel / traveler*—he's been to over twenty countries.
8 I want to visit Jamaica for my next *vacation / visit*, but my sister wants to go to Brazil.

2 Review Read the clues and complete the words about travel. The first letter is given for you.

1 I'm afraid of flying, so I prefer to travel on this.
t __ __ __ __
2 Planes arrive and depart from this place.
a __ __ __ __ __ __ __
3 This person visits new places and goes sightseeing.
t __ __ __ __ __ __
4 Buses arrive and depart from this place.
s __ __ __ __ __ __
5 Many people stay here at night when they are traveling.
h __ __ __ __
6 If you're going to take a car on vacation, you'll need to do this.
d __ __ __ __
7 This is a digital file or printed piece of paper that you pay for and use to travel.
t __ __ __ __ __
8 If it's too far to walk, I usually take one of these.
t __ __ __

3 Review Listen to the sentences. Choose the correct options. 🎧 13

1 *train / plane*
2 *visitors / visits*
3 *traveler / traveling to*
4 *fly / drive*
5 *hotel / station*
6 *train / bus*

4 Unscramble the letters to make words about travel.

1 t m c o u m e   c __ __ __ __ __ __
2 t u o r e   __ __ u __ __
3 e g o y v a   __ __ __ __ g __
4 c s u e i r   __ r __ __ __ __
5 o i t e e d i x p n
   __ x __ __ d __ __ __ __ n
6 d r e i   __ __ __ e
7 p c b a k c a i g n k
   __ __ c __ __ __ __ k __ __ g
8 g f i h l t   __ __ __ __ __ h __

5 Complete the sentences with the correct forms of the words in Activity 4.

1 The ship made the _____ from London to New York in six days.
2 The car _____ through the jungle was long and uncomfortable.
3 My friends are going _____ this summer.
4 We really enjoyed the _____. It actually left on time!
5 I took a different _____ home from the restaurant and got lost.
6 I'd like to take a _____, but I often get seasick.
7 My dad usually _____ to work. The trip takes over an hour.
8 She went on an _____ to Kenya to study lions.

6 Match these verbs with the nouns and phrases they collocate with.

1 get to   **a** the train
2 go for   **b** São Paulo
3 catch   **c** from my house to school
4 get   **d** a long ride in the car
5 get to know   **e** the restaurant

7 Complete the sentences with the correct forms of these words and phrases.

get (x2)	get off (x2)	get to (x2)	get to know (x2)

1 I _____ the bus just in time—I almost missed my stop!
2 I love _____ new cities and new people.
3 What time should we _____ the airport before our flight?
4 I _____ school late because my train was delayed.
5 I'm always worried about _____ lost, so I carry my phone everywhere.
6 _____ the road! There's a car coming!
7 She _____ her way around by talking to the locals.
8 How do I _____ from the port to the center of town?

8 Complete the sentences with these words. There are two words you don't need.

cruise	destination	excursion	expedition
flight	lift	ride	route

1 I'm planning to take a _____ to the Caribbean this summer if I save enough money.
2 On Saturday, we're going on an _____ to a chocolate factory.
3 We need to take another _____ to Mexico City. Ours has been canceled.
4 Would you like to go for a bike _____ this weekend? We could go to Rock Creek Park.
5 According to José, they should reach their _____ by about 5 pm tomorrow.
6 We're going on an _____ into the Amazon for six weeks—we can't wait!

9 **Extension** Match the words with a similar meaning.

1 arrive   **a** leave
2 depart   **b** visitor
3 tourist   **c** journey
4 excursion   **d** land
5 route   **e** way
6 voyage   **f** outing

10 **Extension** Choose the correct options to complete the sentences.

1 Hurry! The plane is about to *depart / arrive*, and the gate is a long *sight / way* from here!
2 We're planning to *leave / stay* our hotel at noon and do some *sights / sightseeing* until dinnertime.
3 It's time to *depart / board* the train. It's on platform 5.
4 I don't *see / know* Chicago very well. I've lived here for a year, and I still get lost.
5 Who are you going to *stay / keep* with while you're in Seoul?
6 I'll meet you at the airport. What time does your plane *land / board*?

LISTENING

11 Match the two words of the compound nouns. Listen and check your answers. Then practice saying the words. 🎧 **14**

1	sky	**a**	park
2	public	**b**	tracks
3	building	**c**	scraper
4	shopping	**d**	top
5	railroad	**e**	sites
6	amusement	**f**	light
7	traffic	**g**	transportation
8	roof	**h**	mall

12 Listen and choose the correct answers to the questions. 🎧 **15**

1 Do the man and the woman know each other?
  a Yes.
  b No.
  c It's not clear.

2 Why does the woman need to ask the man for directions?
  a She's lost her map of the city.
  b She doesn't know where she is.
  c She doesn't have her phone with her.

3 Does the man know where the Stratton Building is?
  a Yes, he gives the woman exact directions.
  b More or less, but he decides to check on his phone.
  c No, he has no idea. He needs to find out on his phone.

4 What word does the woman use meaning *annoy*?
  a bother
  b upset
  c irritate

5 How does the man think the woman should get there?
  a take the subway
  b walk
  c take a taxi

6 What should the woman do when she gets to Central Boulevard?
  a go straight
  b take a right
  c turn left

7 What does the woman need to walk through before she gets to the building?
  a an intersection
  b a park
  c a block

8 What does the man tell her that she can't miss?
  a the Stratton Building
  b lunch in the park
  c Central Boulevard

13 Listen to the lecture. The speaker quotes the poet T. S. Eliot. What do you think Eliot meant? 🎧 **16**
  a Humans should focus more on living than on exploration.
  b Exploration gives us a better understanding of ourselves and our world.
  c We can learn the most valuable lessons from the very first explorers.
  d Exploration doesn't really answer any of our important questions.

14 Listen again and choose the correct answers to the questions. 🎧 **16**

1 What does the speaker mean by "the final frontier"?
  a human exploration
  b the end of exploration
  c unexplored areas

2 What does she describe as "countless"?
  a planets
  b equipment
  c humans

3 Does the speaker agree that space is relatively unexplored?
  a No, she doesn't.
  b Yes, she does.
  c She isn't really sure.

4 What phrase does she use to describe our oceans?
  a a lot closer to home
  b the only final frontier
  c less than ten percent

5 According to the speaker, how much of the Earth is covered by oceans?
  a around 99%
  b less than 10%
  c more than 70%

6 How many people does the speaker say have traveled to the deepest parts of the oceans?
  a many
  b only a few
  c none

7 According to the speaker, what percentage of the living space on our planet is on land?
  a 10%
  b 70%
  c 1%

8 What does she say has yet to be discovered?
  a many kinds of sea life
  b all the oceans of the world
  c the deepest ocean

GRAMMAR Adjectives ending in -ed and -ing

15 Complete the definitions with these words.

annoyed	bored	confusing	depressing
embarrassed	interesting	surprising	

1 _____ = keeping your attention because it is unusual or exciting

2 _____ = not really interested in anything

3 _____ = feeling shy or ashamed

4 _____ = unexpected

5 _____ = difficult to understand

6 _____ = a little angry about something

7 _____ = making you feel unhappy and disappointed

16 Choose the correct participial adjectives to complete the sentences.

1 The Great Pyramid of Giza was *amazing / amazed*. We weren't *disappointing / disappointed* when we finally visited it.

2 It's *surprising / surprised* that the ancient city of Petra was built over 2,000 years ago, but was unknown to the West until 1812.

3 We were all *confusing / confused* to hear the tour guide say that Venice is built on 118 islands.

4 Pompeii was an ancient Roman city that was buried in ash after the *terrified / terrifying* eruption of Mount Vesuvius.

5 No one could sleep last night because we were so *excited / exciting* about seeing the Taj Mahal.

6 We spent a *relaxing / relaxed* afternoon on the banks of the Seine river.

17 Complete the phrases with the correct participial adjectives formed from the verbs in parentheses.

1 that _____ (depress) movie

2 those _____ (exhaust) athletes

3 a _____ (bore) flight that lasted six hours

4 _____ (confuse) tourists who don't speak the language

5 a _____ (frighten) accident involving a large truck

6 _____ (annoy) travelers whose bags were lost

7 an _____ (amaze) cruise in the Caribbean

8 _____ (disappoint) passengers wanting to get home

18 Choose the correct options to complete the text.

Surprised students, surprising day

One day last week, teachers at Funston School told their **(1)** *bored / boring* students to go to the school gym for a meeting. The **(2)** *unexciting / unexcited* students thought that the **(3)** *boring / bored* prinicipal would give out awards for good grades as he did every month. But this time they were wrong. Instead, one hundred **(4)** *confuse / confused* students received a gift—new bikes!

The teachers and students were **(5)** *surprised / surprise* to learn that more than 2,000 generous football players from 80 high schools in Chicago each donated $1 to buy the bikes for the **(6)** *amazed / amazing* pupils at Funston School. It was all part of National Random Acts of Kindness Day.

The students thought it was **(7)** *amazing / amazed* that the players had given them such a great and completely **(8)** *unexpecting / unexpected* gift. Small acts of kindness—giving $1—can add up to a big surprise!

19 Complete the article about Japanese customs with the correct forms of these words.

confuse	embarrass	frighten	insult
relax	terrify	worry	

Traveling to Japan might seem **(1)** _____ if you're not familiar with the customs before you go. But remember this list, and you can remain **(2)** _____ and enjoy your time in the country. Bowing is a way of showing respect. Don't be **(3)** _____ to bow when you meet people. It may sound **(4)** _____, but adding the suffix *-san* to someone's name is another way to show that you respect them. Making noise when you eat noodles shouldn't be **(5)** _____. Slurping shows that you are enjoying your meal. There's no need to leave a tip in a restaurant—in fact, it's kind of **(6)** _____ if you do! Be sure to take off your shoes at the entrance to a restaurant. Don't be **(7)** _____; no one will take them.

2B Urban Explorers

VOCABULARY BUILDING Compound nouns

1 Complete the sentences by making compound nouns with these words. There are two words you don't need.

back	center	horseback	line	park
public	sight	sky	tour	view

1 I'm going _____packing with a couple of friends this summer.

2 Using _____ transportation is much better for the environment than driving a car.

3 The Burj Khalifa, in Dubai, is the tallest _____scraper in the world.

4 We did a walking _____ of Toronto. It was fascinating learning about the history of the city.

5 Wouldn't it be amazing to go _____ riding on the beach?

6 Passengers can relax by the pool after a full day of _____seeing.

7 There was a _____point from the top of the castle. The scenery was breathtaking.

8 Antonia and Rami went on an incredible zip-_____ tour of the forest canopy in Costa Rica.

READING

2 Read the article. Match the information (a–e) with the paragraphs (1–5).

a why sustainable tourism matters _____

b a positive, alternative form of tourism _____

c global tourism facts and statistics _____

d a model of sustainable tourism _____

e higher education and geotourism _____

3 Read the text again and choose the correct options.

1 How many people around the world does the tourist industry provide work for?
   a 1.2 billion
   b 300 million
   c 1.5 trillion
   d 1 in 11

2 How much money does global tourism generate every year?
   a $7 trillion
   b $1.2 billion
   c $1.8 billion
   d $300 million

3 What is the focus of sustainable tourism?
   a developing roads, visitor centers, and hotels
   b using natural and cultural resources
   c changing a place so that tourists are more likely to visit
   d protecting a place and its inhabitants

4 Why is the Midlands Meander a good example of ecotourism?
   a It appeals to people who aren't really interested in change.
   b It includes preservation and educational programs.
   c Visitors can go horseback riding among cattle or ride zip-lines through the forest.
   d It attracts people who are interested in the arts and crafts of the region.

5 Why is ecotourism important?
   a Because you can now study for a degree in sustainable tourism at the University of Missouri.
   b Because The UN General Assembly declared 2017 to be the International Year of Sustainable Tourism for Development.
   c Because it helps develop cultural awareness and benefits local residents by using local workers, services, and products.
   d Because students of ecotourism learn about community planning and environmental education.

4 Read the article again. Are the sentences true (T) or false (F)?

1 Global tourism generates $7 billion of global revenue annually. _____

2 Ecotourists are interested in changing the places they visit. _____

3 The Midlands Meander is a good example of traditional tourism. _____

4 A degree in sustainable tourism includes classes on earth science and global studies. _____

5 The United Nations believes that tourism helps break down barriers between people. _____

6 More than 1.8 trillion people will travel to new places in 2030. _____

Tourism That Helps

1 🎧 **17** Would you like to go backpacking in Nepal? How about taking a cruise to Antarctica? Almost everyone loves to travel. In fact, the business of travel and tourism is considered the biggest industry in the world today. In terms of employment, the tourist industry currently provides work for almost 300 million people around the world—that's one in eleven jobs on the planet! In 2015, global tourism accounted for 1.2 billion international arrivals and billions of additional domestic visits. Overall, global tourism generates about $7 trillion of global revenue annually.

2 Over time, traditional tourism has had a significant impact on the planet. Successful tourism often requires the development of infrastructure, such as usable roads, visitor centers, and hotels. Such development, in turn, affects the natural and cultural resources of the destination visited. Fortunately, sustainable tourism, or *ecotourism*, is an alternative form of tourism that emphasizes the protection of a place and its inhabitants. Also known as *geotourism*, this exciting form of travel appeals to people who prefer to see the places they visit as they are, and aren't really interested in changing them.

3 The Midlands Meander, in KwaZulu-Natal, South Africa, is a good example of sustainable tourism. The organization began as part of a tourism route that attracted people interested in the arts and crafts of the region. Its mission has expanded to include educational programs and farm preservation. Visitors can ride zip-lines through the canopy of the Karkloof Forest, or go horseback riding among Nguni cattle, wildebeests, zebras, and buffalo, and know that they're supporting programs that help maintain the local farming culture and enrich the lives of the area's schoolchildren.

4 Sustainable tourism has become significant enough that you can now study for a university degree in it! The University of Missouri, in the United States, offers an undergraduate* degree in geotourism that includes courses in community planning, earth science, environmental education, geography, and global studies. Students in the program might study weather and climate, the economic aspects of tourism, or conservation issues and problems that occur in response to human use of the natural environment.

5 The United Nations General Assembly declared 2017 to be the International Year of Sustainable Tourism for Development. Why is sustainable tourism so important? As the UN states, tourism breaks down barriers between visitors and hosts. Sustainable tourism promotes cultural diversity and awareness, in some cases actually helping to revive* traditional activities and local customs. When done responsibly, ecotourism benefits local residents by using the local workforce, services, and products of the places being visited. Most importantly, because an estimated 1.8 billion international tourists will be visiting places across the globe in 2030, responsible, sustainable tourism is critical for the health of the planet and of the many wonderful and fascinating places people will travel to.

undergraduate *a college student who has not yet completed a degree*
revive *bring back*

2C Experiences

GRAMMAR Narrative forms

1 Listen and complete the sentences. 🎧 **18**

1 She _____ soccer practice _____.
2 He _____ on the weekends.
3 They _____ the dog _____ a loud crash.
4 I _____ my dad _____ I _____ in Tokyo.
5 Cars _____ as safe as they are today.
6 We _____ breakfast at the hotel because _____ too late.
7 _____ my email, Carol _____ her sister.

2 Complete the chart with the correct forms of the verbs.

Infinitive	Simple Past	Past Continuous	Past Perfect
go			
	ran	was/were running	
talk			
sit			had sat
		was/were taking	
fly			
		was/were catching	

3 Underline the past continuous verbs.

One day last week, I was reading a book and listening to the radio. I was enjoying some great classical music when suddenly, I heard an announcement. There was a huge thunderstorm coming our way! I hurried to close the windows, and called my sister Tami, who was riding her bike to volleyball practice. I told her about the storm, and she asked if our dad was driving home from work and could pick her up. So, I quickly called him to see if he could find Tami before the storm came. He'd left work already and was on his way home, so he said he'd pick her up in about five minutes. Once Tami was in the car with her bike in the back and they were driving home together, the storm hit. There was a lot of rain, thunder, and lightning—I was so glad they were safely on their way home.

4 Underline the past perfect verbs.

When Omar was in high school, he studied math, physics, chemistry, and biology. In his last year, he got an opportunity to take a class at a local college. He was studying all the time, taking tests for his regular classes and at the college! Omar had always enjoyed biology and chemistry in school and wanted to learn more about biochemistry. He'd talked to some of his friends who had done courses at the college while they were still at school, and they all said that they'd learned a lot and had enjoyed it. Omar had been a little worried that his schedule might be too full, but he didn't really mind because he loved the college classes—they were so interesting and the professors were amazing. Omar especially loved being able to use the college library, and did all his homework there. He'd told so many of his friends about his great experience that they all wanted to take classes at the college, too.

5 Choose the correct options to complete the questions and answers.

1 **A** What did you read when you were at the beach last summer?
  B I *read / had read* a book by Barbara Kingsolver.
2 **A** When did you listen to the latest podcast?
  B I listened to it while I *was walking / had walked* to school.
3 **A** How much money did he have when he went into town?
  B He *was having / had* $100.
4 **A** Did you *use / used* to see your grandparents a lot?
  B Yes, we *saw / used to saw* them every summer.
5 **A** Does Pete have a boat?
  B He *used to have / use to have* one, but then he *had sold / sold* it.
6 **A** *Were you trying / Had you tried* pineapple pizza before we went to Pizza Palace last night?
  B No, I *hadn't tried / wasn't trying* it before.
7 **A** How many times did you *take / taken* the test?
  B I *took / was taking* it twice before I finally passed.
8 **A** Did you like living in Los Angeles?
  B It was great! I *used to walk / use to walk* along the beach every day.

6 Complete the second sentence so that it means the opposite of the first.

1 When we went to Milan, we ate breakfast at the hotel every day.
When we went to Milan, _____ every day.

2 My classmates were taking the test when I got to class.
My classmates _____ when I got to class.

3 She made a lot of new friends when she studied in Colombia.
_____ when she studied in Colombia.

4 I was looking for a book by Neil Gaiman.
_____ by Neil Gaiman.

5 I'd eaten my lunch by the time Hiro arrived.
_____ by the time Hiro arrived.

6 They were working in the garden when their neighbor came to say hello.
_____ when their neighbor came to say hello.

7 I used to work at a bank.
_____

8 Renting an apartment in the city used to be so expensive.
_____

7 Choose the option (a or b) that is closest in meaning to the original sentence.

1 Tennis practice had already started when Aliyah arrived.
a Tennis practice started. Then Aliyah got to tennis practice.
b Aliyah got to tennis practice. Then tennis practice started.

2 Before I went to the movie theater, I dropped my little brother off at home.
a I dropped my little brother off at home and then I went to the movie theater.
b I went to the movie theater and then dropped my little brother off at home.

3 Ming's favorite subject used to be geography.
a Today, Ming's favorite subject is geography.
b Today, Ming's favorite subject isn't geography.

4 As they were walking up to the house, Hyun answered his phone.
a They walked up to the house. Then Hyun answered his phone.
b Hyun answered his phone at the same time as they were walking up to the house.

5 After he went camping, he cleaned the tent.
a First he cleaned the tent. Then he went camping.
b First he went camping and then he cleaned the tent.

6 She wasn't studying while she was at the library.
a At the library, she was doing something other than studying.
b She didn't use to study at the library.

7 It started raining while we were having a picnic.
a We had finished our picnic before it started to rain.
b We didn't finish our picnic before it started to rain.

8 Read and listen to the questions. Choose the correct answers. 🎧 19

1 Had you studied another language before you took the English class?
a Yes, I'd studied Japanese.
b Yes, I'd studying French.

2 Did Sally use to work at the hospital?
a No, she didn't use to work there.
b Yes, she use to working there on Mondays and Wednesdays.

3 Did you like the play you went to see with Alicia?
a No, I was hating it!
b No, I hated it!

4 Did you go to the gym while you were on vacation?
a Yes, I went every day except Tuesday.
b Yes, I had gone every day except Tuesday.

5 Did Ms. Liston use to be a chemist?
a Yes, she used to work in a laboratory.
b Yes, she was worked in a laboratory.

6 Had you told your parents about your grades before they saw the teacher?
a Yes, I had tell them last week.
b Yes, I'd told them on Thursday.

7 Had you seen the Himalayas before we went there yesterday?
a Yes, I have seen them last year when I was in Nepal.
b Yes, I saw them last year when I was in Nepal.

PRONUNCIATION *Used to*

9 Listen to the sentences and choose the pronunciation that you hear. 🎧 20

1 /juzd/   /juzt/
2 /juzd/   /juzt/
3 /juzd/   /juzt/
4 /juzd/   /juzt/
5 /juzd/   /juzt/
6 /juzd/   /juzt/

2D Happy Maps

TEDTALKS

AUTHENTIC LISTENING SKILLS

1 Listen to the TED Talk excerpts. Choose the correct option to complete the sentences. 🎧 **21**

1 I just remember a feeling of surprise; surprise at finding a street with no *cars / cause*.

2 However, the app also assumes there are only a handful of directions to the *station / destination*.

3 The result of that research has been the creation of new maps—maps where you *don't only find / don't find* the shortest path, the blue one, but also the most enjoyable path, the red one.

4 Players are shown *pairs of urban scenes / persons on the scenes*, and they're asked to choose which one is more beautiful, quiet, and happy.

5 Based on thousands of *user votes / usable votes*, then we are able to see where consensus emerges.

6 They also *record / recalled* how some paths smelled and sounded.

7 *More generally / Marginally*, my research, what it tries to do is avoid the danger of the single path, to avoid robbing people of fully experiencing the city in which they live.

8 Walk the path full of *people you love / people who love* and not full of cars, and you have an entirely different path. It's that simple.

WATCH ▶

2 Choose the correct options.

1 Why did Daniele feel shame when he discovered a different route to work?
  a He didn't realize his usual route to work was longer.
  b He had only thought about finding the shortest route.
  c He had used the wrong cellphone app to get to work.

2 How did Daniele change after that experience?
  a He changed the focus of his research to create new maps.
  b He used a different app for finding a route.
  c He started to see the city differently.

3 "Logic will get you from A to B. Imagination will take you everywhere." This means…
  a you should travel more if you want to be creative.
  b only logic can get you to where you need to go.
  c it's important to be creative as well as practical.

4 Why did Daniele and his team build a new map of London?
  a They wanted to create a map of the city that was more enjoyable for people.
  b They wanted to make a lot of money from their app.
  c The maps of London were not easy to follow.

5 Besides beauty and quiet, what else did they base the new map of London on?
  a tourist attractions
  b parks
  c smells, sounds, and memories

6 Why does Daniele say that "routine is deadly"?
  a because you may get robbed if you always take the same path
  b because you might end up in heavy traffic
  c because it can make you lazy so you never experience life fully

3 Put the events of Daniele's life in the correct order. Then watch the TED Talk again and check your answers.

a Daniele did a PhD in London. _____
b Daniele then joined Yahoo Labs. _____
c He built a crowdsourcing platform with colleagues at Cambridge. _____
d He changed the focus of his research to creating new city maps. _____
e He moved to Boston and began cycling to work every day. _____
f One day he took a new route to work. _____
g The new bike route surprised him. _____
h With his colleagues, he built a new map of London based on human emotions. _____

VOCABULARY IN CONTEXT

4 Choose the correct options to complete the text.

I live in Seattle and it's very rainy, so I usually **(1)** *team up with / come up with* my colleague Paulo who lives near me, to share a ride to work. Paulo's a little **(2)** *shy / angry* so he's always very quiet in the car. That's fine with me—I never feel like talking first thing in the morning! Last week, the weather was sunny and beautiful. There are only **(3)** *a lot of / a handful of* sunny days in April, so one day I decided to walk to work. The street I live on is **(4)** *lined by / joined by* trees. There were blossoms on them and the sun was shining—it was a beautiful day to walk.

When I got to work, I suddenly realized, to my **(5)** *curiosity / shame*, that I'd completely forgotten about Paulo! Later that morning, he came over to me and said, "**(6)** *Don't get me wrong / Don't talk to me*, Hana, I don't have a problem with you walking, but could you just let me know next time? I was waiting for you!"

2E You Can't Miss It

SPEAKING

1 Put the words in the correct order to make questions and sentences about directions. Then listen and check your answers. 🎧 22

1 the / history museum / know / way / you / the / to / do / ?
_____

2 all the way / you / the intersection / go / to / get / until / .
_____

3 traffic / the / straight / at / light / go / .
_____

4 first / 200 / take / after / traffic circle / yards, / the / off / exit / the / .
_____

5 right / on / past / your / go / a bookshop / .
_____

6 station / is / your / train / the / on / left / .
_____

7 here / very / from / not / it's / far / .
_____

8 more / mile / no / it's / than / away / a / .
_____

2 In English, speakers stress key information to show it is important. Listen again and underline the key information / stressed words in the sentences in Activity 1. 🎧 22

3 Look at the map and complete the conversation with the questions and directions (a–i).

a At the pier, turn right.
b Go straight all the way until you get to the clock tower.
c I'm trying to get to the train station.
d Do you know the way?
e Turn right at the clock tower and go straight on North Street for about five minutes,
f You can't miss it.
g at the first traffic light, turn left.
h It's pretty far away from here—about fifteen minutes' walk.
i so continue along the waterfront until you get to the pier on your left.

A Excuse me, can you help me? **(1)** _____.
B **(2)** _____.
A Oh, OK. **(3)** _____?
B OK, **(4)** _____.
A Right…
B **(5)** _____. Then, **(6)** _____. **(7)** _____.
A The clock tower, yes, OK.
B **(8)** _____, and the station is straight ahead of you. **(9)** _____.
A OK, great, thanks for your help.
B No problem.

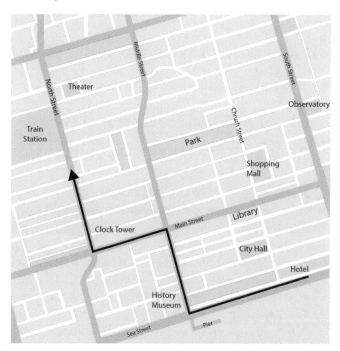

4 Look at the map again. Give directions to a tourist. Make notes. Then listen to the model answers and compare your ideas. 🎧 23

Excuse me, do you know the way…
a from the hotel to the park?
b from the park to the shopping mall?
c from the shopping mall to the pier?

5 Some friends are going on a day trip to the same city and plan to do three things during their visit. Make notes about the good and bad points of each activity, then decide which three things they should do and plan a route. Look at the map and the words below to help you with ideas. Remember to use the useful language. Then compare your notes with the sample answer of two people discussing the task. 🎧 **24**

- pier
- beach
- observatory
- theater
- shopping
- museum
- lunch
- dinner

WRITING A story

6 Read the sentences with *just* and choose the correct options.

1 a Margarita just had left the airport when her phone rang.
  b Margarita had just left the airport when her phone rang.

2 a We had just booked our train tickets, and we were so excited!
  b We had booked our just train tickets, and we were so excited!

3 a The castle looked just as I'd imagined it would.
  b The castle looked as just I'd imagined it would.

4 a There wasn't much to just eat—a few bread rolls and one orange.
  b There wasn't much to eat—just a few bread rolls and one orange.

5 a They were just about to give up when, suddenly, a taxi appeared.
  b They just were about to give up when, suddenly, a taxi appeared.

7 Read the stages of writing a story (a–e). Then match them with the correct section (1–5).

a Develop the main events. Say how you felt and what happened next.
b Bring the story to a close. Say what happened in the end and what you remember most.
c Make notes based on *Wh-* questions, like *What / Where / When / Why / Who*…
d Introduce the main events of the story. Say what happened.
e Set the scene. Let the reader know what the story is about and where it takes place.

1 Planning   _____
2 Paragraph 1   _____
3 Paragraph 2   _____
4 Paragraph 3   _____
5 Paragraph 4   _____

8 Put the parts of the story in the correct order.

a An elderly couple sat next to me on the ferry. I left my seat to buy some coffee, and I was just about to pay, when, suddenly, I couldn't find my wallet. It had all my credit cards and cash, and now it was gone. Just then, I saw the old man who had been sitting beside me. He gave me my wallet! I burst into tears. Without realizing, I'd dropped it under my seat earlier. _____

b I just wanted two things from that trip: a little adventure and a lot of sunshine. Instead, I got a lot of adventure and only a little sunshine! _____

c I stayed on a small island that had no tourists, just local people. Greece is normally hot and dry, so I just packed T-shirts and shorts. Unfortunately, I didn't know that Greek winters are cold and rainy. I was freezing! One day, I decided to travel to another island. _____

d I went backpacking in Greece for a week last winter. None of my friends were free, so I traveled alone. _____

9 Read the story again. Then complete the summary with these words and phrases. There are two you don't need.

a week	alone	adventure	bad weather	begins
concludes	found	lost	sunshine	with friends

The writer traveled **(1)** _____ in Greece for
(2) _____ last winter. The first problem was
(3) _____. The second problem was a
(4) _____ wallet. Luckily, the wallet was
(5) _____. The writer
(6) _____ the story by saying the
trip had more **(7)** _____ than
(8) _____!

10 Write a story that is 150–200 words. Begin with this sentence: *At first, we all thought the journey was fun.*

Tip box

- The story doesn't have to be true. You can make it up.
- Don't use the same story you wrote in Student Book, Unit 2.
- Write some notes to plan your story.
- Write at least four paragraphs.
- In Paragraph 1, set the scene for the story.
- In Paragraph 2, introduce the main events.
- In Paragraph 3, develop the main events. Explain how you felt.
- In Paragraph 4, bring the story to a close.
- Remember to use "just" and different adverbs.
- Have fun writing your story!

Review

1 Match the things (1–6) with the places (a–f) where you would find them.

1 public transportation   a a shopping mall
2 a lot of offices   b an amusement park
3 a clothing store   c a rooftop
4 a roller coaster   d a skyscraper
5 an urban garden   e a subway station
6 beautiful scenery   f a viewpoint

2 Read. Are the sentences true (T) or false (F)? Correct the false sentences.

1 A destination is the place where you begin your journey. ____

2 An expedition is usually a short trip. ____
3 If you commute, your journey to work often takes a long time. ____
4 An excursion is usually a short trip for sightseeing or relaxing. ____
5 If you give someone a ride, you take them somewhere. ____

6 A cruise is a journey on a train. ____

3 Complete the sentences with the correct forms of the words in bold.

1 It's **interest** _____ that in Norway, you always eat with a knife and fork. (Even if you're eating a sandwich!)
2 In Egypt, don't add salt to your food. (It's **annoyed** _____ for the host because it means you don't like their food.)
3 In South Korea, it could be **terrified** _____ for someone if you write a family member's name in red ink. (It means that the person is dead.)
4 In Russia, it's **confused** _____ to give someone you are in a relationship with yellow flowers. (It means that you want to break up with them!)
5 In the Netherlands, your friend might be **worry** _____ if you give scissors or knives as gifts. (It's unlucky.)
6 In Venezuela, it's **surprised** _____ to arrive on time for a party. (Guests who arrive on time seem too eager.)

4 Are the words in bold correct or incorrect? Correct those that are incorrect.

1 I **was fell** asleep in class yesterday. It was so **bored**.

_____

2 Last week he **studied** at the library for eight hours every day. He was really **exhausting**.

_____

3 **Has you ever being** on such an **excited** trip?

_____

4 Leo **had came** home at midnight yesterday. His mother was very **worried**.

_____

5 They **were shocking** when they heard the news.

_____

6 Mr. Hernandez just **had told** Karina that she didn't win the award. It's such **disappointed** news.

_____

7 He hadn't **telling** me his secret until today. It's **amazed** that he's going to Peru for the summer!

_____

5 Choose the correct options to complete the sentences.

1 _____ it a disappointing movie?
   a Was
   b Was being
   c Did be
   d Had been
2 I _____ my neighbor to look after my house while I _____ away on vacation.
   a asking, am
   b was asked, was
   c asked, was
   d ask, had been
3 Were they _____ to the party when they _____, Meg?
   a drive, were calling
   b drove, called
   c been driving, had called
   d driving, called
4 It _____ a difficult test, but Sivan _____ most of the answers.
   a had been, was knowing
   b was, knew
   c was, had know
   d had been, known
5 Renting an apartment in the city didn't _____ to cost so much.
   a used
   b use
   c had been
   d being
6 I had _____ seen the Grand Canyon _____, so my friends and I decided to go.
   a never, before
   b before, yet
   c for, ever
   d ever, before
7 _____ you _____ taken the bus to school before today?
   a Has, never
   b Have, since
   c Had, for
   d Had, ever

③ Active Lives

3A Pushing the Limits

VOCABULARY Sports

① **Review** Read the clues and complete the words about sports. The first letter is given for you.

1 This sport is played with a bat and a ball and each team has nine players. b __ __ __ __ __ __ __

2 This popular Olympic sport happens in a pool. s __ __ __ __ __ __ __

3 People do this sport in the snow and it is popular in cold countries. s __ __ __ __ __

4 This sport can be done on a track or outside over long distances. r __ __ __ __ __ __ __

5 This sport is played on a field and is popular around the world. s __ __ __ __ __

6 People use a mat to do this activity, which is good for the mind and body. y __ __ __

② **Review** Complete the chart with these words.

baseball	basketball	boxing	ice hockey	ice skating
soccer	surfing	tennis	volleyball	yoga

Team sports	Individual sports

③ **Review** Put the words in the correct order to make sentences.

1 baseball / favorite / my / least / sport / is / .

_____

2 can / dangerous / boxing / be / sport / a / very / .

_____

3 more / countries / than / soccer / played / is / in / 200 / .

_____

4 good / heart / running / for / your / is / .

_____

5 swimming / popular / is / Australia / a / in / sport / .

_____

6 doing / makes / feel / yoga / calm / you / .

_____

④ Match the sports (1–6) with the equipment (a–f).

1 tennis	**a** hoop
2 basketball	**b** boat
3 diving	**c** club
4 sailing	**d** board
5 golf	**e** helmet
6 cycling	**f** racket

⑤ Unscramble the letters to make places where people do sports.

1 k r n i   __ __ n __

2 t o r c u   __ __ __ r __

3 d e i f l   f __ __ __ __

4 r c a k t   __ r __ __ __

5 n m t u o i n a   m __ __ __ __ a __ __

6 o l p o   __ __ o __

⑥ Read the paragraph and choose the correct options.

Last weekend, I went to watch my first professional basketball game. I loved it! Even though our seats were far from the **(1)** _____ , we still had a good view. The home team was from New York, and their **(2)** _____ were from Boston. There were over 17,000 **(3)** _____ in the stadium, and it was exciting to watch with so many people.

At one point in the game, the **(4)** _____ of the team from Boston got really angry with the **(5)** _____ about a call he thought was unfair. He was told to be quiet or leave the stadium! It was a very close game. The final **(6)** _____ was 100-96, and the team from New York **(7)** _____ .

1	**a** rink	**b** court	**c** equipment
2	**a** spectators	**b** opponents	**c** coaches
3	**a** opponents	**b** players	**c** spectators
4	**a** opponent	**b** referee	**c** coach
5	**a** referee	**b** coach	**c** player
6	**a** score	**b** win	**c** count
7	**a** played	**b** won	**c** beat

7 Complete the sentences with the correct sports. The first letter is given for you.

1 My favorite sport to watch is d_____, but I'm always worried the athlete will hit the board.

2 G_____ can be done by both men and women and takes incredible strength and skill.

3 The boys take k_____ lessons on Saturdays to learn discipline and self-defense.

4 S_____ can be quite dangerous if the sea is very rough.

5 Ropes and holds are used for c_____.

6 Players are allowed to bounce the ball in b_____.

8 Choose the correct options to complete the sentences.

1 Today, I'm trying to *achieve* / *represent* my personal best in the 100m race.

2 Her goal is to *score* / *beat* the current champion and become the best boxer in the country.

3 The ultimate goal of the team is to *score* / *win* as many medals as possible for their country.

4 It's important to *achieve* / *encourage* everyone to participate in sports.

5 To be a professional athlete, you have to *train* / *represent* almost every day.

6 He *scored* / *achieved* the winning goal in the match against Germany.

7 It's an incredible honor to *achieve* / *represent* your country in the Olympics.

9 Extension Complete the sentences with the correct forms of *play*, *do*, or *go*.

1 I like most sports, but I absolutely love _____ basketball.

2 I have a stressful job, so I relax by _____ yoga.

3 When it's hot outside, we _____ swimming in the lake near our house.

4 I _____ running four days a week, even if I'm tired!

5 He likes to _____ tennis with friends on the weekends.

6 Jerome gets plenty of exercise because he _____ gymnastics every week.

7 Every winter, my family _____ skiing in Colorado.

10 Extension Choose the correct options to complete the sentences.

1 The girls like to go *horseback riding* / *yoga* when we're on vacation.

2 In the winter, tourists can go *ice skating* / *jogging* on a rink in Hyde Park.

3 Racquetball is *done* / *played* in an indoor court surrounded by walls.

4 Do you want to go *diving* / *snowboarding* on the mountain tomorrow?

5 People play *soccer* / *hockey* with a puck and a stick.

6 Would you like to play a game of *table tennis* / *skateboarding*?

7 A flat board with a sail is used for *snowboarding* / *windsurfing*.

LISTENING

11 Listen to the conversation and choose the correct options. 🎧 **25**

1 What, in general, are they talking about?
 a fitness and physical activity
 b favorite games and interests
 c healthy food and drinks

2 What does the woman say she is the first to do?
 a criticize people
 b encourage people
 c discourage people

3 Why is the man feeling unhappy?
 a He doesn't have any interests.
 b He doesn't have many friends.
 c He doesn't think he's in good shape.

4 What does he eat when he plays computer games?
 a salad
 b snacks
 c a picnic

5 How does the young man first react to the idea of a hike?
 a He's enthusiastic.
 b He's confused.
 c He's unsure.

6 What does the young woman mean when she says,
 "…there's no time like the present"?
 a The time for action is now.
 b It's a little late to take action.
 c The present situation is not good.

7 What is the young man afraid that he's turning into?
 a a jealous, angry person
 b a mean, unfriendly person
 c a lazy, unhealthy person

8 What is the best description of the woman's attitude toward the man?
 a She's really frustrated.
 b She's very supportive.
 c She's slightly critical.

12 Listen to the two speakers. Choose the best title for both descriptions. 🎧 **26**
 a Biker Dogs!
 b Let's catch a wave!
 c Skateboards rule!
 d Extreme dogs!

13 Listen to the first speaker again and choose the correct options. 🎧 **26**

1 What word does the woman use meaning "dog"?
 a puppy
 b pooch
 c mutt

2 What do some dogs do "…a thousand feet in the air"?
 a surf
 b paddle
 c cruise

3 What kind of dog is Bandit?
 a a breed
 b a terrier
 c a bulldog

4 What did Bandit learn to do first?
 a ride motorcycles
 b surf waves
 c steal food

14 Listen to the second speaker again and choose the correct options. 🎧 **26**

1 What makes Tillman a natural skateboarder?
 a his attitude
 b his body
 c his owner

2 What did Tillman first learn to do on his skateboard?
 a fall off
 b push it
 c roll along

3 What do you think "mad" means when the owner says "mad skater skills"?
 a extremely good
 b very angry
 c pretty bad

4 What is Tillman's owner most proud of?
 a Tillman's skating skills
 b Tillman's lack of fear
 c Tillman's effect on people

GRAMMAR Simple past and present perfect

15 **Read the sentences and complete the chart.**

1 Have you ever refereed a basketball game?
2 He stayed in shape during the winter by jogging.
3 My cousin has done gymnastics for five years.
4 My favorite football team has already won twice.
5 No one has broken the world record since 2015.
6 Our best player injured herself when she tried to score.
7 The players encouraged the team captain to run faster.
8 They canceled the match because it rained.

Simple past	Present perfect

16 **Choose the correct options to complete the sentences.**

1 When I was younger, I *enjoyed / enjoy / have enjoyed* building sculptures out of things I *found / finded / have find* around the house.
2 Most kids *have did / has done / did* karate or *rode / has ridden / have rode* their bikes, but I just *wanted / have want / have wanted* to make things.
3 One summer, I *have built / build / built* some shelves to hold my comic books.
4 Another time, I *design / designed / have designed* and *make / made / have made* a table for my parents.
5 My friends *have not understood / didn't understand / not understand* that I *have prefer / preferred / have preferred* creating new things, not playing soccer.
6 A few years ago, I *enter / entered / have entered* one of my sculptures in a competition and I *have win / have won / won*!

17 **Complete the sentences with the present perfect forms of the verbs in parentheses.**

1 Paola and Mai _____ (be) friends since they were small children.
2 They _____ (live) next door to each other for fifteen years.
3 Mai _____ (not know) anyone as long as she _____ (know) Paola.
4 Paola _____ (always want) to learn how to play the guitar.
5 She _____ (not practice) as much as her teacher recommended, so she _____ (not improve) very much.
6 Mai _____ (decide) that she wants to go to the same college as Paola.
7 But Paola _____ (not think) about going to college yet.
8 Her parents _____ (tell) her that she needs to be more serious.

18 **Choose the correct options to complete the sentences.**

1 If you *have decided / decided* you want to get in shape, you really should see your doctor to find out if you're healthy enough for exercise.
2 Our friends *joined / have joined* a running club last year and now they run three times a week.
3 She *never skipped / has never skipped* breakfast since the doctor advised her not to.
4 Jack *has now recovered / now recovered* and is exercising again.
5 He *began / has begun* a meditation class last week as a way to deal with stress.
6 My father *only ate / has only eaten* healthy food since he was in the hospital.

19 **Read the article. Complete the sentences with the simple past or present perfect forms of the verbs in parentheses.**

Extreme sports are sports that people consider risky. They usually involve speed, height, and/or extreme physical activity. Here are some examples from around the world:

- **Badwater ultramarathon** For several years, athletes **(1)** _____ (participate) in this race each summer in the hottest place in North America: Death Valley, California. Last year, the athletes **(2)** _____ (run) 135 miles, starting at 280 feet below sea level and ending in the mountains at 8,300 feet.

- **Wingsuit flying world championship** For this competition, athletes wear a jumpsuit that has extra cloth between their arms and legs so they can glide long distances. People **(3)** _____ (call) it "horizontal skydiving" because the athletes often travel long distances. In 2016, in Zhangjiajie, China, the athletes **(4)** _____ (jump) from Tienmen Mountain in Hunan Province and **(5)** _____ (travel) almost a mile to the goal. The winner **(6)** _____ (complete) the race in 23.41 seconds.

- **Street luge skateboarders** These extreme-sports athletes **(7)** _____ (always want) to go faster and faster. In 2014, the twelfth annual competition **(8)** _____ (be) in Brazil, which has the fastest downhill skateboarding track in the world. The world record for street luge, set in 2008, is 97.81 miles per hour!

3B Extreme Sports

VOCABULARY BUILDING Phrasal verbs

1 Complete the sentences with the correct forms of these phrasal verbs.

give up	join in	keep up	knock out
take on	take up	warm up	work out

1 It's important to _____ before you start running, or you could pull a muscle.

2 I'm trying to _____, but you run too fast!

3 I usually either swim or _____ for about an hour after school.

4 She had to _____ running after that problem with her ankle.

5 Which team do you think will _____ Brazil in the semi-final?

6 When you feel more confident, you can _____ for the rest of the game.

7 I was so disappointed when Murray was _____ of the tournament.

8 I'm thinking of _____ karate. I need more exercise, and I like learning new things.

READING

2 Read the text and choose the correct options.

1 What does Steph Davis experience before jumping off a cliff?
   a risk and danger
   b pleasure and peace
   c fear and excitement

2 Which of these sports is often considered risky or extreme?
   a swimming
   b rock climbing
   c running

3 What do researchers believe some extreme-sports athletes are attracted to?
   a taking risks
   b racing down steep slopes
   c dopamine

4 What do some people believe about extreme-sports athletes?
   a They're reckless adventurers.
   b They're not interested in low-risk sports.
   c They don't need to practice.

5 What is one explanation behind the appeal of extreme sports?
   a Some people like to push their own limits.
   b Athletes need something to do in the summer.
   c Some athletes are scared of competition.

3 Choose two possible explanations the writer gives for why people take up dangerous activities.

a People like the feeling of being frightened.
b People who enjoy taking risks may share an adventure gene.
c Many people think yoga and running are boring.
d Some people enjoy the burst of dopamine that comes with extreme activities.
e Some athletes don't really care about the consequences.

4 Choose two points that the writer makes about extreme-sports athletes.

a Many extreme-sports athletes are very well-prepared for what they do.
b Unlike traditional athletes, extreme-sports athletes care about the consequences of what they do.
c Both traditional and extreme-sports athletes prepare carefully for their sports.
d Many extreme-sports athletes have high levels of self-awareness.
e Like traditional athletes, extreme-sports athletes enjoy doing things that feel good.

5 Match the two parts of the sentences.

1 According to recent research, _____
2 Sports, such as surfing and skiing, _____
3 The "adventure gene" _____
4 Many extreme-sports athletes are _____
5 There seem to be _____

a may involve risks and even danger!
b some people may be genetically predisposed to taking risks.
c a number of reasons why people enjoy extreme sports.
d well-prepared, highly-skilled, and aware of what they're doing.
e may influence how some people process dopamine.

Why take the risk?

🎧 27 Just before jumping off a thousand-foot cliff, professional climber, BASE jumper, and wingsuiter Steph Davis admits to experiencing fear and excitement. That's not surprising, since wingsuiting is an extremely risky sport that has claimed the lives of several wingsuiters, including Steph's husband. So why does she do it? Why, in spite of the danger, would Steph want to jump at all, let alone almost every day of the year?

Steph isn't alone in her search for thrills*, and hers isn't the only risky or extreme sport. Surfing, rock climbing, diving from great heights, and even skiing or snowboarding all involve risks and sometimes real danger. Recently, scientists have studied people who pursue these, and other potentially dangerous sports, to learn more about what makes certain individuals take up activities that other people prefer to avoid.

Research suggests that some people attracted to extreme sports may be genetically predisposed* to risky behaviors. According to Cynthia Thomson, a researcher at the University of British Columbia, it's possible that extreme-sports athletes, along with people who enjoy taking risks, share an "adventure gene." This genetic variation may influence how some people process dopamine. Dopamine is a substance that's partially responsible for the feeling of excitement a person experiences when skiing down a steep slope, surfing a giant wave, or even racing down a hill on a bicycle. People with the adventure gene may "need to seek out intense situations to bring up their dopamine levels,"

according to Thomson. That burst* of dopamine might make the individual want to repeat the behavior because it feels so good.

But there's more to extreme sports than dopamine. Researchers compared participants* in low-risk sports, such as yoga and running, to fans of high-risk activities. They wondered whether, as some people believe, thrill-seekers are reckless* adventurers who don't care about the consequences of what they do. What they found is that many extreme-sports athletes are actually very skilled at what they do, train hard, and are responsible and well-prepared when practicing their sport. Eric Brymer is a researcher from Queenstown University of Technology in Brisbane, Australia, who has been studying extreme-sports athletes for years. In his opinion, extreme-sports athletes are "actually extremely well-prepared, careful, intelligent, and thoughtful athletes with high levels of self-awareness and a deep knowledge of the environment and of the activity."

In the end, it seems that there are a number of explanations behind the appeal of extreme sports. For some, it might be the dopamine. Others might be interested in pushing their own limits. One thing is clear, though—extreme-sports athletes like to play hard! As Daron Rahlves, a top downhill-ski racer who spends the summer racing in motocross competitions, puts it: "I'm in it for the challenge, my heart thumping as I finish, the feeling of being alive… I definitely get scared on some of the courses. It just makes me fight more."

thrill *a strong feeling of excitement and pleasure*
predisposed *likely to behave in a particular way*
burst *a sudden outpouring*

participant *someone who is involved in an activity*
reckless *dangerous and not caring about what might happen*

3C Have you ever...?

GRAMMAR Present perfect and present perfect continuous

1 Listen and complete the sentences. 🎧 28

1 How long _____ the piano?
2 I _____ Tina to tell her about the party.
3 _____ to put new batteries in the remote control. It _____ doesn't work.
4 _____ on the phone _____ 45 minutes.
5 How often _____ to the library this week?
6 _____ since five o'clock this morning.
7 He _____ the physics test _____ .

2 Complete the chart.

Infinitive	Present perfect	Present perfect continuous
take		
		have / has been choosing
		have / has been representing
try		
encourage		
		have / has been winning
feel		

3 Choose the correct options to complete the sentences.

1 We've been going to that school _____ 2016.
  a since   c already
  b for   d ever

2 She's lived in Guadalajara _____ two years.
  a since   c already
  b for   d ever

3 Have you started making the sauce _____?
  a ever
  b yet
  c just
  d since

4 I've _____ made a sauce with garlic and mushrooms before.
  a for
  b yet
  c ever
  d never

5 He's _____ listened to the new album five times.
  a already
  b ever
  c since
  d yet

6 Has she _____ met your friend Mia?
  a since
  b yet
  c ever
  d for

7 She's _____ met Mia. They were both at the party.
  a ever
  b already
  c since
  d yet

8 He's _____ started taking driving lessons.
  a ever
  b yet
  c just
  d for

4 Match the questions and answers.

1 How many cookies has Meg eaten? _____
2 How long have you been going to the gym? _____
3 How many Harry Potter books have you read? _____
4 How many times have you been to the hospital for this problem? _____
5 How often does your family go to the theater? _____
6 How long has she been a hairdresser? _____

a At least four, I think.
b I think she's already had three.
c I've read the first five. I love them!
d Oh, for about two years.
e Since she was 21.
f We've been going once or twice a month for the past year.

5 Your roommate is asking what chores you've done in the apartment. Answer the questions using the prompts.

1 Have you changed the light bulb yet?
_____No, I still haven't changed it._____ (no / still)

2 Have you washed the frying pan?
_____ (no / yet)

3 Did you turn on the oven for dinner?
_____ (yes / already)

4 Have you locked the door yet?
_____ (yes / just)

5 Have you put the towels in the washing machine?
_____ (no / still)

6 Have you put the ice cream in the freezer?
_____ (yes / already)

6 Read the sentences and choose the options with similar meanings.

1 I've already been to the gallery to see the new show.
 a I saw the new show at the gallery.
 b I didn't see the new show at the gallery.

2 They've been watching TV for three hours. It's seven o'clock now.
 a They started watching TV at four o'clock.
 b They are not watching TV now.

3 Dylan has just finished his second driving lesson.
 a Dylan took two driving lessons.
 b Dylan has never taken a driving lesson.

4 We hadn't bought tickets before we went to the train station.
 a We had tickets before we got to the train station.
 b We didn't have tickets before we got to the train station.

5 I'd told her to set her alarm, but Natalie was still late for class.
 a Natalie was late for class, even though I told her to set her alarm.
 b I hadn't been telling Natalie to set her alarm, and she was late for class.

6 They've learned about the geography of Morocco, and now they want to learn about its culture.
 a They've learned about Moroccan culture and geography.
 b They learned about Moroccan geography, and they want to learn about its culture.

7 Write a question for each answer using the present perfect or present perfect continuous.

1 _____Have they ever been to South America?_____
No, they've never been to South America.

2 _____
No, I've never seen such beautiful scenery.

3 _____
I've been working on that math question for fifteen minutes.

4 _____
No, he hasn't eaten dinner yet.

5 _____
I've taken the train to school four times this week.

6 _____
No, I've never taken the bus to the airport.

7 _____
She's been reading that novel for a week.

8 Choose the correct options to complete the sentences.

1 Teresa *has been* / *has been going* to Lisbon four times. The last time she went, she stayed for five days.
2 How much luggage has she *brought* / *bringing* with her?
3 I have *disliked* / *been disliking* eggs since I was a child.
4 Have you finished your homework *still* / *yet*?
5 Xavier *has been* / *has gone* to Miami. He'll be back home next week.
6 I've *just* / *ever* returned from Manila. I'm still tired from the flight.
7 You've *deserved* / *been deserving* a promotion for more than six months.
8 We have *never* / *ever* been to that restaurant.

PRONUNCIATION *For*

9 Listen to the sentences and choose the pronunciation that you hear. 🎧 29

1 /fɔr/ /fər/
2 /fɔr/ /fər/
3 /fɔr/ /fər/
4 /fɔr/ /fər/
5 /fɔr/ /fər/
6 /fɔr/ /fər/

3D How I Swam the North Pole

TED TALKS

AUTHENTIC LISTENING SKILLS

1 Complete the text with the signposts. Then listen to the TED Talk excerpts and check your answers. 🎧 **30**

And he came up to me and he said,
And I thought,
And on day four,
And then, after a year of training,

---

(1) _____ I felt ready. I felt confident that I could actually do this swim. So, myself and the five members of the team, we hitched a ride on an icebreaker which was going to the North Pole.

(2) _____ we decided to just do a quick five-minute test swim. I had never swum in water of minus 1.7 degrees before, because it's just impossible to train in those type of conditions. So, we stopped the ship, as you do. We all got down onto the ice and I then got into my swimming costume and I dived into the sea.

I have never in my life felt anything like that moment. I could barely breathe. I was gasping for air…

(3) _____ in two days' time, I was going to do this swim across the North Pole. I was going to try and do a twenty-minute swim, for one kilometer across the North Pole. There is no possibility that this was going to happen…

And my close friend David, he saw the way I was thinking. **(4)** _____ "Lewis, I've known you since you were eighteen years old. I've known you, and I know, Lewis, deep down, right deep down here, that you are going to make this swim. I so believe in you, Lewis."

WATCH ▶

2 Watch the TED Talk and complete the chart. Write no more than two words and/or a number for each answer.

(1) _____ before	Two years before	**(4)** _____ before	**(6)** _____ later
Pugh went to the Arctic for **(2)** _____ time	**(3)** _____ percent of the Arctic Sea ice cover melted away.	Pugh did a **(5)** _____ -minute test swim.	Pugh could feel his hands again.

3 Watch Part 3 of the TED Talk and choose the correct options.

1 Pugh says it took years of training, planning, and _____ to do the North Pole swim.
   a bravery
   b money
   c preparation

2 A couple of hours before his swim, he was feeling _____.
   a frightened and emotional
   b proud and excited
   c happy and relaxed

3 Pugh says the swim was _____.
   a painful
   b worth it
   c fun

4 He thinks that _____ must play its part regarding climate change.
   a every country
   b Britain, America, and Japan
   c the same ship

5 He also thinks that even _____ understand climate change.
   a swimmers like himself
   b rich politicians
   c children in poor countries

6 Pugh believes that people need to _____.
   a believe in themselves
   b spend money to make a difference
   c walk more often

7 Finally, he says we should ask ourselves, _____
   a "What is a sustainable world?"
   b "What type of world do we want to live in?"
   c "Where in the world do we want to live?"

VOCABULARY IN CONTEXT

4 Choose the correct options to complete the sentences.

1 The water was so cold that I couldn't go in and I *barely / easily / really* got wet.
2 She twisted her ankle and within a few minutes it was *grown / expanded / swollen*.
3 Sharks don't live in *fresh water / sea water / salt water*, so I prefer swimming in rivers.
4 His face was painted white and he was wearing this brightly colored clown *equipment / costume / uniform*.
5 I went up to my sister just before the race, smiled and said *"I believe in you, Sis." / "Don't get me wrong, Sis."*
6 What decisions are we going to make today to *ensure / deny / say* that something is done about climate change?

3E School Sports

WRITING An opinion essay

1 Read the sentences and complete the chart.

1 I don't think that swimming pools should be free.
2 I've written a short history of the Olympic Games.
3 In my view, schools should make PE mandatory.
4 Many parks in the UK now have outdoor gyms.
5 Next year, I want to run the New York Marathon!
6 Of course, there's too much advertising in sports.
7 Personally, I think that Lewis Pugh is an inspiration.
8 The World Cup takes place every four years.

Expressing an opinion	Making a general statement

2 Match the two parts of the sentences.

1 In my opinion, cyclists who bike in traffic should have to pass a test
2 I don't think that sports should be taken so seriously
3 I strongly believe that some professional athletes are paid too much money
4 There is no question that we should have better protective clothing in contact sports

a and this sends the wrong message to young people.
b to make sure they understand the rules of the road.
c because some players risk serious injury.
d as their true purpose is just for enjoyment.

3 Complete the opinion essay with the correct sentences (a–f).

Anyone interested in trying a new sport has a lot of choices these days. Of course, people prefer to do sports they know they'll enjoy, and that's a very important factor. **(1)** _____ It's true that most sports are good for us, but in my view, team sports offer additional benefits. They teach us useful lessons both on and off the field. **(2)** _____ In order to be successful, team members have to communicate with each other quickly and clearly.

(3) _____ I strongly believe that team sports improve our ability to understand expectations and to respect others. **(4)** _____ There is no question that they are better at collaborating and working towards a common goal.

(5) _____ It's true that there's the convenience of training in your own time. In addition, some people are more suited to working alone.

(6) _____ In my opinion, sharing

responsibility for success or failure helps us to become better human beings.

a Of course, individual sports have advantages, too.
b Secondly, team sports help us to develop healthy relationships.
c Overall, however, I believe that team sports bring more value to our lives.
d Firstly, I would say that we learn to communicate better when we play team sports.
e Personally, I think that team sports are much better than individual sports.
f Finally, people who play team sports are better at working together.

4 Read the essay again. Choose the correct options to complete the sentences.

1 The writer first expresses her opinion in the *first sentence* / *third sentence*.
2 She believes that team sports offer more *players* / *benefits* than other sports.
3 In her view, *team sports* / *individual sports* improve our communication skills.
4 She thinks that team sports help us to have *good* / *more* relationships.
5 People who play team sports are also good at *winning* / *working* together.
6 The writer mentions some of the *good* / *bad* points about individual sports.
7 She ends the essay with *an opinion* / *a statement* about sharing responsibility.

5 What is your opinion of the following statement?

Some people feel the Olympic Games should not be continued because too many athletes cheat.

Write an opinion essay. Use specific reasons and examples to support your answer.

Tip box
• Spend a few minutes planning your main points.
• Introduce the topic.
• State your opinion in the introduction.
• In the second paragraph, develop your ideas.
• Provide examples to support your opinion.
• Use linking words and phrases (e.g. "However," "In addition").
• In the third paragraph, consider some opposing views.
• Sum up your main idea in the conclusion.
• Restate your opinion at the end.
• Check your spelling and punctuation.

SPEAKING

6 Complete the useful phrases with the missing words. Then decide if the phrase is for agreeing (A) or disagreeing (D).

1 I _____ what you're saying, but… _____
2 He's _____ a good point. _____
3 I _____ what you mean, it's just… _____
4 You're _____ wrong there. _____
5 _____, but… _____
6 I'm _____ sure I agree. _____
7 He's _____ about that. _____
8 That's _____. _____
9 That's a _____ point. _____
10 I _____ agree with you. _____
11 Maybe, _____… _____
12 I _____ up to a point, but… _____

7 Listen to the sentences in Activity 6 and decide if the missing word is higher or lower in pitch than the words near it. Draw an arrow ↗ or ↘ to mark the pitch. 🎧 31

8 Match the sentences (1–6) from Speaker 1 with the replies (a–f) from Speaker 2. Then match the responses (i–vi) from Speaker 3. Then listen to check your answers. 🎧 32

Speaker 1:

1 The government should spend more on sports education in schools.
2 Sports teach everyone about the value of hard work and determination.
3 I think we should have access to a wider variety of sports.
4 I believe sports give young people much better role models than the media or politics do.
5 I think big sports competitions stop people from focusing on the real problems with the country.
6 Athletes are excellent role models for young people.

Speaker 2:

a **That's a good point.** Not everyone likes soccer or swimming.
b **She's got a good point.** They often ignore the serious issues with the economy or infrastructure.
c **Maybe, but** in my opinion there's way too much corruption in sports.
d **I'm not sure I agree.** I think there's too much pressure in sports now.
e **I totally agree with you.** Young people are the future of the country.
f **I agree up to a point, but** the best athletes earn so much that it creates unrealistic expectations!

Speaker 3:

i **He's right about that.** Look at the problems FIFA had with fraud.
ii **I see what you're saying, but** in my opinion, schools need more money for teachers.
iii **I understand what you mean, it's just** that other sports can be expensive. Cheap ones like those are more accessible.
iv **That's true.** Every year, you hear about more new athletes taking risks with steroids.
v **You're not wrong there.** Some of the salaries football players get are unbelievable.
vi **Yes, but** the competitions bring lots of investments, which create jobs and help businesses.

9 How would you respond to these opinions in discussions? Write your ideas and then listen to compare them with the sample answers. 🎧 33

1 **A** I don't think football players should be paid more money than other athletes.
  B _____.
2 **A** There should be more mixed competitions with men and women playing against each other.
  B _____.
3 **A** I don't believe that the government promotes enough alternative sports.
  B _____.
4 **A** It seems strange to me that there's so much focus on sports, but not as much on culture.
  B _____.
5 **A** There are just too many sports on TV these days.
  B _____.

10 Read and discuss. Make notes on your ideas for each question. Then listen to the sample answer and compare your ideas. 🎧 34

We've been talking about issues in sports. Now, I'd like to discuss some more general questions relating to this topic. First, let's consider how sports affect people's lives.

- Do you think there should be more space to do sports in cities?
- How much influence do you think athletes have as role models for young people?

Finally let's think about the role of funding.

- What do you think of the funding of sports by the government?

Review

1 Delete the word or phrase that does <u>not</u> collocate with the verb.

1 beat + *an opponent / a record / a limit*
2 encourage + *a friend / your best / your teammate*
3 achieve + *a goal / exercise / an ambition*
4 score + *your opponent / a goal / a point*
5 represent + *your team / your nation / your goal*
6 train + *hard / for years / a win*

2 Put the words in the correct order to make sentences and questions.

1 she / running / to / stay / only / goes / in shape / .
_____

2 try / limits / my / I / push / to / own / .
_____

3 hard / they / trained / race / before / the / .
_____

4 represent / school / our / who / going / to / is / ?
_____

5 won / medals / has / he / gold / many / gymnastics / for / how / ?
_____

6 coach / our / us / to / encouraged / a team / as / work / .
_____

3 Complete the information about world records with the correct forms of the verbs in parentheses.

1 Chris Walton _____ (hold) the world record for the longest fingernails since 2011. She _____ (not cut) her fingernails for two decades.
2 In 2014, twenty chefs _____ (make) the world's largest dish of fried rice in Turkey. The dish _____ (weigh) over 3,000 kg!
3 The record for the largest wedding party _____ (belong) to a Sri Lankan couple since 2013. Their wedding party _____ (consist) of 126 bridesmaids, 25 best men, 20 page boys, and 23 flower girls.
4 Since 2007, the New York restaurant Serendipity 3 _____ (be) the record holder for the world's most expensive dessert. Their frozen hot chocolate costs $25,000!
5 Japanese fashion designer Kazuhiro Watanabe _____ (hold) the world record for the tallest Mohawk hairdo since 2011. His mohawk is almost four feet tall!
6 Two American men _____ (win) the world record for the longest handshake in 2008. They _____ (shake) hands for 9 hours 30 minutes.

4 Choose the correct options to complete the sentences.

1 Chen *took / has been taking* three science classes last term.
2 *They've been making / They've been made* bread with their grandmother since they were young children.
3 She was checking the ads in the newspaper when she finally found what she *had been looking / looked* for.
4 Leila *had laughing / had been laughing* loudly when the teacher entered the classroom.
5 She *hadn't ever repaired / hadn't repaired* her computer before her essay was due.
6 I *confirmed / had been confirming* the exchange rate and then I bought some perfume at the duty-free shop.

5 Put the words in the correct order to make sentences.

1 sick / I've / since / been / Saturday / last / .
_____

2 on / Adir / an / trying / has / shoes / for / been / hour / .
_____

3 wanted / has / in / live / never / to / Canada / she / .
_____

4 for / I've / Darren / known / years / three / .
_____

5 new / they / yet / met / their / haven't / teacher / .
_____

6 been / has / all / studying / Dinah / day / .
_____

7 moved / Lin and Sarah / Seattle / have / to / already / .
_____

4A Learning to Cook

VOCABULARY Describing food

1 **Review** Unscramble the letters to make words about food.

1 e c k i h c n   c _ _ _ _ _ _
2 a p t a s   _ _ s _ _
3 p s r n a w   p _ _ w _ _ _
4 e e f c f o   c _ _ _ _ _ _
5 l a p e p   _ _ _ _ e
6 l m o e n   l _ _ _ _ _
7 r c r y u   _ _ _ _ _ y
8 t m o a o t   _ _ _ a _ _

2 **Review** What flavor are these foods? Complete the chart. Then add two more foods to each column.

| cake | curry | chilli powder | chocolate |
| French fries | ice cream | potato chips | strawberry |

Sweet	Spicy	Salty

3 Match the opposites.

1 tasty   **a** healthy
2 junk   **b** fresh
3 processed   **c** meat-eater
4 raw   **d** mild
5 vegetarian   **e** disgusting
6 strong   **f** cooked

4 Choose the correct options to complete the sentences.

1 Good sushi is always *fresh / sweet*.
2 I can't eat *wheat / junk food*, so I don't usually eat pasta.
3 Thank you for a *well-balanced / delicious* meal. I loved it!
4 *Raw / Processed* vegetables have a lot of vitamins.
5 Could we go somewhere that is *natural / suitable* for vegetarians?
6 Fast food isn't always *junk / natural* food these days. There are more fast-food places with healthy options.

5 Unscramble the letters to make adjectives that describe food.

1 c k o d o e   c _ _ k _ _
2 s e f r h   _ _ _ s h
3 l e b o i d   b _ _ l _ _
4 f e i r d   _ r _ _ _
5 a s t y t   _ _ _ _ y
6 d e m s a t e   s t _ _ _ _ _ _
7 l a t u n r a   n _ _ _ r _ _

6 Complete the sentences with the words from Activity 5.

1 _____ food can be fried, boiled, or steamed.
2 _____ foods are not processed and they are often good for you.
3 I don't like _____ potatoes. They don't have much flavor.
4 In Vietnam, I picked _____ mangos and oranges for breakfast every day.
5 _____ chicken isn't very healthy, but it's OK to eat it once in a while.
6 I had such a _____ dinner last night. It was delicious!
7 _____ vegetables contain many vitamins.

7 Read and complete the text with one word in each blank.

My father used to eat a lot of **(1)** _____ meals that weren't good for him, and he especially loved **(2)** _____ food, like potato chips and chocolate bars. Then his doctor told him that he needed to change his diet to keep his heart healthy. So he started eating more **(3)** _____ vegetables that had lots of vitamins. He also started eating **(4)** _____ fruit and eggs for breakfast and drinking less coffee. Now, the doctor says his heart is much **(5)** _____, and my dad says the new foods he eats **(6)** _____ delicious!

8 Extension Match the words with their definitions.

1 appetizer
2 grill
3 stir-fry
4 main course
5 diet
6 appetite
7 tasteless

a cook using direct heat
b the biggest part of your meal
c the first thing you eat at a restaurant
d the type of foods that you usually eat
e the feeling of wanting to eat
f having no flavor
g cook by quickly moving around in hot oil

9 Extension These sentences are incorrect. Correct them so that they are true.

1 Eating well-balanced meals is part of an unhealthy diet.
Eating well-balanced meals is part of a healthy diet.

2 An appetizer is the last thing you eat when you are having dinner.
_____

3 A main course is usually a small dish.
_____

4 Vegetarians mainly eat meat.
_____

5 Steaming fish is less healthy than frying it.
_____

6 A cake is a type of appetizer.
_____

10 Extension Complete the chart with these words.

apple pie	bread and butter	chocolate cake
ice cream	mashed potatoes	pasta
roast chicken	salad	soup
steak		

Appetizer	Main Course	Dessert

LISTENING

11 Listen to the speaker. Then complete the text with these words. There are two words you don't need. 🎧 35

bakers	celebrating	century	edible
gingerbread	horrible	oven-baked	spice
sugar	sweet-tasting	wicked	

Have you ever tasted delicious, **(1)** _____ gingerbread cookies? Or have you ever seen, eaten, or even made a **(2)** _____ house? In many countries, gingerbread is an important part of **(3)** _____ winter holidays. You can thank a **(4)** _____ witch for gingerbread houses. Gingerbread has been around since at least the eleventh **(5)** _____. But, in 1812, the brothers Grimm published *Hansel and Gretel*, featuring a witch who lives in a house made of **(6)** _____. The witch used her **(7)** _____ house to attract unsuspecting children. Luckily for Hansel and Gretel, they were clever enough to escape from the witch. After the success of the story, miniature **(8)** _____ homes became popular. The witch's candy-covered home has inspired **(9)** _____ ever since.

12 Listen to the recipe for gingerbread. Put the instructions in the correct order. 🎧 36

a refrigerate the dough for three hours ____

b add the spices—cinnamon, ginger, and allspice—to the mixture ____

c bake the cookies at 375 degrees for seven minutes ____

d mix the butter, sugar, an egg, and syrup ____

e complete the dough by mixing in four cups of flour ____

f use a cookie cutter to shape your cookies ____

g let the cookies cool before you decorate with icing ____

h roll out the dough on a floured surface ____

13 Listen to the speaker and choose the best title for the talk. 🎧 37

a Antarctic Expedition
b Food for Thought
c Breaking Bread Together
d Everybody Loves Candy

14 Listen to the speaker again and choose the correct options. 🎧 37

1 What does the speaker say has always been a part of our human story?
a eating candy
b baking bread
c sharing food

2 What was important about the loaf of bread that was discovered?
a It could easily be divided.
b It was found in Italy.
c It had a circular shape.

3 What does the speaker say that breaking bread symbolizes?
a children imitating adults
b strengthening relationships
c causing disagreements

4 What does the speaker say many people associate with food?
a laughter
b candy
c love

5 Why do people in some cultures leave food at graves?
a to show they remember the person
b to forget all the bad things about the person
c to ask the loved one to give them help

6 What was the name of the Antarctic expedition in 1902?
a The Discovery Expedition
b The Scott Expedition
c The Midwinter Expedition

7 What were the men of the expedition celebrating?
a the cold and the darkness
b the longest night of the year
c the Antarctic regions

GRAMMAR Future plans, intentions, and arrangements

15 Choose the correct options to complete the sentences.

1 I *'ll probably / might probably* meet some friends for coffee after work.

2 I *'m bringing / bring* information about a new restaurant that *opening / opens* next month.

3 We *may decide / are going to decide* to have dinner there with our friends in a few weeks.

4 We *check / 're going to check* the menu to make sure there's something everyone can eat.

5 I'm sure we *'re finding / 'll find* something that everyone will enjoy.

6 After we've checked the menu, we *'re going to make / 'll going to make* a decision.

7 Later, I *'ll email / 'm emailing* the others to let them know when and where we *'re meeting / meet*.

8 I think everyone *will be / is being* pleased with our decision.

9 We *possibly invite / might invite* our teacher, too.

16 Choose the correct options to make the sentences negative.

1 If humans ever travel to Mars, they're going to find plants that can be used for food.
If humans ever travel to Mars, they *aren't going to find / not going to find* plants that can be used for food.

2 Humans will probably grow food the same way they did on Earth.
Humans probably *won't not grow / won't grow* food the same way they did on Earth.

3 They may be able to raise animals the way they did on Earth.
They *may not be / not may be* able to raise animals the way they did on Earth.

4 They'll probably have to develop new ways to grow food.
They *probably might not have to / probably won't have to* develop new ways to grow food.

5 They're bringing food with them on their spacecraft.
They *don't bring / aren't bringing* food with them on their spacecraft.

6 Humans will grow food crops outdoors.
Humans *won't grow / willn't grow* food crops outdoors.

7 The way crops are grown on Mars will work on Earth.
The way crops are grown on Mars *aren't going to work / isn't going to work* on Earth.

8 If scientists discover a way to feed humans on Mars, we'll go there.
If scientists *won't discover / don't discover* a way to feed humans on Mars, we *won't go / don't go* there.

17 Read the sentences and decide which is correct. If both are correct, choose "both."

1 a Our coffee break starts at 2:30.
b Our coffee break will start at 2:30.
c both

2 a Hani is going to teaching me how to make Somali food.
b Hani is going to teach me how to make Somali food.
c both

3 a We will eats something when we get to the park.
b We will eat something when we get to the park.
c both

4 a Mei meet her friend at the pizza place near the river.
b Mei is meeting her friend at the pizza place near the river.
c both

5 a Travis might practice baking cakes next weekend.
b Travis may practice baking cakes next weekend.
c both

6 a Is Leon starting a food blog?
b Will Leon starting a food blog?
c both

7 a Abdul will spend next semester studying food science.
b Abdul will to spend next semester studying food science.
c both

8 a Alejandro is going to text his parents about the new restaurant.
b Alejandro might to text his parents about the new restaurant.
c both

18 Complete the sentences with the simple present or *going to* form of the verbs in parentheses.

1 Sophia _____ (work) part-time at a restaurant this semester.

2 When you _____ (see) Juan tomorrow, tell him that I've made a cake.

3 Giorgio _____ (plan) to attend a cooking school next summer.

4 I think Asha _____ (make) us a salad for lunch.

5 I _____ (steam) some broccoli for the stir-fry.

6 Malcolm and Shani _____ (bake) a birthday cake for their friend.

7 The supermarket is closed now, but it _____ (open) at 8 am tomorrow morning.

8 Dana _____ (come up with) with a menu that everyone will love.

19 Are these sentences correct or incorrect? Correct those that are incorrect.

1 We'll have a party at school and eat food from different cultures.

2 Everyone preparing a dish that is popular in their own country.

3 Chen is going bring his favorite Chinese dish.

4 Marisol will cooking a Mexican dish that's very spicy.

5 Khalid doesn't cook and so he'll ask his mother to prepare falafel for everyone.

6 Kasia may to make a special dessert—if she can remember where the recipe is.

7 If he can find the right ingredients, Milan will to make fish stew.

8 When we will have everything in the cafeteria, it will smell so good.

9 Everyone is going to have a great time together!

Notes: _____
_____
_____
_____
_____
_____
_____
_____
_____
_____
_____
_____
_____

4B Superfood

VOCABULARY BUILDING Compound adjectives

1 Match the words to make compound adjectives.

1			**2**		
a	deep-	baked	**a**	well-	cooked
b	oven-	dried	**b**	old-	finished
c	home-	fried	**c**	good-	fashioned
d	sweet-	made	**d**	over-	known
e	sun-	tasting	**e**	half-	looking

READING

2 Read the text and match the summaries (a–f) with the paragraphs (1–5) next to each statement.

a the real cost of avocados _____
b superfoods and natural resources _____
c the consequences of quinoa's popularity _____
d a description of superfoods _____
e a description of quinoa _____
f the limitations of superfoods _____

3 Read the statements. Are the sentences true (T), false (F), or is the information not given (NG)?

1 Superfoods are packed with benefits that aren't always available in other foods. _____
2 Quinoa can be cooked like rice. _____
3 Quinoa has only recently become known in South America. _____
4 Because quinoa is so rich in nutrients, it's a good substitute for meat. _____
5 Like quinoa, avocados have very specific requirements for growth. _____
6 Superfoods are good for us, and they're also good for the environment. _____

4 Choose the correct options to complete the sentences.

1 Avocados, like quinoa, blueberries, almonds, and salmon, are considered a _____.
   a grain
   b seed
   c superfood

2 These types of food are thought to be rich in nutrients and low in _____.
   a diets
   b calories
   c resources

3 Quinoa is an ancient _____ that, until recently, was unknown outside South America.
   a grain
   b fiber
   c nutrient

4 The _____ of the quinoa plant can be cooked and eaten.
   a flower
   b seeds
   c production

5 A consequence of quinoa's popularity is a change in the _____ of people who've traditionally grown it.
   a price
   b popularity
   c diet

6 Rice and noodles are less _____ than quinoa.
   a tasty
   b nutritious
   c popular

7 The _____ of a kilo of avocados takes more than 800 liters of water!
   a resources
   b advantage
   c production

The Quinoa Conundrum*

1 🔊 38 Do you love avocados? Do you adore almonds? These familiar foods have, among others, recently become known as "superfoods." What makes a food "super"? So-called superfoods are a special category of foods that are considered nutrient-rich, low in calories, and packed with health benefits not always found in other foods. Almonds, avocados, blueberries, and salmon are among the most commonly known superfoods.

2 There are also a number of less familiar foods that fall into the category of superfoods. Among these is an ancient grain called quinoa. Quinoa is a flowering plant that, until very recently, was known and used only in the Andean highlands of South America. The seeds of the quinoa plant can be cooked like rice and other grains, and are unusually well-balanced—the tiny grain is rich in fiber*, amino acids*, vitamins, minerals, and other important nutrients. Although quinoa has been eaten in South America for thousands of years (the ancient Incas referred to it as "the mother grain"), it's only recently become known to the rest of the world as a superfood.

3 One result of the sudden and tremendous popularity of quinoa is a change in the diets of people who've traditionally grown and eaten it. Because their crops are now more valuable and they have more money to spend, some quinoa growers prefer to eat less quinoa and more of the non-traditional and often less nutritious foods that were previously unavailable to them, such as rice or noodles, and even candy and fizzy drinks.

Other quinoa farmers can no longer afford to eat the newly expensive grain they grow and have to find alternative foods to eat.

4 Another issue related to the popularity of this superfood is the availability of resources needed to grow it. As prices for quinoa continue to rise, so do prices for the land on which it's grown. And because the quinoa plant has very specific requirements, there's only so much available land on which to successfully farm it. The same is true for avocados. Avocados are another ancient Latin American food that has become wildly popular after being labeled a superfood. Avocados require water, and lots of it! It takes more than 800 liters* of water to produce a kilo* of avocados. That's like filling a bathtub with water for each avocado you eat! In the state of California, half a billion kilos of avocados are grown annually, and that means billions of liters of water for their production. But California sometimes experiences extended periods of drought*, making the cost of water, like the cost of land, rise dramatically. This makes water-hungry avocados expensive to buy and sometimes too expensive to grow.

5 Are superfoods good for your health, but bad for the planet? As is the case with almost anything we eat or use, sustainability is always an issue. It's becoming clear that we won't always be able to have everything we'd like to eat, at any time of year, wherever we are. Even superfoods come at a cost.

conundrum *a question that has no real answer*
fiber *a substance in plants that helps food pass through the body*
amino acids *acids that occur in living things and that sometimes form proteins*

liter *about a quarter of a gallon*
kilo *about 2.2 pounds*
drought *a long period of time during which there is very little or no rain*

4C Will you...?

GRAMMAR Making predictions

1 Underline the sentences that make predictions about future plans, intentions, and arrangements.

Camila grew up in a small town. Her family had lived there for many years. She loved walking to school with her sisters and cousins, and stopping by her grandparents' house on the way home. When she was in high school, her aunt asked Camila what she wanted to do in the future. Camila said, "I'm going to go to college. I'll probably study biology. I might have to do more training, but then I'm going to be a doctor." Her aunt replied, "That sounds great, Camila! You may have to work very hard if that's your ambition. I wanted to be a doctor when I was younger, but I didn't have enough money for college. I had to work after school. I'm sure you will do well if you study a lot and ask for help when you need it."

2 Choose the correct options to complete the sentences.

1 Amy *will meet / meet* us for a picnic after she *finishes / is going to finish* work.
2 I *'ll / might* probably buy some cheese for my omelet.
3 As soon as she *will get / gets* more business, her store *will be / be* successful.
4 I *won't / willn't* order a cupcake if I have a big lunch.
5 Makoto *going to / may* graduate early if his grades *are / will be* good enough.
6 When I *won't ask / ask* my parents if I can go on the trip, *I'll / I'm* also ask if I can borrow some money.
7 I'm sure Celina will *be taking / be taken* her brother to the barbecue because her dad *won't / isn't* be able to look after him.
8 She's *will / going to* study in Colombia next year so that she'll *have spoken / spoken* a lot of Spanish before graduating.

3 Complete the sentences about future plans, intentions, and arrangements.

does   going to   is   'll   might   she'll   will   won't

1 What time _____ the concert start?
2 This book is so great—I know you _____ want to read it.
3 He really wants to get his own apartment. I think he _____ move back to his parents' house after graduation.
4 What time _____ Paolo's graduation party?
5 Carlos _____ order mashed potatoes with his steak.
6 I imagine Tetsu _____ want to take a shower after jogging in the park.
7 They're _____ be ready to leave at seven thirty.
8 I don't know if _____ have enough time to help me study.

4 Choose the sentence in each pair that is more certain.

1 a We might walk to the post office this afternoon if it doesn't rain.
  b I'm going to order a green tea when we get to the café.
2 a We're going to my parents' house on Monday for my dad's birthday.
  b They may go for a pizza if they haven't already eaten lunch.
3 a We're leaving at six o'clock tomorrow morning.
  b If you arrive by five o'clock, we might have enough time to go out for dinner.
4 a I think she'll be home by 3:30.
  b He won't go to work tomorrow because it's a holiday.
5 a We'll probably take the train to the game.
  b Khalid isn't going to study for the exam this afternoon.
6 a I imagine he'll be disappointed if he doesn't win.
  b Isha will be studying tonight because she has a test tomorrow.
7 a Perhaps we can talk to our coach next week.
  b By the end of the summer, Aurelia will have played soccer for three months.

5 Rewrite each sentence to make it positive.

1 My uncle won't plant more flowers this spring.

_____

2 Mara isn't going to buy balloons for Jed's birthday.

_____

3 I'm not going to listen to the program.

_____

4 We won't have learned about Ancient Rome by the end of this semester.

_____

5 We won't be eating dinner when you arrive.

_____

6 My parents won't buy me a new car after graduation.

_____

6 Put the words in the correct order to make sentences and questions.

1 clap / the / bad, / if / the / play / is / won't / audience / .

_____

2 Tanzania / January / be / to / in / flying / they'll / .

_____

3 going / US / I'm / not / to / next / study / in / the / year / .

_____

4 a / you / for / when / year / will / have / here / worked / ?

_____

5 assignments / collecting / the / Ms. Shultz / be / in / class / won't / .

_____

6 party / the / by the time / downloaded / the / songs / she'll / have / we / get / to / .

_____

7 Match the two parts of the sentences.

1 Are you going _____
2 They'll be _____
3 I expect _____
4 I'm going to _____
5 I think if we all recycle more, there _____
6 I'm going to stay up late tonight, so I'll _____
7 When will you _____

a 'll be less litter around campus.
b have bought the books you need?
c probably be tired tomorrow.
d seeing the movie with Daniel's cousins.
e to read the book before you see the movie?
f watch that documentary about chefs tonight.
g to decorate the classroom for our teacher's last day.

8 Read and listen to the questions. Choose the correct options. 🎧 39

1 Will you invite Zhen to your party?
  a No, I won't possibly invite her.
  b No, I don't think I'll invite her to my party.
2 Will the hockey players be wearing their red or white uniforms?
  a They will have worn the red ones.
  b They're going to wear the red ones.
3 Will Mr. Jackson be hiring more people to work at the library?
  a Yes, he will hiring more people.
  b No, he won't.
4 Will you have listened to the jazz album before your performance?
  a Yes, I'll have listened to it before my performance.
  b No, I won't be listened to it before my performance.
5 When is the violin concert?
  a It will have been playing on Sunday.
  b It's on Sunday.
6 As soon as you get home, will you turn on the oven?
  a No problem. I'll turn it on as soon as I get home.
  b Sure. I turn it on as soon as I will get home.
7 What did you think about the play you saw last night?
  a It's great. You're going to love it!
  b It'll be great. You won't like it.
8 Will he have gotten his driver's license by June?
  a Yes, he's planning to get it at the end of April.
  b Yes, he'll get it last month.

PRONUNCIATION Sentence stress with the future continuous and future perfect

9 Listen to the sentences. Underline at least two words that are stressed in each sentence. Then practice saying the sentences. 🎧 40

1 Anna won't be eating seafood.
2 The chef will be preparing something special.
3 They won't have arrived in Shanghai yet.
4 He'll have left by the time you get there.
5 What will you be doing tomorrow?
6 She won't have finished her work.

4D Why I'm a Weekday Vegetarian

TEDTALKS

AUTHENTIC LISTENING SKILLS

1 Listen to the TED Talk excerpts. Choose the type of pause the speaker uses in each one. 🎧 41

1 So really, any of these angles should have been enough to convince me to go vegetarian. *adverbial time phrase / end of a sentence / commas*

2 On the weekend, your choice. *adverbial time phrase / between a long subject and verb / before an important phrase*

3 After all, cutting five days a week is cutting 70 percent of your meat intake. *commas / before an important phrase / between a long subject and verb*

4 My footprint's smaller, I'm lessening pollution, I feel better about the animals, I'm even saving money. *commas / before an important phrase / adverbial time phrase*

5 After all, if all of us ate half as much meat, it would be like half of us were vegetarians. *end of a sentence / commas / before an important phrase*

WATCH ▶

2 Choose five reasons Graham Hill gives for becoming a vegetarian.

a Eating too much red meat is unhealthy.

b It's easy to become a vegetarian even if you enjoy meat.

c Raising animals for meat causes environmental damage.

d Raising cows for beef uses 100 times the water that vegetables use.

e Giving up meat is an easy way to lose a lot of weight.

f The conditions in factory farms are cruel.

g Steak doesn't taste as good as it used to.

h The emissions caused by meat production are higher than all transport combined.

3 Read the questions and choose the best summaries of Graham Hill's answers.

1 Graham Hill asked himself: "Knowing what I know, why am I not a vegetarian?"

He answered:

a "I had all the facts, but I still kept eating meat."

b "I had no idea how bad meat was."

c "Meat isn't as bad as people say."

2 Graham Hill asked himself: "So why was I stalling?"

He answered:

a "I realized there was no way to change my taste buds."

b "I realized I was only given two options—give up meat entirely or not at all."

c "I realized I never really wanted to eat vegetarian food."

3 Graham Hill asked himself: "Might there be a third solution?"

He answered:

a "Not yet. I'm still thinking about this."

b "Simple. Just stop eating meat altogether."

c "Absolutely. I stopped eating meat on weekdays."

4 Graham Hill asked the audience: "What's stopping you from giving weekday veg a shot?"

He answered:

a "If everyone did their part, it would make a big difference."

b "If only half of you did this, it wouldn't have an effect."

c "Half of you should become vegetarian, and the other half should eat meat."

VOCABULARY IN CONTEXT

4 Choose the correct options to complete the sentences.

1 Eating too much red meat may be a _____ to your health.

a damage   **b** risk   **c** conflict

2 My grandmother lives in the country and _____ chickens on her farm.

a grows   **b** lifts   **c** raises

3 Eating a lot of meat also causes environmental _____ .

a conflict   **b** damage   **c** shame

4 If you haven't _____ a solution by now, you never will.

a come up with   **c** caught up with
b teamed up with

5 My love for animals was _____ my love for fried chicken.

a teamed up with   **c** in agreement with
b in conflict with

6 The amount of greenhouse gas created by meat production is greater than for all forms of transportation _____ .

a surrounded   **c** combined
b joined

4E Future Plans

SPEAKING

1 Look at the photos and match the two parts of the sentences. Then listen and check your answers. 🎧 42

Gena

Tom

Stefan

Gena

1 I'm thinking of…
2 I'm interested in…
3 I'm hoping to…

Tom

4 I'm looking forward to…
5 I'd really like to…
6 I'm aiming to…

Stefan

7 I think I might…
8 I expect to…

a be famous.
b becoming a vegetarian.
c work on the farm next month instead of going on a vacation.
d helping people.
e become a farmer like my dad and grandpa.
f have read several Shakespeare plays by the end of the semester.
g studying theater in college.
h volunteer for a charity.

2 Complete the conversation with the phrases (1–8) from Activity 1. Then listen and check your answers. 🎧 43

A Hey, what's going on with you this summer? Are you going to be around?

B I'm not sure, actually. **(1)** _____ try to find a job. It'll be a long summer without any money.

C Yeah, **(2)** _____ be here. My parents are working, so I don't think we're going on vacation or anything.

A Well, **(3)** _____ going to the coast for a week or two, just camping and having a relaxing time. Are you interested in coming along?

B Hmm, I'm not sure. In the long term, **(4)** _____ study tourism in college, so I think finding a job would be a good idea for me this summer, to give me some practical experience. **(5)** _____ have something worked out by next month, so if I don't, can I let you know then?

A Sure. **(6)** _____ hang out with you this summer so let me know whether you can make it. How about you, Maria? Are you up for it?

C Yeah, **(7)** _____ spending some time by the sea. I love the beach! What are you planning to do while you're there?

A Well, **(8)** _____ learning to surf, so I guess I'll spend a lot of time doing that.

C Oh, really? Me, too! We could practice together.

A That sounds awesome. What do you think, Sal, still can't tempt you to a couple of weeks on the beach?

B Well, maybe. But only if I can't find a job, otherwise I can always come for a day or two. But do you know anyone who's looking for a … ?

3 Think about your hopes and goals for the topics below and write a list. Make notes and then compare your ideas with the sample answers. 🎧 44

Think about:

a school and study
b hobbies and interests
c friends and relationships

I expect to go to college…

4 Answer the question below. Make notes on a separate sheet of paper and give reasons for your ideas. Then listen to the sample answer and compare it with your ideas. 🎧 45

What type of job do you imagine yourself doing in the future?

WRITING A social media update

5 Complete the chart with these examples of tips for writing social media updates.

We enjoyed a fabulous feast.

~~We were furious because the bus left early.~~

Having a wonderful time.

In the next few days, we're hoping to do more sightseeing.

It's amazing here!

This morning, I had the best melon I've ever tasted.

Tip	Example
Leave out the subject in sentences.	
Use exclamation points.	
Use descriptive vocabulary.	
Use emotionally powerful words.	*We were furious because the bus left early.*
Talk about recent events.	
Talk about future plans and hopes.	

6 Complete the tips (1–6) with the reasons for doing them (a–f).

1 It's OK to leave out the subject in some sentences _____

2 It's good to use exclamation marks _____

3 Using descriptive vocabulary is recommended _____

4 Emotionally powerful words improve the post _____

5 It's a good idea to talk about recent events _____

6 Try to mention some future plans and hopes _____

a because they give the reader a very clear sense of how the writer is feeling.

b because this gives readers an idea of what they will find in your next update.

c because they help the reader to recognize surprising or unusual events.

d because readers are interested in what's happening currently.

e because this helps informal posts to sound more like a diary entry or a postcard.

f because it makes the writing much more interesting for the reader.

7 Complete the social media update with these words.

| camping | delicious | magnificent | meat dishes |
| on the way here | planning | terrified | traditional |

South Africa is truly amazing! Left Cape Town yesterday and drove to our camp at Storms River. Oh, **(1)** _____, we stopped to see the wildlife at a national park. The elephants were beautiful, I mean, really **(2)** _____! Some people were frightened when we suddenly saw a lion… it was so close! To be honest, I was pretty **(3)** _____, but later I was glad I'd seen it. The scenery around here is astonishing. We're staying in comfortable but very basic huts (don't like **(4)** _____!). Last night, we went to a **(5)** _____ restaurant for dinner. The local seafood was absolutely incredible, but I didn't try any of the **(6)** _____. Never expected to find crocodile, zebra, and ostrich on a dinner menu, but others in the group said they were **(7)** _____.

For the rest of this week, we'll be hiking along the river and through the forest. Can't wait to see the waterfall. I'm **(8)** _____ to go bungee jumping tomorrow, have never done it before! I'll post a photo. ☺

8 Read the social media update again. Choose the seven things that the writer did.

1 left the subject out of some sentences

2 said how many other people are on the trip

3 used exclamation points

4 mentioned the cost of the trip

5 included descriptive vocabulary

6 talked about some of the food on the trip

7 described the weather

8 used emotionally powerful words

9 complained about some of the activities

10 talked about recent events

11 explained what they're doing next week

12 mentioned future plans and hopes

9 Write at least 250 words on the topic below. Include any relevant examples from your knowledge or experience.

These days, more and more people do not have enough money to buy food. Many supermarkets throw away food items they have not sold. Governments should force all supermarkets to donate food rather than waste it.

What are the advantages and disadvantages of this?

Review

1 Match the words with a similar meaning.

1	tasty	**a**	uncooked
2	healthy	**b**	delicious
3	disgusting	**c**	well-balanced
4	raw	**d**	terrible
5	junk	**e**	unnatural
6	processed	**f**	unhealthy

2 Complete the second sentence so that it means the same as the first. Use no more than three words.

1 I haven't eaten processed food in a long time.

It's been a long time _____ processed food.

2 Don't eat so much unhealthy stuff like chocolate and potato chips!

Don't eat so much _____ food!

3 Fried chicken is popular because of the ease of cooking it.

Fried chicken is popular because _____ to cook.

4 If you don't boil rice long enough, it will be hard.

Rice will be hard if you don't _____ long enough.

5 The food at camp is too unhealthy to eat.

The food at camp isn't _____ to eat.

6 I prefer being a vegetarian to eating meat.

I'd rather be a vegetarian than a _____.

3 Put the words in the correct order to make sentences and questions.

1 arrive / the food / will / in time / for us / to eat / ?

_____

2 making / the chef / is / week / risotto / next / .

_____

3 find out / about / the daily specials / how / the customers / will / ?

_____

4 be / for / everyone / tomorrow / to / get together / might / the best time / .

_____

5 carefully / the ingredients / measure / I / will / very / .

_____

6 are / the inspectors / for / going to / ask / more information / .

_____

7 help / tomorrow / my cousin / at their café / might / his parents / .

_____

8 cold / soon / get / going to / if / we / the soup / is / don't eat / .

_____

4 Complete the conversations about predictions, plans, intentions, and arrangements.

1 A Is Hugo driving to Chicago on Tuesday?

B Yes, he _____.

2 A What's wrong?

B You're driving too fast! You're _____ get a speeding ticket.

3 A Is she stopping at the clinic on the way home?

B I don't remember if she's _____ stop at the clinic.

4 A Will students register for courses online next year?

B No, students _____ be registering online next year.

5 A Daria is eating so much chocolate.

B I think she _____ have a stomach ache tonight.

6 A What time do you want to leave for the movie theater?

B Well, the movie _____ at nine o'clock. So let's leave by eight-thirty.

5 Are the words in bold correct or incorrect? Correct those that are incorrect.

1 I expect that **you'll** want to take a lot of pictures of the beautiful mountains.

2 We don't have time to stop for lunch. You're **will be** hungry when we get to the beach.

3 We're going into town for the game tonight. We **possibly** try the new Vietnamese restaurant.

4 A How long are you **going to staying** in Mexico?

B I'll be there for a week.

5 Until I **will graduate**, I'll live with my parents.

6 By the end of the summer, Ben **will have gone** camping with his friends three times.

7 I **think I won't** pass my exam today.

5A New Ways of Working

VOCABULARY Describing work

1 Review What type of jobs are these? Complete the chart.

accountant	chief executive	firefighter	lawyer
paramedic	police officer	salesperson	store manager

Emergency services	Desk jobs	Retail

2 Review Listen and complete the words for jobs. The first letters are given for you. 🎧 46

1 n _ _ _ _
2 t _ _ _ _ _ _
3 l _ _ _ _ _
4 c _ _ _
5 a _ _ _ _ _ _ _ _ _
6 a _ _ _ _ _ _ _

3 Review Which people often work together? Match the jobs.

1 doctor   **a** police officer
2 lawyer   **b** paramedic
3 firefighter   **c** waiter/waitress
4 salesperson   **d** manager
5 office worker   **e** nurse
6 chef   **f** store manager

4 Match the two parts of the sentences.

1 After he lost his job, _____
2 Being a chief executive is well paid, _____
3 I love being a writer _____
4 The newspaper industry is changing _____
5 Acting is competitive because _____
6 I am very busy at home, _____

a but it is also very demanding.
b because I can be creative.
c he was out of work for six months.
d so I'd prefer a part-time job.
e so many people want to do it.
f because people often get their news online.

5 Choose the correct options to complete the sentences.

1 If you don't have many qualifications, your *career prospects / part-time work* are limited.
2 My job as a doctor is rewarding, but it's also *demanding / well-paid*.
3 Her job is *creative / flexible*. She can work whatever hours she wants.
4 I've been *working on / working for* a new design for six months.
5 He has been in the film *career / industry* for over twenty years.
6 Being a paramedic is *stressful / competitive*. I have to make life-or-death decisions every day.
7 She enjoys being a lawyer, but she's looking for something more *demanding / creative*, like writing or designing.

6 Match the words and phrases with a similar meaning.

1 stressful   **a** unemployed
2 industry   **b** with a good salary
3 out of work   **c** business
4 job   **d** work
5 well-paid   **e** responsible for
6 in charge of   **f** demanding

7 Complete the sentences with *in*, *for*, or *on*.

1 I work _____ my parents at their ice-cream shop every summer.

2 The architect has been working _____ a new building in the city center.

3 I've been working _____ my new book for months, but I have writer's block!

4 He's been working _____ the publishing industry for years. He's a great editor.

5 She doesn't like her job as a lawyer, but she does it _____ the money.

6 My friend was working _____ an exciting project when she lost her job.

7 I used to work _____ the office five days a week, but now I work from home on Tuesdays.

8 Put the words in the correct order to make sentences.

1 being / I / of / a / like / charge / in / team / large / .

_____

2 out / work / he / been / has / of / three / months / for / .

_____

3 big / for / me / working / projects / is / on / stressful / .

_____

4 writer / such / a / is / being / creative / a / job / .

_____

5 with / job / for / I / looking / career / am / a / prospects / .

_____

6 wants / work / the / in / entertainment / she / industry / to / .

_____

7 aren't / jobs, / so / many / competitive / very / it's / there / .

_____

9 **Extension** Complete the sentences with the correct forms of *find*, *need*, or *quit*.

1 I have to _____ a job soon—I really need the money.

2 She finally _____ her job as a doctor after seven years.

3 My friend _____ her job as a salesperson by looking at the store's website.

4 Do you know anyone who _____ a part-time job? We're hiring at our restaurant.

5 I don't do this job because I _____ it. I do it because I love it!

6 Why did you _____ your job? Was it too stressful?

10 **Extension** Read the statements. Are the sentences true (T) or false (F)? Correct the false statements.

1 A rewarding job makes you feel like you are doing something important and useful. _____

2 An open position is a job that is no longer available for someone to do. _____

3 A challenging job is a job that doesn't require much effort. _____

4 If you resign, you quit your job. _____

5 A supervisor is in charge of other members of staff. _____

6 A person who is retired is at the beginning of their career. _____

7 A trainee is a person who is learning to do a job. _____

LISTENING

11 Listen and complete the sentences. 🎧 47

1 You _____ look for a job that gives you a feeling of satisfaction.

2 The referee at a soccer match _____ enforce the rules.

3 The dog trainer _____ stop the dog from biting people.

4 Police _____ drive faster than the speed limit when they _____ .

5 I _____ understand how some people _____ work such long hours.

6 He _____ apply for the job. His father owns the company.

12 Listen to the speaker. Are the sentences true (T) or false (F)? 🎧 **48**

1 Cesar Millan is a dog trainer. _____
2 Millan couldn't tell Kisses and Kitten apart. _____
3 The dog was the color of cotton candy. _____
4 The name of Millan's TV show is *The Whisperer*. _____
5 A "whisperer" can talk to animals. _____
6 Millan tries to fix behavioral challenges. _____
7 Millan thinks dogs often behave badly. _____
8 Millan trains both the dog and the owner. _____

13 Listen and choose the correct options. 🎧 **49**

1 What breed is the pink dog?
   a Kisses
   b Maltese
   c Millan
2 Was Kisses' problem very unusual?
   a Yes, it was a first for Millan.
   b No, not for young, female dogs.
   c No, it happens with all dogs.
3 What word does the speaker use to mean *a learned response*?
   a a routine
   b a pattern
   c a habit

4 What does Millan always try to do for his audience?
   a teach a lesson
   b answer questions
   c fix their problems
5 How does Millan change dogs' behavior?
   a He teaches their owners to punish them more.
   b He rewards the owners when they succeed.
   c He teaches them new responses to situations.
6 How would you describe Millan's training method?
   a patience and punishment
   b repetition and rewards
   c respect and patience
7 What is another word for *reward* that the speaker uses?
   a a sweet
   b a cookie
   c a treat

14 Listen and choose the correct options. 🎧 **50**

1 What two animals are mentioned as "service animals"?
   a dogs and sheep
   b elephants and dogs
   c monkeys and dogs
2 What do service animals do?
   a control other farm animals
   b assist blind and deaf people
   c provide transportation
3 What was Gavin the dog's previous job?
   a working for the military
   b working for the police
   c controlling other animals
4 What was Gavin's biggest problem?
   a He was afraid of other dogs.
   b He was a workaholic.
   c He needed a new job.
5 What did Millan do for Gavin?
   a He taught him to be calm and relax.
   b He gave him a new purpose in life.
   c He helped him to start a new family.
6 What was Gavin's first new job?
   a protecting a mother dog and her puppies
   b adopting a new human family
   c learning not to fear loud sounds
7 What is the joke in the last sentence?
   a a dog chewing on shoes and couches
   b a dog taking a human for a walk
   c a dog chasing a Frisbee or ball

GRAMMAR Verb patterns: verb + -ing or infinitive with to

15 Complete the chart with these sentences.

He's the kind of person who doesn't like disappointing people.

I think the owner is planning to hire more people.

I've promised to talk to the bank about a business loan.

Remember to check your spelling before you submit the application form.

She'll go on searching for a job until she finds something.

We agreed to continue the discussion tomorrow.

We only hire people who don't mind accepting challenges.

Why don't you try looking on the company website?

Verb + -ing	Infinitive with to

16 Choose the correct options to complete the sentences.

1 I'm planning *looking / to look* for a part-time job when I can finally drive.
2 I'd consider *to work / working* at a shopping mall.
3 I've spent hours *to apply / applying* for jobs online and *asking / to ask* my friends if they know of any.
4 I haven't managed *to get / getting* any interviews so far.
5 I hope *finding / to find* a job sometime soon because I really need the money.
6 My friends invited me *to travel / traveling* across Spain with them and I want *going / to go*.
7 We want *flying / to fly* to Barcelona and visit some friends there.
8 I'll keep *looking / to look* for a job until I find one that I really like.

17 Complete the sentences with the correct forms of the verbs in parentheses.

1 Office workers often have to get used to _____ (spend) all day in front of their computers.
2 But many of them don't mind _____ (sit) at their desks, _____ (send) emails, and _____ (talk) on the phone.
3 Some people even manage _____ (go) outside during their lunch break.
4 They'd like _____ (spend) more time outdoors, but they can't.
5 People who work outside often dislike _____ (work) in the winter.
6 Some of them hope _____ (find) office jobs so they can be more comfortable.
7 But then they realize that they would miss _____ (be) in the fresh air.

18 Complete the sentences with the correct forms of these verbs.

be	give	miss	solve	talk	tell	work

1 Would you mind _____ me directions to City Hall?
2 I can't afford _____ another day of work.
3 We all pretended _____ really busy when the boss walked in.
4 Please stop _____ me how to do my job!
5 How did you end up _____ here?
6 Thankfully, we managed _____ the problem.
7 Do you enjoy _____ to new people?

19 Find and correct the mistakes. There is one in each sentence.

1 Our hard-working and creative employees have learned producing smartphone apps more efficiently.
2 Neither of my parents likes to working long hours.
3 I don't want be in charge of people who don't do their jobs well.
4 Most college graduates expect finding well-paid jobs.
5 I agreed attending the training course because we want the company to remain competitive.
6 Have you considered to research jobs in the tech industries?
7 Customers often go on to complaining even when you've told them there's nothing you can do.

5B An Unusual Job

VOCABULARY BUILDING Ways of seeing

1 Choose the correct options to complete the sentences.

1 I hadn't seen Javier for years—I hardly *recognized* / *identified* him.
2 Over a two-month period, researchers *observed* / *spotted* schoolchildren in three different countries.
3 I didn't have time to read the report in detail—I only *glanced* / *caught* at it.
4 Has the driver of the vehicle been *noticed* / *identified* yet?
5 Ava's leaving work early—I just *observed* / *spotted* her getting into her car.
6 We suddenly *noticed* / *recognized* that the door had been left open.

READING

2 Read the text and choose the correct options to answer the questions.

1 How did Krithi Karanth first become interested in wildlife conservation?
   a She saw a tiger in the wild when she was three years old.
   b Her father started taking her to work with him when she was very young.
   c She grew up on the Indian subcontinent.
   d She went on an expedition to track tigers.

2 According to paragraph 2, why are conflicts between people and wildlife in India inevitable?
   a Much of the wildlife in India lives in protected national parks.
   b Conservation workers and local communities disagree about preserving wildlife.
   c People and wildlife must share limited space along park borders and edges.
   d Wildlife conservation efforts are directed mostly toward tigers and elephants.

3 According to paragraph 3, approximately how many of the households surveyed by Krithi Karanth were affected by conflicts with wild animals?
   a about 80%   **c** 2,000
   b all of them   **d** 15%

4 How does the Wild Seve project help villagers affected by conflicts with wild animals?
   a They leave a voice message with details about the incident.
   b They teach local people to use cellphones to report conflicts with wildlife.
   c They compensate Indian citizens for losses caused by protected wildlife.
   d They help the Indian government track animals.

5 Why is it helpful to be flexible in order to work as a wildlife conservation scientist?
   a Wildlife conservation scientists aren't very well-paid.
   b Wildlife conservation scientists must sleep outside.
   c A wildlife conservation scientist must learn to use sophisticated technology.
   d A wildlife conservation scientist must be happy to work both in an office and outdoors.

3 Read the statements. Are the sentences true (T), false (F), or is the information not given (NG)?

1 Krithi Karanth spotted her first leopard when she was only a year old. _____
2 People and wildlife are in conflict in India because space for both is shrinking. _____
3 Roughly 65% of households surveyed by Krithi Karanth lost valuable animals as a result of conflicts with wildlife. _____
4 The Indian government is looking for ways to move elephants that are involved in conflicts with villagers. _____
5 Elephants in India do more damage than feral pigs. _____
6 A wildlife biologist must know how to use technology and how to survive in the field. _____

4 Choose the correct options to complete the sentences.

1 Krithi Karanth first _____ a leopard in the wild at the age of two.
   a held   **c** observed
   b rescued   **d** photographed

2 Krithi and other researchers are _____ for ways to help humans and animals avoid conflict.
   a listening   **c** looking
   b noticing   **d** recognizing

3 Researchers _____ to identify households that had suffered losses as a result of conflicts with wildlife.
   a were allowed   **c** were able
   b didn't need   **d** don't have

4 The Wild Seve project teaches people _____ situations in which villagers and wildlife come into conflict.
   a to compensate   **c** to encourage
   b to report   **d** to call

5 Krithi's daughter _____ her first leopard in the wild at the age of four.
   a spotted   **c** caught
   b described   **d** helped

A Wild Job

1 🎧 **51** Her father, one of India's most well-known conservationists and tiger experts, started taking her into the jungle with him when she was just a year old. She spotted her first leopard in the wild at the age of two. By the time she was eight, she was going along on expeditions to track tigers. Today, conservation scientist Krithi Karanth works to help some of the world's most familiar species, including tigers and Asian elephants, to coexist* with the approximately one billion people who live on the Indian subcontinent.

2 Much of India's wildlife lives in protected national parks. Because humans and wildlife must share space along park edges and borders, conflicts are inevitable*. As Krithi says, "Spaces for wildlife are shrinking, and therefore you are putting people in closer contact with wildlife." Krithi, a National Geographic Explorer, is looking for ways to address conflicts between wildlife conservation efforts and local communities that are affected by wild animals, particularly tigers and elephants.

3 As part of that effort, Krithi and other researchers initially surveyed nearly 2,000 households within 10 kilometers (about 6.2 miles) of a nature reserve. They found that roughly 65% of those households had suffered crop losses due to feral* pigs and elephants, while another 15% lost livestock* to tigers, leopards, foxes, and wild dogs. Krithi also found cases of human injury or death caused by the animals the reserves are meant to protect.

4 While the Indian government compensates* Indian citizens for losses caused by protected wildlife, the process can be complicated for farmers and compensation is sometimes not enough. As a result, according to one of Krithi's colleagues: "the level of distrust between conservation officers and local villagers is extremely high." Wild Seve, an action-based research project that Krithi helped create, is hoping to help. The Wild Seve project teaches farmers and local people to use cellphone technology to report and hopefully resolve conflicts with wildlife. After a wildlife encounter, villagers are encouraged to call a toll-free phone number and are prompted to leave a voice message with details about the incident. Field staff from Wild Seve then visit the site, view and document the damage, file a claim on behalf of the farmer, and track the claim until the farmer is compensated.

5 A wildlife conservation scientist must be flexible enough to work long hours both in the field and in a lab or office. He or she must be comfortable with sophisticated technology and with sleeping in a tent or on the ground. It's not an extremely well-paid job and it's very demanding, but it can be a deeply satisfying career for someone who loves wildlife and the outdoors. Krithi is passing her passion for wildlife on to her own child, who glimpsed* her first leopard at the age of four. "We were with my parents, and all three generations of us sat in absolute silence, taking in the moment, watching this amazing leopard. There are not enough words to describe that memory."

coexist *to live together*
inevitable *sure to happen*
feral *describing a farm animal or pet that has become wild*

livestock *farm animals such as cows and pigs*
compensate *to give money in return for something*
glimpse *to see something for a very short time*

5C Advice

GRAMMAR Present and past modals

1 Listen and complete the sentences. 🎧 52

1 My parents are working, so I _____ dinner for my little brother.

2 They _____ their friends while they're having breakfast.

3 Our team really _____ this game.

4 They _____ three more points to win.

5 We _____ Julia to come to the concert with us.

6 I _____ the dog for a walk before I go out.

7 You _____ her some flowers when you visit.

2 Complete the chart with these sentences.

Do you think she'll be able to help with the project?

I think you should ask him for help with your resume.

Ron couldn't take a day off because he didn't have enough vacation time.

I could pay for lunch if you like.

She isn't allowed to use the phone at work.

Should I ask her for an interview?

You shouldn't eat lunch at your desk.

Can you send an application after the closing date?

You should come to the office party.

Ability or possibility	Advice	Prohibition

3 Do these sentences refer to permission (P), no ability/possibility (NA/P), or deduction/speculation (D/S)?

1 Are you allowed to drive your parents' car? _____

2 I couldn't send the email before I left—there wasn't enough time. _____

3 She really likes science. She may decide to study biology in college. _____

4 Sorry, but I wasn't able to talk to José because he was in a meeting. _____

5 The train leaves at six o'clock. We might want to eat dinner at five thirty. _____

6 They aren't able to deal with this today. It'll have to wait until tomorrow. _____

7 They must have won the contract—they look so happy! _____

8 You can come with us if you drive. _____

4 Put the words in the correct order to make pieces of advice.

1 read / should / before / the / you / chapter / class / .

_____

2 aren't / you / eat / in / allowed / to / class / .

_____

3 the teacher / you / class / listen / in / talks / when / should / .

_____

4 understand / ask / you / need to / don't / the teacher / for / help / if / you / something / .

_____

5 may / classmates / to / you / with / your / study / want / .

_____

6 in / miss / semester / you / can't / classes / more / than / three / a / .

_____

7 you / in / chat / with / friends / shouldn't / class / your / .

_____

8 three / books / you / can / check out / each / from / the / library / week / .

_____

5 Rewrite the sentences in the present tense.

1 We weren't allowed to talk in class unless the teacher asked us to.

We aren't allowed to talk in class unless the teacher asks us to.

2 We couldn't miss more than three classes during the semester.

_____

_____

3 He didn't have to tell his teacher if he wasn't going to be in class.

_____

_____

4 They could talk to their friends after class.

_____

_____

5 I needed to borrow the car to drive to work.

_____

_____

6 Tomas had to finish the report before 5 pm.

_____

_____

7 I couldn't go to Bangkok with Mikasa.

_____

_____

8 She had to work, so she couldn't to go to the museum with us.

_____

_____

6 Complete the sentences with these modals. Read the hints in parentheses.

can	can't	isn't allowed to	might
need to	should	shouldn't	

1 We _____ clean our apartment before the party. (obligation)

2 You _____ bother watching that show—it was really boring. (advice)

3 She completed the training, so now she _____ use the new equipment. (permission)

4 If Raul has enough vacation time, he _____ be able to travel to Sri Lanka next year. (speculation)

5 He hasn't passed his driving test, so he _____ drive on the highway. (prohibition)

6 You _____ hear Sam play the drums—he's really good! (advice)

7 We _____ forget our tickets when we leave for the airport. (prohibition)

7 Choose the correct options to complete the sentences.

1 Do you think I ought *to catch* / *catch* an earlier train?

2 Can we *to take* / *take* the test on Monday?

3 Are advanced students allowed *to skip* / *skip* a class?

4 You must *to hand in* / *hand in* your projects by Tuesday.

5 Our team might *to win* / *win* the championship.

6 You should *to study* / *study* at a school in Mexico and learn Spanish.

7 Those flowers don't look good. Do you think we should *to throw* / *throw* them out?

8 I asked Kari, but she wasn't able *to help* / *help*.

8 Match the two parts of the conversations.

1 I'm hungry. _____

2 Can you come with us to the festival tomorrow? _____

3 Does Manuel know about the party? _____

4 Is Yen doing well at school? _____

5 I need to lose a little weight. _____

6 Do you think I should apologize to my sister? _____

7 What are you doing tomorrow? _____

8 Ooh, that salad looks delicious! _____

a I'm not sure. We may go to the festival at the park.

b No, and you can't tell him—it's a surprise!

c No, I can't. I have to work.

d Yes, really well—she must be studying a lot.

e Yes. You should call her right away.

f You can't eat it now—it's for the party.

g You should join a gym.

h You should try this melon—it's really fresh!

5D Why the Best Hire Might Not Have the Perfect Resume

TEDTALKS

AUTHENTIC LISTENING SKILLS

1 Listen to the TED Talk excerpts. Choose the type of contrast the speaker uses in each one. 🎧 53

1 We call A "the Silver Spoon," the one who clearly had advantages and was destined for success. And we call B "the Scrapper," the one who had to fight against tremendous odds to get to the same point.
contrasting words / repeating structures

2 A series of odd jobs may indicate inconsistency, lack of focus, unpredictability. Or, it may signal a committed struggle against obstacles.
repeating structures / replacing with opposites

3 Getting into and graduating from an elite university take a lot of hard work and sacrifice. But if your whole life has been engineered toward success, how will you handle the tough times?
contrasting words / replacing with opposites

4 One person I hired felt that because he attended an elite university, there were certain assignments that were beneath him, like temporarily doing manual labor to better understand an operation. Eventually, he quit. But, on the flip side, what happens when your whole life is destined for failure and you actually succeed? *contrasting words / repeating structures*

5 They don't think they are who they are in spite of adversity, they know they are who they are because of adversity. *contrasting words / repeating structures*

WATCH ▶

2 Watch Part 2 of the TED Talk and choose the correct answers to the questions.

1 What does Regina Hartley do when a resume reads "like a patchwork quilt"?
  a She stops and considers the person.
  b She throws it away.
  c She thinks about her own life story.

2 Hartley feels that a Scrapper deserves an interview because
  a he/she may be unpredictable.
  b he/she may have struggled against obstacles.
  c he/she may have a lack of focus.

3 Hartley believes that graduating from an elite university
  a does not guarantee you can handle tough times.
  b means that your life is engineered towards success.
  c means that you are destined for failure.

4 How did the person she hired, who'd attended an elite university, feel when he was asked to do manual labor?
  a He thought it was a good learning opportunity.
  b He wanted to learn more about the operation.
  c He felt he was too intelligent for it.

5 Why does she urge the audience to interview the Scrapper?
  a She was one herself and overcame obstacles.
  b She finds their stories interesting.
  c She wants to give them a chance in life.

6 What did Hartley say that successful business people had in common?
  a Many of them went to elite business schools.
  b Many of them had early hardships in life.
  c Some of them were adopted.

7 According to Hartley, what type of resume did Steve Jobs have?
  a a resume that most people wish they had
  b the resume of the Silver Spoon
  c the patchwork quilt resume of a Scrapper

3 Watch Part 3 of the TED Talk. Match the entrepreneurial traits with the consequences.

1 dyslexia _____
2 believing that you have control over yourself _____
3 a sense of humor _____
4 good relationships _____
a becoming a better listener and learning to pay greater attention to detail
b getting you through tough times and changing your perspective
c having people mentor and encourage you helps you overcome adversity
d never giving up because challenges give you a sense of purpose

VOCABULARY IN CONTEXT

4 Complete the sentences with these words and phrases.

a piece of cake	assignment	count on
term	tough	turn out

1 Job interviews are _____ for me. I never know what to say.
2 Her first _____ was to write a report.
3 Did your presentation _____ well?
4 If you need help with that project, you can _____ me. I'm here for you.
5 The staff invented the _____, "bulldog," for their boss. He wasn't a nice person.
6 For some people, getting a job is _____. They just have good interview skills.

5E Going for the Job

SPEAKING

1 Put the words in the correct order to make sentences and questions. Then listen and check your answers. 🎧 54

1 was / I'd / creative person / I / a / say / pretty / .

_____

2 work / I'm / to / long / willing / hours / .

_____

3 people / to / at / pretty / talking / good / I'm / .

_____

4 restaurant / I've / of / experience / a lot / had / .

_____

5 English / working / I'm / my / on / .

_____

6 wanted / always / work / outdoors / to / I've / .

_____

7 think / job / me / I / this / new / would / skills / give / .

_____

8 what / job / the / involve / does / ?

_____

9 would / just / have to / I / was / if / wear / wondering / I / a uniform / .

_____

10 to / we / wear / allowed / jewelry / are / ?

_____

2 Complete the interview with phrases and questions from Activity 1. Then listen and check your answers. 🎧 55

Interviewer Hi, Tomas. Thank you very much for coming in.

Tomas It's good to meet you.

I What attracted you to work for Market Finance?

T Well, **(1)** _____ work at a financial company and I've been very interested in the company for a long time—it has an excellent reputation.

I Great. And why do you think you're right for this job?

T Well, I like to think I'm not afraid to work hard, and this is an entry-level position, so **(2)** _____ the opportunity to understand a lot of new things, and **(3)** _____ learning new skills.

I Now, as I'm sure you're aware, the job is very demanding.

T Yes, **(4)** _____ enthusiastic person and able to deal with difficult situations and new challenges.

I I see.

T And **(5)** _____ work long hours when necessary to get the work done.

I OK, so, that all sounds very good. And what are your main strengths?

T Well, **(6)** _____ with people; I used to be a waiter working at a busy restaurant in the tourist part of town. And my English is pretty good.

I Yes, your English is very good!

T And, as I mentioned, I learn new things quickly and I'm well organized.

I And what about negatives? What do you need to improve?

T Well, I know I can sometimes be a perfectionist, like when I was designing the school magazine, I spent too long on the design work, so **(7)** _____ my time management skills.

I So, do you have any questions you'd like to ask?

T Err, I do have a couple. **(8)** _____ wear a suit to the office every day?

I Generally, yes, we expect everyone to wear business attire.

T Right. And just one other thing, **(9)** _____ take work home if we want to get ahead with something?

I No, that's against company policy. Company information needs to stay in the office and all your work should be completed within working hours.

3 Prepare your own interview questions and answers for a job that you would like to get. Then compare your ideas with the sample interview above.

4 Make notes on your answers to the questions below. Remember to use the useful language. Then listen to the sample answer and compare your ideas. 🎧 56

- *Why are you learning English?*
- *Do you think it will be useful for your future career?*

PRONUNCIATION Showing confidence

Remember to speak slowly and use an even tone to sound confident in conversations.

5 Listen to the sentences and decide whether the speakers are confident (C) or not confident (NC). 🎧 57

1 _____ 3 _____ 5 _____ 7 _____
2 _____ 4 _____ 6 _____ 8 _____

WRITING A cover letter

6 Read the sentences from a cover letter and choose the correct functions.

1 I am writing to apply for the job of part-time assistant at the veterinary clinic.
  a giving the reason for wanting the job
  b clearly stating the reason for writing
  c giving details of relevant experience

2 Last summer, I volunteered at the local animal shelter.
  a giving details of relevant experience
  b providing school qualifications
  c providing information on availability

3 I am a responsible person and absolutely dedicated to the care of animals.
  a asking for information about the job
  b giving information on education
  c describing relevant personal qualities

4 I would value this experience as I plan to study Veterinary Medicine in college.
  a giving information about availability
  b describing formal qualifications
  c giving the reason for wanting the job

5 I look forward to hearing from you soon.
  a describing past experience
  b asking politely for a reply
  c giving the reason for writing

7 Label the parts of the cover letter.

asking about the job	formal greeting
full mailing address	information about availability
personal qualities	polite ending
reason for writing	relevant experience
requesting a reply	today's date

(1) _____ 818 Doris Avenue
2059 North Sydney

(2) _____ June 4, 2018

(3) _____ To Whom It May Concern:

(4) _____ I am writing to apply for the role of waiter at Squash Juice Bar, which I saw advertised on your website. I feel I would be a very good candidate for this job.

(5) _____ While I do not have the direct experience of working at a juice bar, I was a waiter for two months last summer at The Bay Leaf in town.

(6) _____ I would say I was a fast learner who enjoys working in a team. In addition, I have received very positive feedback from my former manager and customers at The Bay Leaf.

(7) _____ I was just wondering if I would have to work every weekend or just some weekends?

(8) _____ I would be free to begin after June 25th and am available until mid-September. I hope that you will consider me for the job.

(9) _____ I look forward to hearing from you soon.

(10) _____ Sincerely,
Luis Campo

8 Read the letter again. Are the statements true (T) or false (F)?

1 Luis knows the person he is writing to. _____
2 He saw the job on the Squash Juice Bar website. _____
3 Luis doesn't have any experience as a waiter. _____
4 He mentions relevant points about his personality. _____
5 One of his qualities is teamwork. _____
6 He includes a question about the salary. _____
7 He is not available to begin work until mid-May. _____
8 He ends the letter appropriately. _____

9 Underline six mistakes in this cover letter. How would you correct them?

11 Lindsay Street
Edinburgh
EH23 6BD
June 2018

Hi Mr. Yoon,

I'm writing to apply for the job of part-time assistant at the veterinary clinic, which I saw advertised online.

I have some relevant experience. Last summer, I volunteered at the local animal shelter where I learned a lot about managing animals.

It's obvious that I am the perfect candidate for this job. Also, I would say that I was a very responsible person, dedicated to the care of animals.

I finish school in June and will be free until September. Drop me a line with some more details about the job.

Thanks,

Agustina Garcia

10 Follow the instructions.

• This is part of a letter you received from a Polish friend:

> I just spotted a cool summer job. It's in Chicago, based at O'Hare Airport. I'm excited because I really want to work in the tourism industry! The job involves meeting and greeting passengers, checking their documents, that kind of thing. Do you think I should apply?

• Write a letter (about 100 words) giving your friend advice about what to include in their cover letter.

Review

1 Match the opposites.

1 temporary   **a** relaxing
2 part-time   **b** employed
3 out of work   **c** low-paid
4 demanding   **d** permanent
5 well-paid   **e** easy
6 challenging   **f** full-time

2 Listen to the sentences and choose the most appropriate adjective. 🎧 **58**

1 *demanding / competitive / flexible*
2 *creative / competitive / well-paid*
3 *creative / flexible / stressful*
4 *creative / stressful / competitive*
5 *well-paid / permanent / creative*
6 *flexible / stressful / well-paid*

3 Complete the sentences with the correct forms of these verbs.

count	give	help	lock	quit	take	work

1 My cousin doesn't regret _____ her job at the newspaper. It was very stressful.
2 I told them that I'd miss _____ with such great people.
3 If you forget _____ your time sheet to payroll, then you won't get paid.
4 Do you remember _____ the front door when you left last night?
5 My boss asked someone else _____ that difficult customer.
6 Did Juan decide _____ the job at the café or is he working somewhere else?
7 We didn't finish _____ all the stock last night, so we'll have to do it tonight.

4 Find and correct the mistakes in the words in bold. Two sentences are correct.

1 You **can't to forget taking** your medicine before you go to bed.
2 She **should try studying** with friends.
3 He **might to remember calling** Tom if he writes himself a note.
4 They **shouldn't continuing taking** pictures once the play starts.
5 When I was younger, I **wasn't allowed stop to have** piano lessons.
6 She **might regret skipping** breakfast.

5 Choose the correct options to complete the sentences.

1 You can _____ me anything. I won't be angry.
  a ask
  b to ask
  c asking
  d had asked

2 Scientists _____ tell us a lot about climate change.
  a should
  b isn't able to
  c can
  d should to

3 You might _____ that new exhibition at the art gallery.
  a like
  b to like
  c liking
  d had liked

4 Natalie _____ come on vacation with us last year.
  a may
  b couldn't
  c wasn't able
  d didn't need

5 You _____ study in India. It would be such an interesting experience.
  a are able
  b might to
  c ought
  d should

6 You should _____ at least two new languages.
  a learn
  b to learn
  c learning
  d have learned

7 _____ I ask you about your job?
  a Should to
  b Be able to
  c Ought
  d Can

8 I couldn't _____ for the job.
  a apply
  b to apply
  c applying
  d applied

UNIT 1

Review

afraid (adj)	/əˈfreɪd/
angry (adj)	/ˈæŋgri/
bored (adj)	/bɔrd/
excited (adj)	/ɪkˈsaɪtɪd/
pleased (adj)	/plizd/
unhappy (adj)	/ʌnˈhæpi/
upset (adj)	/ʌpˈsɛt/
worried (adj)	/ˈwɜrid/

Unit Vocabulary

annoyed (adj)	/əˈnɔɪd/
anxious (adj)	/ˈæŋkʃəs/
ashamed (adj)	/əˈʃeɪmd/
confused (adj)	/kənˈfjuzd/
delighted (adj)	/dɪˈlaɪtɪd/
embarrassed (adj)	/ɪmˈbærəst/
lonely (adj)	/ˈloʊnli/
nervous (adj)	/ˈnɜrvəs/
relaxed (adj)	/rɪˈlækst/
scared (adj)	/skeərd/
stressed (adj)	/strɛst/

Extension

cheerful (adj)	/ˈtʃɪrfəl/
disappointed (adj)	/ˌdɪsəˈpɔɪntɪd/
grateful (adj)	/ˈgreɪtfəl/
impatient (adj)	/ɪmˈpeɪʃənt/
jealous (adj)	/ˈdʒɛləs/
proud (adj)	/praʊd/
selfish (adj)	/ˈsɛlfɪʃ/

Vocabulary Building

confused (adj)	/kənˈfjuzd/
confusion (n)	/kənˈfjuʒən/
depressed (adj)	/dɪˈprɛst/
depression (n)	/dɪˈprɛʃən/
disappointed (adj)	/ˌdɪsəˈpɔɪntɪd/
disappointment (n)	/ˌdɪsəˈpɔɪntmənt/
embarrassed (adj)	/ɪmˈbɛrəst/
embarrassment (n)	/ɪmˈbærəsmənt/
excited (adj)	/ɪkˈsaɪtɪd/
excitement (n)	/ɪkˈsaɪtmənt/
exhausted (adj)	/ɪgˈzɔstɪd/
exhaustion (n)	/ɪgˈzɔstʃən/
friendliness (n)	/ˈfrɛndlinɪs/
friendly (adj)	/ˈfrɛndli/
happiness (n)	/ˈhæpinɪs/
happy (adj)	/ˈhæpi/
loneliness (n)	/ˈloʊnlinɪs/
lonely (adj)	/ˈloʊnli/
nervous (adj)	/ˈnɜrvəs/
nervousness (n)	/ˈnɜrvəsnɪs/
sad (adj)	/sæd/
sadness (n)	/ˈsædnɪs/
selfish (adj)	/ˈsɛlfɪʃ/
selfishness (n)	/ˈsɛlfɪʃnɪs/

Vocabulary in Context

characteristic (n)	/ˌkærɪktəˈrɪstɪk/
curiosity (n)	/ˌkjʊəriˈɒsɪti/
gender (n)	/ˈdʒɛndər/
homesick (adj)	/ˈhoʊmˌsɪk/
joy (n)	/dʒɔɪ/
wrinkle (n)	/ˈrɪŋkəl/

UNIT 2

Review

airport (n)	/ˈɛərˌpɔrt/
bus (n)	/bʌs/
drive (v)	/draɪv/
fly (v)	/flaɪ/
holiday (n)	/ˈhɒlɪˌdeɪ/
hotel (n)	/hoʊˈtɛl/
plane (n)	/pleɪn/
station (n)	/ˈsteɪʃən/
tourist (n)	/ˈtʊərɪst/
train (n)	/treɪn/
travel (v)	/ˈtrævəl/
traveler (n)	/ˈtrævələr/
visit (v)	/ˈvɪzɪt/
visitor (n)	/ˈvɪzɪtər/

Unit Vocabulary

car (n)	/kɑr/
catch (v)	/kætʃ/
commute (v)	/kəˈmjut/
cruise (n)	/kruz/
destination (n)	/ˌdɛstɪˈneɪʃən/
excursion (n)	/ɪkˈskɜrʒən/
expedition (n)	/ˌɛkspəˈdɪʃən/
flight (n)	/flaɪt/
get (v)	/gɛt/
get off (phr v)	/ˌgɛt ˈɔf/
get on (phr v)	/ˌgɛt ˈɒn/
get to (phr v)	/ˈgɛt ˌtu/
get to know (phr)	/ˈgɛt tə ˈnoʊ/
go for (a bike ride) (phr)	/ˈgoʊ fər (ə ˈbaɪk ˌraɪd)/
go on (a flight) (phr)	/ˈgoʊ ɒn (ə ˈflaɪt)/
lift (n)	/lɪft/
ride (n)	/raɪd/
route (n)	/rut/
ship (n)	/ʃɪp/
take (v)	/teɪk/
voyage (n)	/ˈvɔɪɪdʒ/

Extension

board (v)	/bɔrd/
depart (v)	/dɪˈpɑrt/
journey (n)	/ˈdʒɜrni/
know (v)	/noʊ/
land (v)	/lænd/
leave (v)	/liv/

Vocabulary Building

backpacking (n)	/ˈbækˌpækɪŋ/
horseback riding (n)	/ˈhɔrsˌbæk ˈraɪdɪŋ/
public transportation (n)	/ˈpʌblɪk ˌtrænspɔrˈteɪʃən/
sightseeing (n)	/ˈsaɪtˌsiɪŋ/
skyscraper (n)	/ˈskaɪˌskreɪpər/
viewpoint (n)	/ˈvjuˌpɔɪnt/
walking tour (n)	/ˈwɔkɪŋ ˌtʊər/
zip-line (n)	/ˈzɪp ˌlaɪn/

Vocabulary in Context

a handful of (phr)	/ə ˈhændfʊl əv/
don't get me wrong (phr)	/ˈdoʊnt ˌgɛt mi ˈrɒŋ/
shame (n)	/ʃeɪm/
shy (adj)	/ʃaɪ/
surrounded by (trees) (phr)	/səˈraʊndɪd baɪ (ˈtriz)/
team up with (phr v)	/ˈtim ˈʌp ˌwɪθ/

UNIT 3

Review

baseball (n)	/ˈbeɪsˌbɔl/
basketball (n)	/ˈbæskɪtˌbɔl/
boxing (n)	/ˈbɒksɪŋ/
football (n)	/ˈfʊtˌbɔl/
ice hockey (n)	/ˈaɪs ˌhɒki/
ice skating (n)	/ˈaɪs ˌskeɪtɪŋ/
rugby (n)	/ˈrʌgbi/
running (n)	/ˈrʌnɪŋ/
skiing (n)	/ˈskiɪŋ/
surfing (n)	/ˈsɜrfɪŋ/
swimming (n)	/ˈswɪmɪŋ/
tennis (n)	/ˈtɛnɪs/
volleyball (n)	/ˈvɒliˌbɔl/
yoga (n)	/ˈjoʊgə/

Unit Vocabulary

achieve (v)	/əˈtʃiv/
beat (v)	/bit/
board (n)	/bɔrd/
boat (n)	/boʊt/
climbing (n)	/ˈklaɪmɪŋ/
club (n)	/klʌb/
coach (n)	/koʊtʃ/
court (n)	/kɔrt/
diving (n)	/ˈdaɪvɪŋ/
encourage (v)	/ɛnˈkɜrɪdʒ/
equipment (n)	/ɪˈkwɪpmənt/

Vocabulary in Context (UNIT 1, right column top)

outing (n)	/ˈaʊtɪŋ/
sight (n)	/saɪt/
sightseeing (n)	/ˈsaɪtˌsiɪŋ/
stay (v)	/steɪ/
way (n)	/weɪ/

field (n)	/fild/
gymnastics (n)	/dʒɪmˈnæstɪks/
helmet (n)	/ˈhɛlmɪt/
karate (n)	/kəˈrɑti/
mountain (n)	/ˈmaʊntən/
net (n)	/nɛt/
opponent (n)	/əˈpoʊnənt/
player (n)	/ˈpleɪər/
pool (n)	/pul/
racket (n)	/ˈrækɪt/
referee (n)	/ˌrɛfəˈri/
represent (v)	/ˌrɛprɪˈzɛnt/
rink (n)	/rɪŋk/
score (n)	/skɔr/
spectator (n)	/ˈspɛkteɪtər/
surfing (n)	/ˈsɜrfɪŋ/
track (n)	/træk/
train (v)	/treɪn/
win (v)	/wɪn/

Extension

do (v)	/du/
go (v)	/goʊ/
go ice skating (phr)	/ˌgoʊ ˈaɪs ˌskeɪtɪŋ/
go horseback riding (phr)	/ˌgoʊ ˈhɔrs‚bæk ˈraɪdɪŋ/
play (v)	/pleɪ/
play polo (phr)	/ˈpleɪ ˈpoʊloʊ/
snowboarding (n)	/ˈsnoʊ‚bɔrdɪŋ/
table-tennis (n)	/ˈteɪbəl ‚tɛnɪs/
windsurfing (n)	/ˈwɪnd‚sɜrfɪŋ/

Vocabulary Building

give up (phr v)	/ˈgɪv ˈʌp/
join in (phr v)	/ˈdʒɔɪn ˈɪn/
keep up (phr v)	/ˈkip ˈʌp/
knock out (phr v)	/ˈnɒk ˈaʊt/
take on (phr v)	/ˈteɪk ˈɒn/
take up (phr v)	/ˈteɪk ˈʌp/
warm up (phr v)	/ˈwɔrm ˈʌp/
work out (phr v)	/ˈwɜrk ˈaʊt/

Vocabulary in Context

barely (adv)	/ˈbɛərli/
costume (n)	/ˈkɒstum/
ensure (v)	/ɛnˈʃʊər/
fresh water (n)	/ˈfrɛʃ ˈwɔtər/
I believe in you (phr)	/ˈaɪ bɪˈliv ɪn ˈju/
swollen (adj)	/ˈswoʊlən/

UNIT 4

Review

apple (n)	/ˈæpəl/
cake (n)	/keɪk/
chicken (n)	/ˈtʃɪkɪn/
chili powder (n)	/ˈtʃɪli ‚paʊdər/
chocolate (n)	/ˈtʃɒkəlɪt/
coffee (n)	/ˈkɔfi/
curry (n)	/ˈkɜri/
French fries (n)	/ˈfrɛntʃ ˈfraɪz/
ice cream (n)	/ˈaɪs ‚krim/

lemon (n)	/ˈlɛmən/
pasta (n)	/ˈpɑstə/
potato chips (n)	/pəˈteɪtoʊ ‚tʃɪps/
prawn (n)	/prɔn/
strawberry (n)	/ˈstrɔ‚bɛri/
tomato (n)	/təˈmeɪtoʊ/

Unit Vocabulary

boiled (adj)	/bɔɪld/
cooked (adj)	/kʊkt/
delicious (adj)	/dɪˈlɪʃəs/
disgusting (adj)	/dɪsˈgʌstɪŋ/
fresh (adj)	/frɛʃ/
fried (adj)	/fraɪd/
healthy (adj)	/ˈhɛlθi/
junk food (n)	/ˈdʒʌŋk ‚fud/
meat-eater (n)	/ˈmit ‚itər/
mild (adj)	/maɪld/
natural (adj)	/ˈnætʃərəl/
processed food (n)	/ˈprɒsɛst ˈfud/
raw (adj)	/rɔ/
steamed (adj)	/stimd/
strong (adj)	/strɒŋ/
suitable for (phr)	/ˈsutəbəl fɔr/
sweet (adj)	/swit/
tasty (adj)	/ˈteɪsti/
vegetarian (n)	/ˌvɛdʒəˈteəriən/
well-balanced (adj)	/ˈwɛl ˈbælənst/

Extension

appetite (n)	/ˈæpə‚taɪt/
apple pie (n)	/ˈæpəl ˈpaɪ/
bread and butter (n)	/ˈbrɛd ən ˈbʌtər/
cake (n)	/keɪk/
chocolate cake (n)	/ˈtʃɒkəlɪt ˈkeɪk/
diet (n)	/ˈdaɪɪt/
grill (n)	/grɪl/
main course (n)	/ˈmeɪn ˈkɔrs/
mashed potato (n)	/ˈmæʃt pəˈteɪtoʊ/
roast chicken (n)	/ˈroʊst ˈtʃɪkən/
salad (n)	/ˈsæləd/
soup (n)	/sup/
starter (n)	/ˈstɑrtər/
steak (n)	/steɪk/
stir-fry (n)	/ˈstɜr ‚fraɪ/
tasteless (adj)	/ˈteɪstlɪs/

Vocabulary Building

deep-fried (adj)	/ˈdip ˈfraɪd/
good-looking (adj)	/ˈgʊd ˈlʊkɪŋ/
half-finished (adj)	/ˈhæf ˈfɪnɪʃt/
home-made (adj)	/ˈhoʊm ˈmeɪd/
old-fashioned (adj)	/ˈoʊld ˈfæʃənd/
oven-baked (adj)	/ˈʌvən ‚beɪkt/
over-cooked (adj)	/ˈʌvən ‚kʊkt/
sun-dried (adj)	/ˈsʌn ‚draɪd/
sweet-tasting (adj)	/ˈswit ‚teɪstɪŋ/
well-known (adj)	/ˈwɛl ˈnoʊn/

Vocabulary in Context

combined (adj)	/kəmˈbaɪnd/
come up with (phr v)	/ˈkʌm ˈʌp ‚wɪθ/
damage (n)	/ˈdæmɪdʒ/

in conflict with (phr)	/ˌɪn ˈkɒnflɪkt ‚wɪθ/
raise (v)	/reɪz/
risk (n)	/rɪsk/

UNIT 5

Review

accountant (n)	/əˈkaʊntənt/
architect (n)	/ˈɑrkɪ‚tɛkt/
chef (n)	/ʃɛf/
chief executive (n)	/ˈtʃif ɪgˈzɛkjətɪv/
doctor (n)	/ˈdɒktər/
firefighter (n)	/ˈfaɪər‚faɪtər/
lawyer (n)	/ˈlɔjər/
nurse (n)	/nɜrs/
office worker (n)	/ˈɔfɪs ‚wɜrkər/
paramedic (n)	/ˌpærəˈmɛdɪk/
police officer (n)	/pəˈlis ‚ɔfɪsər/
salesperson (n)	/ˈseɪlz‚pɜrsən/
store manager (n)	/ˈstɔr ‚mænɪdʒər/
teacher (n)	/ˈtitʃər/
waiter (n)	/ˈweɪtər/
waitress (n)	/ˈweɪtrɪs/

Unit Vocabulary

business (n)	/ˈbɪznɪs/
career prospects (phr)	/kəˈrɪər ‚prɒspɛkts/
competitive (adj)	/kəmˈpɛtɪtɪv/
creative (adj)	/kriˈeɪtɪv/
demanding (adj)	/dɪˈmændɪŋ/
flexible (adj)	/ˈflɛksəbəl/
in charge of (phr)	/ˌɪn ˈtʃɑrdʒ əv/
industry (n)	/ˈɪndəstri/
job (n)	/dʒɒb/
out of work (phr)	/ˈaʊt əv ˈwɜrk/
responsible for (phr)	/rɪˈspɒnsəbəl fɔr/
stressful (adj)	/ˈstrɛsfəl/
unemployed (adj)	/ˌʌnɪmˈplɔɪd/
well-paid (adj)	/ˈwɛl ˈpeɪd/
work (n)	/wɜrk/
work for (phr v)	/ˈwɜrk ‚fɔr/
work in (phr v)	/ˈwɜrk ‚ɪn/
work on (phr v)	/ˈwɜrk ‚ɒn/

Extension

challenging (adj)	/ˈtʃælɪndʒɪŋ/
find (v)	/faɪnd/
need (v)	/nid/
quit (v)	/kwɪt/
resign (v)	/rɪˈzaɪn/
retired (adj)	/rɪˈtaɪərd/
rewarding (adj)	/rɪˈwɔrdɪŋ/
supervisor (n)	/ˈsupər‚vaɪzər/
trainee (n)	/ˌtreɪˈni/
vacancy (n)	/ˈveɪkənsi/

Vocabulary Building

glance (v)	/glæns/
identify (v)	/aɪˈdɛntə‚faɪ/
notice (v)	/ˈnoʊtɪs/
observe (v)	/əbˈzɜrv/

recognize (v)   /'rɛkəg,naɪz/
spot (v)   /spɒt/

Vocabulary in Context

a piece of cake (phr) /ə 'pis əv 'keɪk/
assignment (n)   /ə'saɪnmənt/
count on (phr v)   /'kaʊnt ,ɒn/
term (n)   /tɜrm/
tough (adj)   /tʌf/
turn out (phr v)   /'tɜrn 'aʊt/

Photo Credits:

5 (cl) Berna Namoglu/Shutterstock.com, **7** (tl) Spotmatik Ltd/Shutterstock.com, **7** (tc) Monkey Business Images/Shutterstock.com, **7** (tc) wong yu liang/Shutterstock.com, **7** (tr) Ollyy/Shutterstock.com, **9** (t) Goran Bogicevic/Shutterstock.com, **15** (br) Chad McDermott/Shutterstock.com, **17** (cr) Krishna.Wu/Shutterstock.com, **19** (br) Ella Sarkisyan/Shutterstock.com, **20** (bl) Mihai Simonia/Shutterstock.com, **23** (bc) Emir Simsek/Shutterstock.com, **28** (tl) Blackregis/Shutterstock.com, **29** (br) KYTan/Shutterstock.com, **31** (t) Pavel Burchenko/Shutterstock.com, **27** (tr) Photodisc/Getty Images/Houghton Mifflin Harcourt, **39** (tr) Ruth Black/Shutterstock.com, **43** (t) Elena Schweitzer/Shutterstock.com, **44** (tl) racorn/Shutterstock.com, **47** (tl) Syda Productions/Shutterstock.com, **47** (cl) Elena Dijour/Shutterstock.com, **47** (bl) Syda Productions/Shutterstock.com, **42** (bl) © Valentyn Volkov/Shutterstock.com, **52** (tl) s_bukley/Shutterstock.com, **55** (br) Kadur, Sandesh Vishwanath/National Geographic Creative, **50** (bl) Golden Pixels LLC/Shutterstock.com, **67** (t) Pool/Getty Images, **71** (tl) Blend Images - KidStock/Getty Images, **71** (tr) ©Joey Schusler, **71** (cr) Bloomberg/Getty Images, **64** (tl) Impact Photography/Shutterstock.com, **74** (bl) leungchopan/Shutterstock.com, **76** (tl) v.schlichting/Shutterstock.com, **76** (tl) RTimages/Shutterstock.com, **76** (tr) Robynrg/Shutterstock.com, **76** (cl) sumire8/Shutterstock.com, **76** (cl) Sergiy Kuzmin/Shutterstock.com, **76** (cr) Mariyana M/Shutterstock.com, **76** (bl) nld/Shutterstock.com, **76** (bl) Early Spring/Shutterstock.com, **76** (br) elenovsky/Shutterstock.com, **79** (t) 06photo/Shutterstock.com, **84** (cl) razorbeam/Shutterstock.com, **84** (cr) Dja65/Shutterstock.com, **81** (tr) Minerva Studio/Shutterstock.com, **88** (tl) Virginia Polytechnic Institute and State University/National Geographic Creative, **91** (t) LookTarn.ss/Shutterstock.com, **98** (cr) Nejron Photo/Shutterstock.com, **100** (tl) muratart/Shutterstock.com, **100** (cl) muratart/Shutterstock.com, **100** (bl) PHOTOCREO Michal Bednarek/Shutterstock.com, **103** (tl) Roxana Gonzalez/Shutterstock.com, **111** (tl) Dragon Images/Shutterstock.com, **115** (tl) PhotoDisc/Getty Images,

Text Credits:

39 "Chew on This," by Kay Boatner, National Geographic Kids, December 2013–January 2014, p. 6., **40** "The Joy of Food: Bringing Family and Friends Together," by Victoria Pope, National Geographic Magazine, December 2014, p. 37+., **52** "The Dog Whisperer," by Ruth A. Musgrave, National Geographic Kids, March 2012, p. 26+., **64** "No Arms, Amazing Feet," by James Dennehy, et al., National Geographic Kids, December 2011-January 2012, p. 28+., **88** "The Maasai: Changed, for Better or Worse, by Cell Phones," by Daniel Stone, National Geographic Magazine, March 2016, p. 24., **100** "City of Bones," by Bekah Wright, National Geographic Kids, October 2009, p. 24+. **103** "Cuba's Young Artists Embrace a New World," by Daniel Stone, National Geographic, December 12, 2016. "Rhythm in Your Blood: Meet the Young Artists Keeping Cuba's Traditional Music Alive," by Marisa Aveling, Pitchfork, June 13, 2016.